America's Early
Women Celebrities

America's Early Women Celebrities

*The Famous and Scorned
from Martha Washington to
Silent Film Star Mary Fuller*

ANGELA FIRKUS

McFarland & Company, Inc., Publishers
Jefferson, North Carolina

This book has undergone peer review.

LIBRARY OF CONGRESS CATALOGUING-IN-PUBLICATION DATA

Names: Firkus, Angela, 1967– author.
Title: America's early women celebrities : the famous and scorned
    from Martha Washington to silent film star Mary Fuller /
    Angela Firkus.
Description: Jefferson : McFarland & Company, Inc., Publishers, 2021. |
    Includes bibliographical references and index.
Identifiers: LCCN 2020056726 | ISBN 9781476680231
    (paperback : acid free paper) ∞
    ISBN 9781476641843 (ebook)
Subjects: LCSH: Women—United States—Biography. | Women—
    United States—History—19th century. | Women in popular culture—
    United States—History—19th century.
Classification: LCC HQ1412 .F557 2021 | DDC 305.4092/273 [B]—dc23
LC record available at https://lccn.loc.gov/2020056726

BRITISH LIBRARY CATALOGUING DATA ARE AVAILABLE

ISBN (print) 978-1-4766-8023-1
ISBN (ebook) 978-1-4766-4184-3

Front cover image: Elizabeth Patterson Bonaparte (1785-1879).
Thomas Sully used watercolor on ivory to create this miniature copy
of the triple portrait by Stuart Gilbert. Sully painted it sometime between
1805 and 1810. Watercolor on ivory (Metropolitan Museum of Art)

Printed in the United States of America

McFarland & Company, Inc., Publishers
  Box 611, Jefferson, North Carolina 28640
  www.mcfarlandpub.com

Table of Contents

Preface

I intended to write a book about female heroes in American history but found myself drawn to women whose actions were at times rather selfish. I realized that what the women who most intrigued me shared was a quest for celebrity, and I found that historians had begun to use that word often when describing some women of the past. I use for this book the concept that celebrity is a status negotiated between someone famous and her fans. She may have gained fame through a particular skill, become notorious from scandalous action, or simply garnered publicity by being in the right place at the right time. She became a true celebrity, however, by fostering a relationship with her public or by being the focus of such a promotional campaign. In this way, she became known by many more people than actually read her books, attended a performance, or had any obvious reason to be interested in her. The motive for her action might be to make money from the sale of tickets, books, or merchandise but not necessarily. Likewise, the celebrity could present a contrived public identity or represent herself fairly accurately. She might maintain celebrity for the rest of her life or it might be short lived. What is certain is that she would not be loved by all; while a hero produces adoration, a celebrity creates a mixture of reactions. I think the value in presenting women of the past as the Oprah Winfrey, Taylor Swift, Kim Kardashian, or Ruth Bader Ginsburg of their time is that it gives us a sense of their impact on society. It helps us to see these women so we can take inspiration from the fact that they took incredible chances to survive and thrive. Certainly this is heroic but mostly these women refused to sacrifice themselves in a sense of duty.

I easily identified some of the subjects for the following chapters. I have admired Lydia Maria Child, Sojourner Truth, and Jane Addams for years. I needed to search for others of these women like Elizabeth Patterson Bonaparte, Adah Menken, and Mary Fuller since, while they were celebrities in their own time, they somehow fell out of our collective

1

popular culture memory. I turned to sources such as Cora Castle's 1913 "Statistical Study of Eminent Women" to find some of their names.[1] Other women, such as Jenny Lind, Lola Montez, and Victoria Woodhull, demanded inclusion, appearing again and again in sources I consulted for other chapters.

They were no less demanding of attention in their own time. Fans, journalists, critics, and publicists helped make these women celebrities but they did not force them into the spotlight. During much of the period I cover in this book, it was easy for a woman to be obscure and very difficult to generate and then garner the lasting interest required to be a celebrity. One traveler from England noted that in the United States women were "guarded by a seven-fold shield of habitual insignificance."[2] In addition, attracting attention was synonymous with being scandalous. There was little space in which to operate to foster celebrity. Most women would not have dreamed of living in that place. These women dared to do it and faced the consequences in a world generally unaccepting of female influence. For nearly all of them it was a matter of survival; they could make much more money as a celebrity than in any other occupation available. Some also seemed to crave fame and influence. A few additionally fought for social justice.

Women could, however, exercise power in ways other than celebrity. I have left out of this study influential women of this period who strictly avoided notoriety: women such as Abigail Adams, Dolley Madison, Lucy Stone, and Carrie Chapman Catt. My focus is on the women who sought fame, flirted with infamy, and actively engaged with their fan base. I provide some background information on the women but my main focus is their celebrity not actual selves. A reader interested in learning more about each of these women can turn to a number of excellent biographies, many of which I cite as sources and in a bibliography after each chapter. Instead I try to explain why these women needed recognition as well as how they felt about and dealt with being known. I have presented, then, a book of short (somewhat intertwined) biographies and have not attempted to tell a history of celebrity, although I make some connections in the conclusion.[3] Neither have I provided a comparison with male celebrities of the same time period. I know that such analysis would deepen our understanding of these women and of fans, but I chose to make the women the sole focus of my study. I look forward to more scholarship that connects the dots and that tackles gender comparisons.[4]

These early celebrities faced all of the challenges familiar to stars today. They were on the front lines of battles over privacy, name and image licensing, free speech, libel, gender double standards, and body image. Nearly all of them had a love/hate relationship with their fame. While they wanted to be *known of* they did not necessarily want to be *known*: they tried to maintain some form of privacy. Many of these celebrities developed a public persona (or many) to distance themselves from fans. This negotiation between celebrities and their fans continues to evolve but clearly was already evident in early America.

I hoped I would find more information about fans (and anti-fans) but I am pleased with the stories I have included. Colonists displayed engravings of Martha Washington in their homes. A sailor published a poem in honor of Phillis Wheatley. Romantics cried at the gravesite of fictional character Charlotte Temple. A man tried to disrupt a Fanny Wright lecture by placing a burning drum of turpentine at the door. A devoted fan sent Lydia Maria Child an expensive hair comb that matched one that Child included in a novel. A ballet enthusiast wore a shoe from Fanny Elssler around his neck. A woman paid half a month's wages to hear Jenny Lind sing. A critic called Jane Addams an ass.

Authors of recent biographies explore fan interaction and some of these celebrities told stories of their encounters with the public. The media as it existed at the time also found excessive fan behavior to be news worthy. Those articles have also been important. Many researchers have uncovered diaries and letters from fans but I fear I have just skimmed the surface of what is available. Hopefully we will be able to more clearly over time hear the voice of the fan of this period. Longing for a connection to someone we admire from afar seems to be an element of our modern-world sensibilities. Fans existed long before they called themselves that. The word only became common in the early twentieth century but I have used it throughout this book because it conveys so much that no other word can duplicate. I also use star and celebrity, mostly interchangeable, before they too were commonly used nouns.

I have been fascinated by celebrities my whole life and thoroughly enjoyed discovering more about these women. My research led me to uncanny connections between some of the women's stories, which I recount in this book. In this endeavor I had help from many people and I thank them all. My husband Steven Wagner was a constant supporter and early reader of the manuscript. My mother and sisters have always provided encouragement. Cottey College students, faculty, and staff provided aid in so many ways. Layla Milholen and everyone at McFarland made this book possible. Librarians at the Maryland Historical Society, the Fred W. Smith National Library for the Study of George Washington, and the Medford Historical Society and Museum provided invaluable assistance. The online sources Chronicling America,

Hathi Trust, Google Books, Media History Digital Library, and Internet Archive allowed me easy access to more than I could have imagined and most of the primary sources I cite are from them.

The technology available to fans has also certainly changed, but celebrity did not need social media or even a national media. In the United States before 1920, celebrity culture was vibrant. Women used all the means available to make and maintain a name for themselves. Fans sought a connection to those they adored and devised ways to participate in popular culture; anti-fans searched for ways to denounce celebrities they found undeserving. These impulses of celebration and scorn changed over time but are still very much with us today.

ONE

◇◇◇◇◇◇◇◇◇◇◇◇

Phillis Wheatley and
Martha Washington

Symbols of Genius and Amiability

The two most prominent female celebrities of the American colonies possibly met in a small drawing room of a Cambridge, Massachusetts, house amidst war. In 1776 poet Phillis Wheatley was admired on both sides of the Atlantic and Martha Washington had just risen to prominence as the most important wife in the colonies. Wheatley lived her own life, having escaped enslavement three years earlier, but Washington found herself constrained by the demands of the career of her husband. Their meeting would have been brief and cordial but also complicated by the fact that General Washington and his lady owned enslaved people. No matter the atmosphere of the gathering, 1776 was a turning point for the celebrity of each of the women. After the meeting, Washington became more famous and her public self even more constructed, while Wheatley faded from view just as she acquired the right to unquestionably dictate her own image. The women served well, however, as symbols sorely needed by a nation fighting for independence: Wheatley as a genius poet and Washington as an amiable wife.

That a young enslaved girl would be the emerging nation's first celebrity is fantastic. Born in West Africa she was renamed after the ship (the *Phillis*) on which she survived the trip to the Americas. To be reminded of that forced journey every time she signed her name, received a letter from a friend, or was introduced to yet another possible patron is unimaginable. Possibly, the young girl failed to remember much about being captured, sold, and transported into slavery. She was only about seven years old in 1761 when she was on display for sale; she was small and had just lost her front baby teeth. John Wheatley, a

5

prosperous Boston merchant, brought her home to his wife Susanna and his two teenaged children Mary and Nathaniel.[1]

Wheatley either absorbed the learning taking place in the house or was educated purposefully (possibly due to the family's religious conviction that all should be able to read the Bible). She quickly showed an aptitude for literature and the Wheatleys encouraged her study. The young enslaved girl learned Latin and absorbed the classics as well as works of geography, politics, and history while living in a society where most free women acquired only a minimal education. She wrote her first poem by 1765 and published a piece about two merchants shipwrecked on Cape Cod in the *Newport Mercury* in 1767. Wheatley attained fame, however, with her second publication, a poem honoring and lamenting the death of possibly the most famous religious personality of the time: British evangelist George Whitefield. Her elegy called him a "great Saint" who could "inflame the soul, and captivate the mind"; Wheatley may have heard him preach in Boston the week before he died or might have even met him since her owner Susanna Wheatley had many Methodist connections.[2] Charismatic Whitefield traveled more than half a dozen times to the American colonies to conduct revivals and to perform charity work. Wheatley felt a sense of loss, whether she actually knew him or not, and wrote a poem that captured that sad mood: "What can his dear America return? But drop a tear upon his happy urn." Published cheaply as a single sheet broadside and also as a short pamphlet, her poem was distributed in 1770 and 1771 throughout New England but also in New York, Philadelphia, and London.[3] Wheatley was now widely known and would soon be a celebrity.

Historians have long explored the history of fame but have only recently argued that celebrity too developed long ago. We can easily see that stars of early movies acted as and were treated like our current-day celebrities. Can we really use the word celebrity to label women who came to prominence before a national media even existed? An increasing number of historians are arguing yes. They point out that in the eighteenth century the increase in consumerism, the spread of republican ideas, the growth of newspapers and other print media, and a focus on individual identity combined to allow actors and writers (many of them women) to attract Lady Gaga–like scrutiny. Actors Sarah Siddons, Charlotte Clarke, George Ann Bellamy, and Mary Robinson have all reclaimed their celebrity.[4] Wheatley also performed on stage in a sense and marketed her identity to increase demand for her work. She actively sought a relationship with her audience. Fans admired her poetry but also elevated her as a symbol of promise for the revolution.

After Wheatley gained attention with her poem for Whitefield, she published other works, nearly all marking the deaths of prominent people and their family members. Praise followed. The *Boston Evening Post* printed her tribute to doctor Samuel Marshall. Wheatley's poem on the death of Temperance Clap Pitkin, daughter of a former president of Yale and wife of a wealthy minister in Connecticut, was printed as a broadside. Benjamin Rush, a prominent Philadelphia doctor, wrote admiringly of Wheatley in his 1773 antislavery pamphlet. Rush called Wheatley's talent "singular genius" and reported that her poems were being "read with pleasure by the public."[5]

So how did one show admiration for a genius poet? Read everything she has written, recommend her writings to friends, and travel to see her to request additional pieces. While the former methods might have been used for anyone, since Wheatley was a young enslaved woman from Africa, in the minds of white colonials, justification for adoration needed to be confirmed. Was she really writing these pieces, they wondered, or was the whole thing a sham? Thus it is fitting that fans referred to Wheatley's poems, especially those written in response to a specific prompt, as performances (although the word at the time was commonly used to refer to any written work). People flocked to the Wheatley house on King Street and invited the poet to their homes. They wanted to see for themselves whether or not she was capable of writing the poems they loved, but many also wanted their own personal piece of Wheatley's mind. The still enslaved young woman seems to have risen to each occasion, increasing her celebrity.

While out visiting in late 1771, Wheatley was challenged by a young woman to write a piece about memory because she said she did not know of a poem about that subject. Wheatley wrote an examination of the powers of the god of memory with "exhaustless treasures of his secret stores." Wheatley clearly wrote this poem without consulting her mythology books because Mneme or Mnemosyne is actually the *goddess* not god of memory, but the piece was warmly received even with incorrect pronouns. "The long-forgot thy gentle hand conveys, returns, and soft upon the fancy plays," Wheatley wrote.[6] An anonymous contributor sent the poem to the *London Magazine*, which published it in March of 1772; newspapers in the colonies reprinted it the next year. The source included a short biography of Wheatley, a description of why Wheatley came to write the poem, and a reprint of the note Wheatley wrote to the young lady who requested the poem. The contributor called Wheatley a genius and may have been the now grown and married Mary Wheatley Lathrop, daughter of Wheatley's owner. Wheatley too was probably involved in the campaign to publicize both her poem and her image.[7]

It seems that it was women who were most drawn to Wheatley and who commonly asked her to write poems for them. Deborah Cushing sent works by Wheatley to her husband Thomas, a prominent politician, and told him that some women she knew (Mrs. Dickerson, Mrs. Clymer, Mrs. Bull, and others) had asked Wheatley to "compose some pieces for them" and were pleased by her "performances."[8] During this early period Wheatley wrote poems with titles such as "To a Lady on her Remarkable Deliverance in a Hurricane" and "To a Lady on her coming to America for her Health"; could these also have been performance pieces?

Ruth Barrell Andrews, a Boston poet, gives possibly an additional example. When Andrews's one-year-old nephew died in the fall of 1772, Wheatley wrote a piece consoling the parents that their child was now in heaven. It is not known whether or not Andrews or another family member requested Wheatley write the poem, but it is certainly possible. Andrews had the piece sent to her brother through her husband John who was a prominent lawyer in the city and who had previously sent Wheatley's writings to his in-law. John called this particular piece a "masterly performance."[9] While the specific circumstances are unknown, eighteen of the most prominent men in Boston, including the governor and lieutenant governor of Massachusetts as well as signer of the Declaration of Independence John Hancock, also attested that they believed that she had written the poems being published under her name. "She has been examined by some of the best Judges, and is thought qualified to write them," the testimonial proclaimed. Most scholars doubt that Wheatley appeared in person to the men as a group. Could it have been the wives of some of these men who actually sat with Wheatley as she composed verses for them?[10]

Wheatley performed for men also as her celebrity spread. In the fall of 1772 Thomas Wooldridge visited Wheatley. Wooldridge worked for the Earl of Dartmouth, who had recently been appointed to the post of secretary of state for the American colonies. He traveled widely in the colonies, making reports to Dartmouth back in London on various colonial topics. He heard about Wheatley and wanted to evaluate her for himself. At the house on King Street in Boston, he asked Wheatley if she could write a poem on any theme. She assured him that she could. He then asked her to perform for him by writing about the Earl of Dartmouth, of whom she had already heard. When he sent Dartmouth the poem and letter that Wheatley wrote, Wooldridge called Wheatley "extraordinary." He also assured Dartmouth that he had watched her write and could confirm that the pieces were "her own production."[11]

Similarly, minister Bernard Page reported to the Countess of Huntingdon, also in London, that Wheatley's "Presence and Conversation demonstrate the written Performances, with her Signature, to be hers." When he returned to the Wheatley house though he actually saw the poet write and "took the opportunity to watch her narrowly; by which I found she wrote a good & expeditious hand." Wheatley may have written lines from "Thoughts on the Works of Providence," which she had recently completed. Obviously smitten, Page summed up Wheatley as "humble serene & graceful; her Thoughts, luminous & sepulchral, ethereal & evangelical and her Performances most excellent, yea almost inimitable. A WONDER of the Age indeed!"[12]

Colonists failed to reinforce this support and adoration with cash however. Celebrities of the time could and did find themselves poor despite their elevated status.[13] By 1772, Wheatley had written enough poems to fill a volume and attempted to publish a book by subscription. She failed to raise the money as not enough of her fans came forward to pledge their support. Some felt that continuing suspicion about the truth of Wheatley's abilities may have doomed the venture. Although Wheatley and her supporters advertised the details of the planned book multiple times (including listing the titles of twenty-eight poems to be included), the campaign fell short of the three hundred subscribers needed. Not surprisingly Boston fans Ruth and John Andrews paid the four shillings required and expressed disappointment that the project failed. Wheatley withdrew her manuscript from the Boston printer she had chosen and sent it to London where she hoped she might find more support.[14]

London printer Archibald Bell agreed to publish the poems and visited the Countess of Huntingdon to obtain her patronage as well as her permission to have the volume dedicated to her ladyship. By now, the countess had heard good reports about Wheatley from many within her religious circle as well as having enjoyed both a letter and the elegy of her personal pastor George Whitefield directly from the poet herself. Bell read the new poems to her and she declared parts of them "very fine!" The countess agreed to Bell's plan and only requested that an illustration of Wheatley be added to the front of the volume, which he agreed to do.[15]

While publication seemed to be going smoothly, Wheatley traveled to London in the spring of 1773 to oversee the printing, for health reasons, or possibly mostly for a publicity tour. Newspapers all across the northern colonies reported the departure of the "ingenious negro poet" and at least eight printed her poem "Farewell to America," some by request of a patron.[16] London welcomed Wheatley as a celebrity. Admiration seemed to be conveyed differently than in the colonies; we have no accounts of Wheatley performing while she was in London for about six weeks. Instead, her admirers gave her a celebrity-style grand tour of the city. They treated her to expensive shows, VIP admission to exclusive museums, and entrance into the prestigious social call circle. She met everyone who was anyone: politicians, artists, scientists, ministers; namely she had conversations with both Lord Dartmouth and Benjamin Franklin, who would remain in London on behalf of the colonies for another two years. Two prominent people she failed to meet were King George III, possibly because her stay was too short to allow for the request of an audience to be granted, and the Countess of Huntingdon who was in Wales recuperating from an illness.[17]

In addition to giving her star treatment, her admirers sent her home with many gifts. These were mostly in the form of literature. Fans in the colonies had given her books (the Rev. Charles Chauncy gave her a copy of his own *Daily Devotions* in 1772 that she re-gifted two years later), but the volumes she received in London demonstrated how her new acquaintances appreciated her intellect and wished for her further development; amazingly she was still only twenty years old. Lord Dartmouth, in particular, gave Wheatley five guineas and recommended that she buy the works of Alexander Pope and of others. As she prepared for her return trip, she packed her trunks with Pope's complete works (in nine volumes) as well as his translations of Homer's *Iliad* and *Odyssey*, John Milton's *Paradise Lost*, Miguel de Cervantes' *Don Quixote* in translation, John Gay's *Fables*, and many others.[18] For someone who loved words as much as Wheatley did and who was herself legally property, owning these books must have seemed impossible.

Published according to Act of Parliament, Sept.ʳ 1. 1773 by Archᵈ Bell.
Bookfeller Nº 8 near the Saracens Head Aldgate.

Phillis Wheatley (ca. 1753–1784). Wheatley included this engraving in her book *Poems on Various Subjects*. It is the only known likeness of her from when she was alive (Library of Congress, LC-USZC4-5316).

Her book, *Poems on Various Subjects, Religious and Moral,* was published by the time Wheatley arrived back in Boston in September of 1773. At least eight regional and local newspapers reported on the return of the "extraordinary," "celebrated" "Poetical Genius." Some of the same newspapers also printed dispatches of her adventures in London.[19] While the American press ran advertisements for her book, critics only reviewed it in European periodicals. Within those pages it received ample publicity (most reprinted at least an excerpt of one of the poems) but only measured praise. The *London Magazine,* which had previously published a piece by Wheatley, for example, reprinted "Hymn to the Morning." The review expressed "admiration of talents so vigorous and lively," though admitted to doubting the poems showed any "astonishing power of genius." The review in the *Scots Magazine* reprinted the poem "To Maecenas" and did call Wheatley's talent "genius." The *Critical Review* judged that while the poems are "not remarkably beautiful, they have too much merit to be thrown aside, as trifling and worthless effusions" especially since Wheatley had been only a few years earlier "an illiterate barbarian."[20]

Wheatley remained in the spotlight in 1774 and acquired symbolic status for many. French philosopher Voltaire wrote to a correspondent that he believed that author Bernard Le Bovier de "Fontenelle was wrong to say that there would never be any poets among the Negroes: there is currently a Negress who makes some very good English verse." Poet Mary Scott used Wheatley as an example to prove that women could write well in her "The Female Advocate: A Poem," which was written in response to Duncombe's "Feminead."[21] Most widely distributed, however, was a letter Wheatley wrote to the Rev. Samson Occom in February of 1774 lamenting the plight of enslaved people in the Americas. Wheatley herself had enjoyed freedom since shortly after her return from London and she explained in the letter that in every being "God has implanted a Principle, which we call Love of Freedom; it is impatient of Oppression, and pants for Deliverance." Someone, probably Occom, sent the letter to the *Connecticut Gazette* and it as well as nine other newspapers printed the letter in the spring of 1774, amid revolutionary fervor. Many of the papers printed it both because of its message of freedom and, they reported, "as a Specimen of her Ingenuity."[22]

As before, word of mouth and sharing performances among friends seems to also have been a large part of Wheatley's fame. Now, however, with so many more poems to indulge in (nearly forty printed in her book and more appearing in periodicals) an additional form of adoration emerged: imitation. Fans took up their own pens and wrote. They wrote both of and to Wheatley, inspired by her amazing story and unlikely success: a young pious enslaved woman had published a book of poems that was the talk of the English and French speaking world. Also colonists wrestled with an emerging American identity as their cities pulsed with rebellion (the Boston Massacre of 1770 occurred just blocks from where Wheatley lived and the Boston Tea Party happened a few months after she returned from England). Wheatley represented hope that the colonies had enough brains to survive whatever happened next. So why shouldn't everyone make an effort at genius and see what happened? Boston poet Jane Dunlap declared Wheatley to be her inspiration and rival for acclaim when she wrote her own elegy to minister George Whitefield:

> Shall his due praises be so loudly sung
> By a young Afric damsels virgin tongue?
> And I be silent! And no mention make
> Of his blest name, who did so often speak.[23]

Naval officers seemed especially moved by Wheatley to write verse. Sailor John Prime Iron Rochfort wrote in the *Royal American Magazine* of Wheatley's talent and lamented at his own feeble attempt to praise her:

> For softer strains we quickly must repair
> To Wheatley's song, for Wheatley is the fair;
> That has the art, which art could ne'er acquire:
> To dress each sentence with seraphic fire.
> Her wondrous virtues I could ne'er express!
> To paint her charms, would only make them less.[24]

John Paul Jones, of "I have not yet begun to fight!" fame, wrote Wheatley a poem that focused even more acutely on her charms. Jones directed his piece to be given to "the celebrated Phillis the African favorite" of the muses, but expressed adoration of Wheatley's physical not intellectual attributes. Possibly inspired by the profile illustration of Wheatley published with her poems since we have no record that the two actually met, he wrote "The loveliest form, the fairest face, The brightest eye, the gentlest mind, And every virtue, charm and grace, Should be to endless fame consigned."[25]

Wheatley carefully crafted a persona her fans found inspiring. She demonstrated humility as well as genius. Wheatley rarely included herself in her poems except as a stand in for a muse or to humbly protest that she was not extraordinarily talented. She wrote by request and often in the form of elegies to praise God and to offer comfort to the bereaved, thus showing her piety and lack of ambition for herself. Also Wheatley argued in the preface of her book of poems that she never intended to publish her poems but wrote them for her own amusement. She only agreed to have them printed, she continued, after the urging of her "most generous Friends; to whom she considers herself, as under the greatest Obligations." She concluded that "with all their Imperfections, the Poems are now humbly submitted to the Perusal of the Public."[26]

Wheatley was, however, an ambitious woman not the passive recipient of a series of favors from friends. She certainly directed the extended campaign that resulted in the publication of her book of poems, even personally signing each one so that it would be easy to spot unauthorized editions.[27] Wheatley also probably negotiated for her freedom as the condition for her return to Boston from London; in England, she was not only free but the law prevented her forced return to slavery.[28] She demonstrated her ambition best by writing letters to prominent people. Always worded very humbly but demonstrating quite a bit of confidence, these letters advanced her career enormously. She wrote to the Countess of Huntingdon, for example, sending her a copy of her elegy of George Whitefield, and was subsequently given permission to dedicate her book of poems to her ladyship.

As part of this ambitious campaign, Wheatley sent a poem to George Washington but it was likely Martha Washington who was most moved and occasioned their visit. In a letter of October of 1775, Wheatley flattered the general that his recent appointment as head of the Continental Army and "the fame of your virtues, excite sensations not easy to suppress." These sensations apparently caused her to write a poem declaring him "Fam'd for thy valour, for thy virtues more" and foretelling victory for the colonies as she warned Great Britain that it would "Lament thy thirst of boundless power too late." Wheatley concluded with predictions of even more than victory: "A crown, a mansion, and a throne that shine, With gold unfading, WASHINGTON! Be thine."[29]

General Washington responded to Wheatley's letter and ode in late February of 1776, after his wife had joined him in army winter camp in Cambridge, Massachusetts. By then, Martha Dandridge Custis Washington was herself a celebrity, serving as a symbolic amiable wife. She experienced a bit of unwelcome local fame early in life, when John Custis, the father of her first husband, openly opposed the match in eccentric ways. Reportedly before the wedding, he carted the family silver to town and declared that he would give it away on the street rather than allow the daughter of his lowly neighbor to have it.[30] The two married anyway and the shame of that rebuke was replaced by the dignity of becoming the mistress of one of the wealthiest families of Virginia. She would have probably remained a wife and mother out of the limelight but for Daniel Custis's death in 1757 and her subsequent marriage to George Washington.

When Washington stayed behind as the general left to take up his commission in 1775, she initially felt safe and content to remain at Mount Vernon or at the home of friends in the area. She changed her mind when British General Lord Dunmore began raiding plantations in the area and the press declared her a tory who disapproved of her husband siding with the patriots.[31] In November Washington gathered her family for a journey to Massachusetts, determined both to protect them and to prevent harm to her husband's reputation. When she arrived outside of Philadelphia, the newspapers reported, "the Lady of his Excellency General Washington" was welcomed by a military honor guard that escorted her carriage into the city. In a letter, Washington referred a friend to that report rather than recount the events: "I dont doubt but you have see the Figuer our arrival made in the Philadelphia paper." By the time that Washington left Philadelphia a week later, she had made herself a star. She won over the patriots by trading her expensive gowns for homespun clothing to show support for boycotting British goods. She also dissuaded the society women from holding a ball in her honor since the Continental Congress had recommended colonists refrain from "extravagance and dissipation." The press trumpeted her departure and she wrote to that same friend that she exited the city "in as great pomp as if I had been a very great somebody."[32] She again acquired a military guard and experienced ringing bells and cheering crowds in each town through which she passed.

In camp at Cambridge, Washington organized and held a traditional Twelfth Night celebration (January 6 was also the Washingtons' wedding anniversary so the occasion was special for them). It is during this time of early 1776 that she may have come across Phillis Wheatley's letter and poem. Washington read a wide variety of material though she has often been portrayed as too busy to read or unable to enjoy books for pleasure while her husband lived. She certainly read the newspapers and as an informed hostess probably also kept up with literary publications; wealthy women were expected to be well informed and intelligent in the 1770s. Her library included religious works, sleazy novels, popular collections such as *The Beauties of Milton, Thomson, and Young,* and books of poetry.[33] She probably lacked knowledge of Wheatley, however, since the poet was not famous in the South in the early 1770s like she was in New England.

Washington learned of Wheatley once she arrived in Cambridge though. Like other women, Washington wanted to meet Wheatley; as the owner of enslaved people, she may have been even more curious than most to make the acquaintance of the poet genius. It is possible that she prompted the general to reply to Wheatley, now rather belatedly, to thank and praise her. The letter does not betray any familiarity with other of Wheatley's writings but praises the sent ode as proof of her "poetical talents." The Washingtons also invited Wheatley to visit the army camp.[34] It is hard to imagine ambitious Wheatley passing up the opportunity even though the presence of the British Army made it dangerous.

Wheatley may have escaped the occupation of Boston by the British by moving temporarily to Chelsea, just north of the city. She could have visited with the Washingtons in one of the parlors of their Cambridge home for the winter, the Vassall Mansion, which had been abandoned by a family fleeing to England and which was later owned by author Henry Wadsworth Longfellow. Washington excelled at putting her guests at ease and one can imagine her doing the same with Wheatley. Since arriving in Cambridge, Washington made the acquaintance of prominent local women, some of whom undoubtedly knew Susanna Wheatley, who had died in 1774. Washington and Wheatley may have chatted about these common friends, about poetry, or on religious matters. There is no evidence that Wheatley performed for the Washingtons and in fact she may have been the one treated to a gift. This could have been a book, which Wheatley often received, or a memento from General Washington, such as a miniature portrait or a lock of his hair.[35]

At the time of this meeting, the celebrity of the two women was moving in opposite directions. Wheatley started to fade from the public eye during the American Revolution even though her poem to General Washington and the exchange of letters was printed in multiple locations in 1776. She attempted in 1779 to publish a second volume of poems by subscription but failed to generate enough interest though she placed at least six advertisements in newspapers.[36] By this time Wheatley had again transformed her identity. She was not only free but married and possibly pregnant. Her ties to the important Methodist community were definitely reduced by the death of Susanna Wheatley but also by her refusal to take up a position as a missionary wife in Africa.[37] She published a few more pieces, elegies and poems on liberty, but Wheatley died poor December 5, 1784, unable to interest the public in her new identity. Somehow she failed to still serve as a symbol of the new country. Boston newspapers printed short notices of her death. A poet who signed the name Horatio felt it only fitting that one who wrote so many elegies should receive one of her own. This poet felt unqualified for the task like so many others inspired by Wheatley: "Then should these lines in numbers soft array'd, Preserve thy mem'ry from oblivion's shade; But O! how vain the wish that friendship pays, Since her own volumes are her greatest praise."[38] Wheatley was buried in an unmarked grave.

Washington returned home to Mount Vernon in the spring of 1776 but increased her celebrity by spending at least part of each winter of the American Revolution with her husband in army camp, experiencing even the awful conditions at Valley Forge. Newspapers continued to report her travels and crowd reactions. As the general's wife, she became especially popular with the soldiers, who cheered her entrance into camp with shouts of "God Bless Lady Washington!" They knew her arrival was not simply symbolic but also meant an easing of at least some of their conditions since she always tried to improve their rations and organized knitting circles to provide them with socks and other apparel. Her support of a women-led fundraising effort for the troops in 1780 undoubtedly contributed to its great success; erroneous assumptions that she had written the fundraising call to action "Sentiments of an American Woman" may have increased circulation of the broadsheet.[39] She herself gave six thousand pounds to the cause and Phillis Wheatley gave seven shillings six pence.[40] The men saw her as a mother figure and noted her kindness; one soldier reported to his brother that he was honored to serve as one of Washington's guards since she was "the most amiable woman upon Earth."[41] Another confided to his diary that she combined in "an uncommon degree great dignity of manner with the most pleasing affability."[42]

Fans celebrated Washington with depictions in popular culture that mostly adhered to this image of amiability. Celebrities did not yet own rights to their image or name, so admirers or those just wanting to make money could produce items for sale honoring great people or just capitalizing on their popularity. Boston artist Joseph Hiller, Sr., printed a portrait of Washington that was available for sale. Fans could buy the nine by twelve-inch broadside of Washington looking very glamorous and regal, not at all the grandmotherly image that later came to dominate her image. In this portrait, Washington wears a string of pearls in her hair and a very low-cut dress that exposes considerable cleavage and elegant arms. Her dress is partially hand colored blue, a color of royalty. Hiller labeled the portrait *Lady Washington*.[43] Musicians also wrote songs in her honor and these more closely reflected the image of her importance as a wife. They sold lyrics sheets for ballads such as "Saw You My Hero, George," which depicts Washington arriving in the North in the summer of 1778, only to find the general engaged in battle. In the song, she searches for him on the battlefield, hearing of his heroic deeds of the day, until finally she hears the shouts of praise, knowing he is safe in the end. Another musician composed the "Lady Washington's Reel," which became very popular for balls.[44]

Washington received many honors and gifts during the war that demonstrated not only her popularity but her actual and symbolic importance to the cause. The Continental Navy christened one of their first ships *Lady Washington* and others, including privateers, honored her in the same way. By the winter of 1778, one regiment had renamed itself "Lady Washington's Dragoons" and paraded in white uniforms with blue trim. Congress authorized the spending of funds to buy a carriage for Washington's journeys to and from Mount Vernon although it was chronically short of cash during the war.[45] Apparently Congress was spared that expense, however, since the Pennsylvania Assembly gave her one that had belonged to Governor Penn. She accepted a porcelain piece from diplomat to France Arthur Lee and a gold medallion from the city of Williamsburg, Virginia. She failed, however, to receive an unknown present from Marie Antoinette, the Queen of France, because it was apparently intercepted by the British.[46] Also not received were boxes of tropical fruit and pounds of tea sent by the widow of a British officer in New York who had heard in 1781 that Washington was ill. General Washington sent it all back assuring the woman that his wife was feeling just fine.[47] What a propaganda blow it would have been to the patriot cause for the press to report that Washington was sipping tea and eating pineapple, all courtesy of the British.

LADY WASHINGTON.

Martha Washington (1731–1802). This engraving by Joseph Hiller, Sr., was for sale around 1777. The lower part of Washington's dress was hand colored blue (Metropolitan Museum of Art. Bequest of Charles Allen Munn, 1924).

After the war, the presents continued, particularly from military men, and she remained a celebrity symbol of amiability. The Marquis de Lafayette sent her andirons for her white Italian marble fireplace and a pair of Chinese pheasants that she let loose in the yard. The Society of the Cincinnati, created by the American and French officers who served in the Revolution, presented her with a set of China.[48] Her name continued to be used for boats, now merchant vessels that carried goods around the world, and for other business ventures such as the Lady Washington Inn on Third Street in Philadelphia.[49]

When her husband transitioned from General Washington to President Washington in 1789, she was called on once again to be a public partner. "The Lady of the President" (First Lady was not yet in use) traveled separately from the president to the then capital of the nation at New York, allowing for people of the towns and cities along the route to show admiration for her specifically. Reporters followed along in their own carriage for part of the trip and many newspapers ran detailed accounts of the military honor guards, thirteen-gun salutes, ringing bells, distinguished welcoming committees, and cheering crowds, "who had assembled to testify their joy on this happy occasion."[50] Two events distinguish this procession from the ones Washington made during the American Revolution. First, when she arrived in Philadelphia she stood up in the carriage to express her gratitude to those who had assembled to greet her; this was possibly the only time she made a public speech. Second, she was met by her husband at Elizabethtown, New Jersey, and sailed with him to New York, past Battery Park, on the federal barge. The *New York Daily Gazette* announced that the landing would be at Peck's Slip and slyly encouraged a large crowd: "we make no doubt but our citizens will show their usual respect on this happy occasion."[51]

Washington continued to represent amiability as she took on her new status and even embarked on a campaign to strengthen this image. She and others knew that in a "world turned upside down" a symbol of continuity in the form of a supportive wife was invaluable. Newspapers printed articles in late May of 1789 that emphasized her good qualities and supportive role. She was labeled a "truly respectable personage" by the *New York Daily Gazette,* a "much respected personage" with an "exalted rank" and "amiable virtues, which distinguish and adorn her character" by the *Pennsylvania Mercury and Universal Advertiser*, and again "amiable" by the *Gazette of the United States* out of New York. The Pennsylvania newspaper also engaged in very early celebrity analysis. It questioned why Washington was being honored with such fanfare and concluded that though she had not actually done anything, she had still helped bring independence. The article surmised that the "affectionate respect" everyone felt for her was due to how "by her presence, she contributed to relieve the cares of our beloved Chief, and to soothe

the anxious moments of his military concern."[52] Clearly the writer of the article ignored or was unaware of all the actual work she accomplished aiding the soldiers during the war. Whether or not these articles were part of a direct publicity campaign is unknown but the consistency of message seems to suggest so. Tobias Lear, long-time secretary for the president, wrote letters for Washington, managed her image, and may have helped with her publicity also.[53]

Others, however, strengthened the image. Enos Hitchcock dedicated his 1790 book about women's education to her with the hope that because of her "unrivalled sway in the hearts of a grateful country," her example would have "influence in forming the female character."[54] At a 1792 celebration of George Washington's birthday at the Virginia Coffee House in Cornwall, England, one gentleman toasted "Mrs. Washington, and the fair daughters not only of America, but of all the world, and may they imitate her virtuous example."[55] Her reputation for amiability caused many people down on their luck to write her with requests for assistance. They addressed her as Madam, the Honorable Lady Washington, Your Excellency, and "patroness of distress'd merit" as they asked for money or a job.[56] Responses to these letters have not been found but one group of needy visitors we know she never refused: soldiers. George Washington Parke Custis remembered his grandmother entertaining poor veterans often. Washington would talk with them as well as give them food and sometimes money.[57]

Washington continued to receive gifts while her husband was in office. In 1796 American-Dutch merchant Andreas Everardus van Braam Houckgeest designed and presented her with a set of China bearing her "MW" monogram, the Latin phrase "glory and defense come of it," laurel wreaths, and the names of the fifteen states joined by links into a chain.[58] Former army officer John Lamb often sent the household food stores, such as apples, preserved ginger, and salmon.[59] When Washington received personal items from the public, she often sent them back, as was the case with a screen (for a fireplace probably) sent to her by Mary Ann Aitken of Philadelphia. Washington had a note sent with the returned gift praising the piece for its "taste and beautiful execution" but informing Aitken that she could not receive such favors.[60] She did, however, characteristically, keep likenesses of her husband. Doing this seemed acceptable because it showed patriotism and respect for the esteem others held for President Washington. American artist John Trumbull gave her an engraved print from his military painting *Washington at Trenton*.[61] The Countess of Buchan (Margaret Fraser) sent her a plaster medallion containing the likeness of her husband.[62] Mrs. Van Berckel presented her with the most elaborate gift. It was a painting of the president surrounded by three women: one was spinning the thread of his life, another was winding the thread, but a third, who was poised to cut the thread with scissors, was being held back by the Genius of Immortality, allowing the thread of his life to drift off into eternity. Mrs. Van Berckel wrote a poem to accompany the portrait in case the message was lost on the viewer:

> In Vain the Sisters ply with busy care,
> To reel off years from Glory's deathless Heir.
> Frail things may pass—His fame shall never die,
> Resc'd from Fate by Immortality.[63]

Washington's fame, however, was not completely unsullied. She faced criticism for some of the etiquette precedence she set though she was given very little latitude in these matters. Congress decided that it would be both impractical as well as injudicious for the Washingtons to participate in the normal cycle of calling in New York society. Barred from visiting with individual families, Washington entertained anyone who was considered properly dressed on Friday evenings. She usually served plum cake, tea, and coffee and reportedly ended the evening abruptly at exactly nine o'clock. Some portrayed these events as more fitting for a queen than for the wife of the president of a republic. Others, however, were appalled at what seemed to them to be a lack of proper decorum when Washington traveled about town. One congressman, after encountering her carriage, complained that it lacked a large enough entourage.[64] Finding a balance was clearly a difficult task, especially when all knew that every action was setting a precedent. Washington escaped any serious scorn. It is hard to criticize someone who exists so much as a symbol and not as a real person.

As after the revolution, once the Washingtons returned again to Mount Vernon, their fame did not fade. In fact, now there were even more visitors and letters and Washington continued her campaign of amiability. After becoming a widow for the second time, Washington faced the duty of replying to the condolences but was assisted by her husband's long-time secretary Tobias Lear. The task was so monumental that Congress voted unanimously to allow her free postage so she would not need to bear the cost alone.[65] Some of the sympathy correspondence also demonstrated Washington's own fame as a supportive wife. One of General Washington's former military aids counseled her that "it ought not to be indifferent to you that Posterity too will know, that, in all your social relations & in discharging all the duties of your sex, the whole tenour of your conduct has been highly exemplary and worthy of the most unreserved approbation."[66] A Society of Females wrote first requesting a lock of her hair and again in thanks for the memento, though apologetically: "Pardon this second intrusion on your goodness," they wrote.[67]

One admirer gushed and perhaps could see through the carefully crafted amiable wife public image.

> You in particular, who have Shared his glory in so distinguished a manner; who perhaps have been the hidden Spring of his great actions, for whose sake perhaps he won so many trophies, you at whose feet he has laid all the laurels he has been so deservedly crowned with, will undoubtedly enjoy forever the love and veneration of the inhabitants of America & with Sincerity of Heart, I beg leave to assure you that I am deeply impressed with these Sentiments, & think it a peculiar advantage in having an opportunity to inscribe myself, Madam, Your most humble, obedient & respectful Servant.[68]

She found this fame and adoration useful almost immediately. When Congress requested that her husband's body be moved to the new capital in Washington, D.C., she responded with a carefully worded letter (employing what we would now label a passive-aggressive technique) containing a very reluctant acquiescence to the plan. Accustomed to never "oppose my private wishes to the public will—I must consent," she wrote; but, she continued, "in doing this I need not—I cannot say what a sacrifice of individual feeling I make to a sense of public duty."[69] Newspapers across the country printed the letter in the middle of January of 1800 and as a result the former president's body remained at Mount Vernon. Clearly she had given and suffered enough for the public good. There was no need to separate her further from her beloved husband by moving his body to the capital.

Washington lived fewer than three years after her husband died. Newspapers across the country reprinted an obituary from the *Washington Federalist*. It lauded her as the "widow of the late illustrious General George Washington" with the usual descriptors but it also acknowledged some additional qualities. The notice read in part "To those amiable and Christian virtues, which adorn the female character, she added dignity of manners, superiority of understanding, a mind intelligent and elevated.—The silence of respectful grief is our best eulogy."[70] The *Philadelphia Repository* ran a piece that elevated her to her husband's level and possibly above with its more lengthy obituary. It argued that "she was the worthy partner of the worthiest of men, and those who witnessed their conduct, could not determine which excelled in their different characters."[71] The *Spectator*, however, printed an original notice that only emphasized Washington's supportive role and her "amiable qualities."[72]

Washington took drastic steps to preserve the image she and those around her had crafted during her life. She burned her personal correspondence and urged her relations to do the same. If she kept a diary, it did not survive her.[73] Thus there is little but a few scraps to contradict a portrait of an amiable contented wife. She wrote to her niece Fanny in 1789 (a letter that miraculously survives), "I never goe to the publick place—indeed I think I am more like a state prisoner than anything else, there is certain bounds set for me which I must not depart from—and as I can not doe as I like I am obstinate and stay at home a great deal."[74] The toll that such a life of duty exacted was clear by 1791 when she lamented to a friend, "I have been so long accustomed to conform to events which are governed by the public voice I hardly dare indulge any personal wishes which cannot yield to that."[75] Along with preserving her amiability image, she had also destroyed any evidence that might have existed of her contribution to her husband's successes that went beyond the support of a dutiful wife. Did they discuss politics? Did she advise him on diplomacy? Did he rely on her assessment of character? If so, she wanted it all to remain unknown so that he would receive all the credit.

While Washington and Wheatley lived very different celebrity lives, they did have this in common: they existed for most as symbols that represented their carefully crafted public images. In the process they left just enough evidence of their true selves to be endlessly intriguing to us. The requirements of celebrity have changed drastically but this fact remains. The nation's first female stars knew from the beginning that a public persona was something to create and not a reflection of their true self. At the end of the eighteenth century, Americans were satisfied with knowing of a genius poet and an amiable wife. They relished personal encounters; they gave gifts; they cherished mementos and performances. They did not, however, clamor for secrets or heap scorn on them. Celebrities could remain symbols and maintain their privacy while in the public eye.

Select Bibliography

Barker-Benfield, G.J. *Phillis Wheatley Chooses Freedom.* New York: New York University Press, 2018.

Brady, Patricia. *Martha Washington: An American Life.* New York: Penguin, 2005.

Braudy, Leo. *The Frenzy of Renown: Fame and Its History.* New York: Vintage Books, 1986.

Brooks, Joann. "Our Phillis, Ourselves." *American Literature* 82 (June 2010): 1–28.

Bryan, Helen. *Martha Washington: First Lady of Liberty.* New York: John Wiley and Sons, 2002.

Carretta, Vincent. *Biography of a Genius in Bondage.* Athens: University of Georgia Press, 2011.

Ennis, Daniel. "Poetry and American Revolutionary Identity: The Case of Phillis Wheatley and John Paul Jones." *Studies in Eighteenth-Century Culture* 31 (2002): 85–98.

Fawcett, Julia. *Spectacular Disappearances: Celebrity and Privacy, 1696–1801.* Ann Arbor: University of Michigan Press, 2016.

Fields, Joseph, comp. *"Worthy Partner": The Papers of Martha Washington.* Westport, CT: Greenwood Press, 1994.

Gates, Henry Louis. *The Trials of Phillis Wheatley: America's First Black Poet and Her Encounters with the Founding Fathers.* New York: Basic Books, 2003.

Isani, Makhtar Ali. "The Contemporaneous Reception of Phillis Wheatley: Newspaper and Magazine Notices during the Years of Fame, 1765–1774." *The Journal of Negro History* 85 (Fall 2000): 260–273.

Jenner, Greg. *Dead Famous: An Unexpected History of Celebrity from Bronze Age to Silver Screen.* London: Orion, 2020.

Lange, Allison. "Picturing Tradition: Images of Martha Washington in Antebellum Politics." *Imprint* 37 (Autumn 2012): 22–39.

Lilti, Antoine. *The Invention of Celebrity: 1750–1850.* Cambridge: Polity Press, 2017.

Marcus, Sharon. *The Drama of Celebrity.* Princeton: Princeton University Press, 2019.

McPherson, Heather. *Art & Celebrity in the Age of Reynolds and Siddons.* University Park: The Pennsylvania State University Press, 2017.

Robinson, William H. *Phillis Wheatley: A Bio-bibliography.* Boston: G.K. Hall, 1981.

Shields, John C., ed. *The Collected Works of Phillis Wheatley.* New York: Oxford University Press, 1988.

Shields, John C., and Eric D. Lamore, eds. *New Essays on Phillis Wheatley.* Knoxville: University of Tennessee Press, 2011.

Wheatley, Phillis. *Poems on Various Subjects, Religious and Moral.* London: A Bell, 1773.

Two

〈〈〈〈〈〈〈〈〈〈〈〈〉〉

Susannah Rowson and
Elizabeth Patterson Bonaparte
Bad Girls at a Good Time

Charlotte Temple and Elizabeth Patterson Bonaparte never met as Wheatley and Washington did, but their wax figure likenesses shared space in a Cincinnati museum in 1827. We know they were not acquainted because Temple did not exist; she was the title character of the best-selling novel of early America who bore a child out of wedlock. Bonaparte was real and the single mother of Napoleon's nephew; she became known widely as The American Beauty and shocked society with her skimpy French fashion. It would seem that Americans would have been content to imagine these two bad girls as part of the museum's other top draw: a terrifying depiction of Dante's Inferno with flashing lights and screaming, writhing figures in hell. The women suffered some scorn but were largely adored for decades. Bonaparte maintained popularity for her lifetime, but Charlotte Temple acquired a celebrity status that transcended life and reality.

Charlotte Temple was supposedly born in Portsmouth, England, but actually in the mind of Susanna Haswell Rowson. In 1791 London, Rowson attempted to support her family however she could. She realized after five years of marriage that her husband lacked marketable skills but loved drinking alcohol. While the couple did not have children, they supported her elderly father and his sister's family. Rowson, who traveled and enjoyed the opportunity to read widely from the age of five through about twelve, found that she could make money turning these experiences and knowledge into performances. She published three novels and two books of poetry before selling *Charlotte: A Tale of Truth* to Minerva Press of London, which published it anonymously.[1]

While Rowson incorporated many of her own experiences into her novels, she did little of that with *Charlotte*. The plot is a simple one. At boarding school, young Charlotte Temple falls in love with a soldier and runs away with him as he sails for war in the American Colonies. In New York she is abandoned and dies after giving birth to his child. Her father arrives in time to speak with her and vows to raise the baby girl. The one strong connection between the plot and the author's life is that Rowson's own mother died after giving birth. In addition, though born in Portsmouth, England, Rowson had first-hand knowledge of the colonies. She lived comfortably with her father and his second family near Boston, Massachusetts, for ten years of her childhood, until the American Revolution forced them all to return to England; Lieutenant Rowson of the British Royal Navy (retired) and crown appointed revenue collector would not renounce the king.[2]

Back in England, the family was now impoverished, having had their possessions confiscated by the colonial patriots. Rowson could no longer indulge in unlimited explorations of literature but possibly served as a governess, wrote, and also used her atypical life experiences to prepare for performances on the stage. Her acting career took her and her husband first to Edinburgh and then, two years after publishing *Charlotte* in 1791, to Philadelphia, Pennsylvania. While Rowson had worked steadily in the British Isles she had not achieved much fame or fortune.[3] She set out to change that in her adopted country.

Rowson assaulted the American art scene, hammering it with the sheer volume of her work. In her three years with the company of the New Theatre (also known as the Chestnut Street Theatre) she appeared in nearly ninety productions, some of which she wrote or to which she contributed song lyrics.[4] After she moved to Boston to join the Federal Street Theatre she performed in forty more plays in about a year before retiring from the stage in 1797.[5] In addition, she published novels and poetry, as well as contributed to magazines. She also arranged to have many of her previous publications available to her new American audience. By the end of 1794 four reprints were available for sale.[6] Specifically, she approached Mathew Carey, publisher based in Philadelphia, with a copy of *Charlotte*, which she now wanted published under her own name. He printed both the first and second edition in 1794 because it sold out so quickly.[7]

Rowson's efforts to attract attention were a well-coordinated quest for celebrity. Her books, for example, clearly identified her as a stage performer and author of her other works, serving nicely as cross-promotional pieces. Her position with the New Street Theatre Company allowed for her name to be printed nearly daily in the newspaper advertisements for plays. Rowson also worked hard to make sure each additional piece offered her public something new, some novel personal information they could use to create their own image of Mrs. Rowson, star. In her book prefaces, for instance, she revealed autobiographical information and explained the parts of each novel that were based on her own life. Also, though she published for her own popularity, she tried to maintain respectability by arguing that her main concern was to provide moral lessons to young vulnerable girls.[8] In the text of some of her works she even directly addressed her audience with questions or to chat about a side item, attempting a personal, intimate connection. She used this technique with *Charlotte*, but she had written this previously; an example from her American career is her performance of the epilogue of her play *Slaves in Algiers*. In it, Rowson appeared as herself and directly asked the audience how they liked the play though presumably she did not pause her monologue to wait for a reply.[9]

The Mrs. Rowson she presented to her public was both humble and confident. In the prefaces to her books, Rowson dismissed her own talent and her ambition, explaining that she lacked a thorough education and now simply wrote in her leisure time for her own amusement. She argued that she had only agreed to publish her work because her friends had urged her to. She also, however, confidently tried to forestall criticism by lamenting that some "sage critic" would probably declare her work inferior without even reading much of it and all because she was a woman.[10] In her epilogue to *Slaves in Algiers* she continued the theme of humility by feigning nervousness: "Bless me! I'm almost terrified to death. Yet sure, I had no real cause for fear, since none but liberal, generous friends are here. Say, will you kindly overlook my errors? You smile. Then to the winds I give my terrors." Rowson possessed years of experience and likely felt comfortable on stage. She demonstrated her true confidence by continuing her monologue with six more stanzas, some containing feminist statements surely meant partly in jest but controversial nonetheless: "Women were born for universal sway; men to adore, be silent, and obey."[11]

Rowson continued her campaign for celebrity in 1794. In April, about the time that the American edition of *Charlotte* was first available, she placed advertisements for a new novel that she would publish by subscription. While those interested could make payments to Mathew Carey or publishers in a half dozen other cities, Rowson listed herself as the principal distributer; theater attendees could buy a subscription from Rowson at a location very near the theater.[12] This is possibly how Martha Washington, Lady of the President, ordered her advance copy of

Trials of the Human Heart, published in 1795. The book includes a list of subscribers, including Washington. Martha and George attended many plays. The President even selected the program at the New Theatre for February 29, 1796, probably as a birthday celebration, and it included Rowson "playing Miss Pickle in *The Spoil'd Child.*"[13] One can imagine Lady Washington, having been moved by a play performance and having read *Charlotte,* chatting with Rowson about Philadelphia, the theater, and sentimental fiction. Rowson would have been a very intriguing guest at one of Washington's drawing room gatherings but there is no evidence she attended. Actors enjoyed renown but also notoriety; they should have been allowed to attend if properly dressed but Rowson might have found the experience uncomfortable.

Rowson's publicity campaign failed to make her a celebrity and even attracted negative comment. William Cobbett belittled Rowson in a lengthy letter to the *American Monthly Review* that was published in February of 1795. Writing under the pseudonym of Peter Porcupine, Cobbett sarcastically praised Rowson's efforts at fame: "The inestimable works that she has showered (not to say *poured,* you know) upon us, mend not only our hearts, but if properly administered, our constitutions also." He felt personally offended by her feminist statements such as the previously quoted flipping of gender dominance; Cobbett was not one to "adore, be silent, and obey" or apparently to take a joke. Possibly unaware that she had spent much of her childhood in the colonies, Cobbett seemed incensed that she would try to comment on American politics: "Before we were so happy as to have *a Rowson* amongst us, we were, or seemed to be, ignorant of our real consequence as a nation." Ironically, Cobbett was actually more the outsider since he had only been in the United States since 1792.[14]

John Swanwick came to her defense. Swanwick, politician and poet using the pseudonym Snub, published a pamphlet criticizing Cobbett and praising Rowson in 1795:

> How callous and lost to sensibility, is the heart that would extort tears from female eyes by such envenomed shafts! I hope the lady has too much fortitude to weep; and that she may not anticipate the stings of future malice, the heroic Snub will ever interpose his shield in her defence, because he regards her as a bright ornament to female science. Though he cannot boast of the pleasure of a personal intimacy with the lady, yet he has derived ineffable satisfaction from the labours of her pen; labours well calculated for the improvement of a heart susceptible of literary refinement.[15]

He clearly did not know Rowson if he thought for one moment that she would cry over the criticism.

As hard as Rowson and others worked to make her a celebrity, she could not quite attain the stature she apparently sought. Her half-brother Robert Haswell reported to her in 1796 that Boston women loved her for her books.[16] The less than enthusiastic response to her subscription campaign for her novel *Trials of the Human Heart*, however, demonstrated the limit of her appeal. Fewer than half of the three hundred subscribers needed are listed in the published book, which was altered to allow it to be printed at all.[17] *Rebecca* sold well, but others of her books did not. She seemed bitter that her more nuanced later books could not match the popularity of *Charlotte*. She complained through one of her characters that love was the only subject for novels that publishers were interested in. "I wonder," the unnamed author said, "that the novel readers are not tired of reading one story so many times, with only the variation of its being told different ways."[18] Her song "America, Commerce and Freedom" was a huge hit, sung at celebrations throughout the country and included in sixty-three songbooks between 1795 and 1820.[19] But it did little to boost her own profile. Most Americans probably did not even know she had written it. There would be no wax figures made of Susanna Rowson, as there were of Charlotte Temple and Elizabeth Patterson Bonaparte.

After retiring from the stage, however, she accomplished maybe an even greater feat than becoming famous: she became a thoroughly respectable lady of Boston society. In order to have a more consistent income (she made little money from the impressive sale of *Charlotte* because she sold her rights) and possibly a more lasting fame, in 1797 Rowson founded and operated a successful school for young girls. Though a concern for the morals of youth was a major part of the persona of Mrs. Rowson and possibly actually of the real Rowson, parents had many reasons to be reluctant to entrust their children to her. As both an actor and a writer of novels, she was engaged in two of the more scandalous occupations open to women. Her married status and her exceptional talents must have allowed many to overlook these obvious concerns; by the end of the first term one hundred girls were enrolled with her.[20] She remained a prolific writer (even performing when friends requested poems on specific subjects like Wheatley had) but now she published many more textbooks than novels. She became active in local charities, contributed essays to Boston magazines, and wrote patriotic songs and poems.

When she died in 1824 she was mourned locally but she seemed to be quickly forgotten. New England newspapers printed complimentary obituaries that emphasized her "talents, virtues and intelligence."[21] The *Columbian Centinel* published an elegy, possibly written by a former student, which celebrated the Mrs. Rowson image:

Who can measure all her worth, or find
A rival to her industry, or tell
What deeds her needle, pencil, or her pen
In leisure hour performed?[22]

Within just a few decades, though, even the specific location of her body was unknown. Visiting Rowson's grave on a literary figures tour of Boston would be a bit complicated. She was initially interred in the family vault of her friend and music teacher at her school, Gotlieb Graupner, under St. Matthew's Church in South Boston. When the church was torn down in 1866, her body was transferred to Mount Hope Cemetery; apparently the label had fallen away from Rowson's coffin so since the contents were unknown, she was buried in a mass grave. When descendants established a family plot with a large headstone in Forest Hill Cemetery at the turn of the twentieth century it was impossible to locate her remains.[23]

The family memorial in Forest Hill Cemetery identifies Rowson as the author of *Charlotte Temple* (as the book became known after 1797) but she could never match the popularity of her creation. Though she was largely forgotten, her book remained a best seller right into the twentieth century. By 1797 the book had gone through four printings and sold more than twenty-five thousand copies (people have recently paid thousands of dollars for some of those early books).[24] By 1812, its main publisher estimated that well over fifty thousand had been bought, making it in his estimation the best-selling work of fiction ever, and he was quickly printing three thousand more.[25] The *Columbian Centinel* agreed that *Charlotte Temple* had unrivaled success, pointing out that one bookseller in the South had reported selling thirty thousand copies just from his shop.[26] The reach of the novel cannot only be told through sales though, since many people of that time did not own books but still had access to them. People borrowed from friends and though lending libraries were not widespread yet, they did exist; one researcher has found forty that before 1830 owned copies of *Charlotte Temple*. Some libraries did not carry novels because of the lingering stigma against wasting time with something that could impair your morality, but each inventory found that included any novels at all, included Rowson's book on the list.[27] Over the next century there were more than two hundred editions printed.

Americans of nearly all kinds embraced Charlotte Temple and her story. It seemed to transcend class, gender, and even race in a surprising way. Cathy Davidson examined more than four hundred copies of *Charlotte Temple* and has created a compelling argument for the near universality of intimacy with the story. She explains that through inscriptions in the books she has found that "copies were given by mothers and fathers to their sons as well as to their daughters, by brides to their new husbands or by young men to their fiancées, by sisters to brothers and by brothers to sisters, and even by a grandmother to a grandson." In addition, Davidson found "copies owned by Northern farmers and Southern belles, by affluent readers in Eastern cities and by lonely pioneer women desiring some solace from the arduous task of settling the Western prairies." And while she speculates that most of the owners she has located were white, "there is evidence of a group of young black women in Ohio who, in the first years after Emancipation, learned from *Charlotte Temple* how to read their way to independence."[28]

What is it that drew people to this sentimental book? First of all, Rowson skillfully unfolded a tale of universal appeal. She largely rejected the epistolary style, which was common in fiction at the time and which told the story through a series of letters among the principal characters. Instead, she used a combination of narration and dialogue to more clearly and directly lay out the series of events. This allowed Rowson to tell a simple story with many side twists in a concise manner. Though the book was initially sold as two volumes, it was short in comparison to other novels of the time. In addition, Charlotte is sympathetic because she finds herself in impossible situations not completely her fault. Charlotte remains pitiable because she seems to accept responsibility for her downfall even though she knows she alone was not to blame. An early reviewer labeled Charlotte a martyr and it seems that is how many of her audience saw her as well.[29] Readers could put themselves in her circumstances easily, but then too, accept the believability of other main characters as well since nearly all share some blame for what happens to Charlotte.

And this believability is equally important to understanding the appeal since Rowson and countless others promoted the book as being based on a real case of seduction and abandonment. Rowson sold her story in London as *Charlotte: A Tale of Truth* and even after the title was changed for editions printed after 1797, her preface continued to assert that the events had occurred. There is no evidence it did happen and some inconsistencies exist that expose the story as false. The point is, however, that millions believed that Charlotte was real. Rowson continued to say up to her death that she had not imagined the story and her descendants furthered the defense. Authors such as Nason, Halsey, Dall, and Brandt perpetuated the myth in Rowson biographies or in their introductions to editions of *Charlotte Temple*.[30]

Rowson changed the names of the principal characters but people close to her revealed them to be Charlotte Stanley and Rowson's own cousin, Colonel John Montresor. Stanley, the story goes, was the daughter of a minister and a member of the family of the Earl of Derby. Montresor was an engineer in the Royal Navy and the son of Rowson's aunt (sister of her father). Many argued that these nobility and family connections necessitated use of fictional names. Supposedly in 1774, Montresor convinced Stanley to elope with him to New York, though in reality he was already in the American colonies by that time. There he abandoned her and she gave birth and died as Rowson recounted in *Charlotte Temple.* Researchers have failed to find an appropriately aged Charlotte Stanley but facts uncovered about Colonel Montresor actually make this fictional tale darker than the novel; in 1774 Montresor was not only married but thirty-eight years old, turning the story from one of young love gone bad to one of malicious seduction and abandonment.[31] It is amazing that the family did not object to the persistent rumors linking Montresor to the novel's seducer.

Readers not only believed the tale but many became true fans needing to act on their obsession with Charlotte, an obsession that did not necessarily include the author. Thus, they turned Charlotte into the celebrity and not Rowson. While an increase in the number of women becoming pregnant outside of marriage might not be proof of readers acting in sympathy with Charlotte other examples show her popularity.[32] Race horses were named for her and amateur performances of the story were performed all across the country, allowing countless young women to actually be Charlotte for a short time.[33] Some readers were moved to write odes in honor of her; predictably, not all attempts were successful. The editor of the *Wilmingtonian* advised Octavian to put more work into the next piece submitted to a newspaper. He judged the submission about Charlotte Temple "not only exceeding lame" but also lacking the "style of even ordinary poetry." Even with this harsh criticism, Octavian may have been pleased that the editor printed one stanza:

> Ah cruel man, can you indifferent view
> The spot where lies the victim you deceived,
> Tore her from parents, friends, who loved her true,
> Relentless doomed her to a clay cold grave.[34]

Others were content to keep their odes private, often writing them in their copies of the book. One preserved a poem, in an edition from 1832, vindicating Charlotte's actual purity by declaring that a "virtuous mind will bloom forever." Another reader clearly moved to expression wrote a jumbled piece in a book published in 1812 that referred to Charlotte as fair, sweet, a young lamb, misled, betrayed, and unfortunate as she "Cros'd the awful final ocean." M.W. Green emphasized his own emotional disappointments, presumably felt more acutely after reading the book, in the long piece he wrote in his 1818 copy.[35]

Readers entrusted their prized copies of *Charlotte Temple* with other examples of their private selves. They often wrote on the final page of the book, demonstrating how finishing the story was an occasion needing to be commented upon. Sally B. felt compelled to write "So true a tale" on the last page of her 1814 copy.[36] Eliza Netterville advised there "Virgins take a warning" in what one researcher has argued might be a sign of sarcasm and boredom with the morality of the book rather than a serious acknowledgment of the message.[37] Some more sincere fans added art work or hand colored the portraits of Charlotte printed in their copy. Betsey Sweet meticulously decorated and signed her knock-off 1802 edition; it was printed so carelessly that the publisher even spelled author Rowson's name wrong. Sweet prized the copy anyway, years later writing her married name among her doodles.[38]

Celebrity status, as we have seen, is not a constant but needs to be challenged and updated. Sometimes this work is not done by a publicity campaign but happens spontaneously. While Charlotte Temple remained extremely popular, her reputation was not always intact. Some, like the editor of the *New York Dispatch*, continued to believe that reading *Charlotte Temple* was appropriate, especially for what he called "rosy country lasses," because a girl that reads in between her chores "is never killed by 'sentiment.'"[39] Lydia Maria Child, one of the most prolific authors of the time, however, argued that few other books did "so much harm to girls of fourteen or fifteen." Child may have never met Susannah Rowson, but she lived in Medford, Massachusetts, as a child while Rowson operated a school there. In her *Mother's Book*, published in 1831, Child advised parents to choose novels for their children that were moral throughout instead of simply containing a moral message at the end. She nicely explained the dangers of reading *Charlotte Temple*:

> Vices the juvenile reader never heard of, are introduced, dressed up in alluring characters, which excite their admiration, their love, their deepest pity; and then they are told that these heroes and heroines were very naughty, and that in the end they were certain to die despised and neglected. What is the result? The generous bosom of youth pities the sinners, and thinks the world was a cruel world to despise and neglect them.[40]

Child well understood the appeal and the impact. Just as Child explained, fans pitied the sinning Charlotte and needed additional tangible methods to honor her memory. They sought ways to go beyond the words on the page to make a connection with her. Very specifically they needed to visit her grave and the other sites of her tortured years in

New York. Since Charlotte had not actually existed and Rowson failed to name any specific locations in the book, it seems that this would have been impossible; fans found a way. It is unclear exactly how or when, but within twenty years of the publication of the book, a grave commonly believed to be the burial site of Charlotte Stanley existed in Trinity Church Cemetery in Manhattan, New York. Conveniently, the early records of the church burned in 1776. Apparently, Charlotte's daughter Lucy spent her childhood in England and was adopted by her grandfather's wealthy friend. In 1800 she traveled to New York to see her mother's grave. Finding a small headstone there, she replaced it with a large slab that contained a silver plate inscribed "to the memory of Charlotte Stanley, aged 19." The plate had disappeared by 1850 and sometime after that, the name Charlotte Temple was etched into the slab. Whether or not Charlotte Stanley was still buried there was in question since many believed that Lucy had actually taken her mother's remains with her back to England and had left the slab to commemorate where her mother had remained for so long.[41]

Fans turned visiting this site into a pilgrimage. They treated the grave as if it held the remains of a friend or family member by leaving flowers. But they also showed their emotional affinity with Charlotte by leaving mementos of love, whether it be lost, ongoing, or aspirational. Fans left ashes of burned love letters, locks of hair, and other intimate objects. Apparently the most commonly left items, however, were tears. Witnesses, who observed the grave over the years in the nineteenth century, commented on how frequently visitors publicly cried at the site for the young girl robbed of her life by love, ignoring monuments to notables such as Alexander Hamilton.[42]

Visiting the grave was free but many tried to make money from the celebrity of Charlotte. Authors wishing to cash in on the enthusiasm simply added references to her in their work. P.D. Manvill, in her 1807 book *Lucinda; or the Mountain Mourner*, which was actually based on fact, used *Charlotte Temple* as the example of a story that might distract girls from their own problems.[43] Thomas Man included Charlotte Temple among the famous figures mentioned in his "To the Ghosts of Dead Renown"; he also honors the "wife of General Washington" but not Susanna Rowson or Phillis Wheatley.[44] Authors also published stage versions of the story. Most famously, P.T. Barnum's American Museum in New York performed the "pathetic story of 'Charlotte Temple'" in the 1850s. The great showman seemed to enjoy the affect that the play had on audience members such as one elderly woman from Portland, Maine, who even though she was "quite familiar with the sad history of Miss Temple" still cried.[45] Some suspect that it was Barnum who had the name Charlotte Temple etched into the slab in Trinity Church Cemetery, which was only six blocks from his theater, as a publicity stunt.[46]

Even more interesting examples of the commodification of the celebrity of Charlotte Temple are the life-sized displays. Fans of early America flocked to museums, taverns, and gardens to see up close wax figures of their favorite celebrities, nearly all actual people, for about twenty-five cents (children for half price). Daniel Bowen included Charlotte Temple among the early figures on display first in New York, then Boston, and eventually on tour through the country in 1818 and 1819. Fans visited the Uniontown Museum in Pennsylvania, the Market House in Columbus, Ohio, the Illinois Hotel in St. Louis, Missouri, or Mrs. McCammant's Inn at Washington, Pennsylvania, to both shed a tear with Charlotte and hiss at Montraville for abandoning her. In 1822 customers at Letton's Museum in Cincinnati, Ohio, witnessed a more hopeful scene as these two characters from the book were joined by Charlotte's father holding his newborn grandchild. Joseph Dorfeuille and his Western Museum, Letton's competitor in town, displayed both Elizabeth Patterson Bonaparte and Charlotte Temple, this time sitting with her baby in her lap and a letter in her hand. Samuel Hadley remembered that as a boy (in about 1840) he was able to, for free, get a "good long peep" at Charlotte Temple as she arrived in Lowell, Massachusetts, by canal boat for display at Wyman's Exchange.[47]

Temple and Bonaparte wax figures may have shared exhibit space as early as 1805 but the advertisement for that display in Washington, D.C., is unclear. Moulthrop and Bishop announced showing a collection that included, in addition to the many political figures, "The Zealous Father frowning upon the wantonness of his daughter with her gallant"—which could be Charlotte Temple, her father, and Montraville—and "The Beauty of America, represented as being far superior to any physiognomy ever exhibited."[48] This was without a doubt, Bonaparte because her marriage to Napoleon's brother Jerome in 1803 had not only made her a celebrity but had consolidated recognition of her as the most beautiful woman in the country.

Bonaparte's life could have been a tale straight out of a sentimental novel, except that she unlike the easily-led Charlotte had a will of iron. She met a handsome uniformed seducer (he was suspected of having ruined many women already by the time he was nineteen) and was abandoned with child. Bonaparte obtained a marriage certificate unlike the characters in the novels that she read when young. She also acquired written assurance of the right to one third of her new husband's assets and to an equal share of the inheritance of her disapproving father's vast holdings. Bonaparte knew the story of Charlotte Temple and loved romantic English poetry, though she was also inclined to read the Greek epics of Homer and feminist writings of Mary Wollstonecraft.[49] Temple's fate would not be the fate of this smart, ambitious, beautiful young woman. She did not know, however, how fragile promises could be even when they were in writing and widely known.

Bonaparte's wedding and honeymoon propelled her into the limelight but she seized celebrity with her beauty and style. By all accounts Bonaparte was incomparably gorgeous. Her beauty was classical as many noted her Roman nose, small mouth, large dark eyes, and statue-like rounded shoulders. Famous artist Gilbert Stuart painted a triple portrait of her (profile, straight on, and slightly turned with a faint smile), as if he was doing a study of beauty itself, and people flocked to his studio to see it.[50] Wealthy merchant Thomas Law called it a "new captivating trinity."[51] Bonaparte also carefully crafted a style sure to maintain her celebrity. The dress she wore for her Christmas Eve wedding was typical of the type of French gown she would popularize in the United States to the shock of many Americans. The scandal came not from its low neck line; ladies of the period confidently exposed ample cleavage (Lady Washington had been portrayed that way in her Revolutionary War portrait). Rather, Bonaparte's wedding gown was high-waisted and cut fairly close to her body (reminiscent of classical dress and what has become known as empire style). It was made of thin muslin material. Wearing few undergarments with this dress allowed Bonaparte to show off her physique much more clearly than if she was wearing a gown of a heavier material. When she walked, one could discern the outline and some said even the color of her thighs, and when she laughed, the movement of a breast would be easily observed if one watched.[52]

And many watched as closely as they dared and imitated her if they could. The honeymooners traveled from Baltimore to Niagara Falls, and then back south to Washington, D.C., where many held parties in their honor. Gawkers waited for her to arrive and then watched through the windows when they could. Grown men stared at her breasts but most attendees seemed too shy to look at her except when they felt she would not notice. Some daring women in Washington, most notably the Caton sisters, also began wearing French fashions (and eventually marrying aristocrats from Europe as well). Within a decade, her style was widely imitated but with limited success. Sarah Seaton confided to her diary in 1813: "Madame Bonaparte is a model of fashion, and many of our belles strive to imitate her" but they cannot match her since she possessed the "most transcendently beautiful back and shoulders that ever were seen."[53]

Many expressed their views on Bonaparte openly. The *American*

Elizabeth Patterson Bonaparte (1785–1879). Thomas Sully used watercolor on ivory to create this miniature copy of the triple portrait by Stuart Gilbert. Sully painted it sometime between 1805 and 1810 (Metropolitan Museum of Art, Purchase, Dodge Fund and funds from various donors, 2000).

published a piece addressed to Bonaparte that praised her for her "charms which deck thy form" and "the graces of thy soul."[54] Aaron Burr, vice president of the United States, reported to his daughter Theodosia that Bonaparte was a "charming little woman," who dressed with "taste and simplicity," and who had "sense, and spirit, and sprightliness."[55] Louisa Catherine Adams wrote to her mother-in-law and former first lady Abigail Adams that of course everyone knew that Bonaparte was the most beautiful woman in America.[56] Others criticized. Writer Margaret Bayard Smith admitted to her sister in New Jersey that everyone agreed that Bonaparte was very beautiful but that she feared she had "made a great noise" in Washington. She described the dress she wore to one event in detail and declared her "almost naked." Smith delighted in reporting that some women (including the newlywed's aunt) had told Bonaparte that if she wanted to be invited to the next gathering she "must promise to have more clothes on."[57]

Some of the gossip became malicious. The *American* piece

addressed to Bonaparte linked her to what the author called a "despotic empire reign."[58] A poem that circulated privately in Washington in 1804 labeled Bonaparte a "concubine" and worse. It read in part:

> Well! What of Madame Bonaparte
> Why she's a little whore at heart
> Her lustful looks her wanton air
> Her limbs revealed her bosom bare.[59]

Bonaparte cared little for public approval and continued wearing her beloved dresses. She remained a sought-after guest for parties because she was good company, her family was one of the wealthiest in the country, and even though she dressed in a daring way, she was never suspected of truly scandalous behavior such as an affair.[60] She worried though about condemnation from family members. Her in-laws the Bonapartes never accepted her. Napoleon refused to acknowledge the marriage, ordered his brother back to France where he would have an annulment, and banned Elizabeth Patterson Bonaparte from his empire. When the couple, plus a baby on the way, parted in Lisbon, Portugal, it was effectively the end of their marriage. Bonaparte gave birth to a boy at a house outside of London. Although he continued to pledge his love and loyalty to his first wife, in 1807 Jerome Bonaparte remarried and became King of Westphalia (a country created for him by Napoleon out of parts of Germany). Bonaparte's father betrayed her also. He disapproved of the wedding, expected her to remarry when it did not stick, and when he died in 1835 bequeathed her very little though he had agreed to her having an equal share with her siblings. He also made sure the snub was public by declaring that the will be printed in the newspapers. She wanted the money since what she obtained from her in-laws was not enough to sustain her (and ceased after the defeat of Napoleon in 1815) even though she possessed excellent money management skills. She was equally upset by her father's reasons for reducing her share, which were also printed in the newspapers. He called her disobedient and argued that her "folly and misconduct" had not only caused him "more anxiety and trouble" than all of his other thirteen children combined, but had cost him money so it would not be "reasonable, just, and proper" for her to have an equal share.[61] While everyone, even close friends, thought Bonaparte must be the happiest woman in the world, being so admired and sought after, she suffered because of these betrayals and the failed relationships they represented.[62]

After the annulment of her marriage, Bonaparte looked to Napoleon—to the annoyance of many Americans—to ensure the future of her and her son. American newspapers ridiculed and criticized Napoleon for his treatment of a woman of "superior rank and virtue."[63] Bonaparte wrote to the emperor and French government officials anyway to enter into negotiations. In the meantime, she dressed the part of an aristocrat, even wearing a tiara, and openly supported the emperor's efforts. Bonaparte carefully avoided scandal but spent much time with two prominent Englishmen who were both interested in marrying her; Napoleon hated the prospect of a Bonaparte being raised by an English stepfather at a time of hostility between France and Great Britain. Americans were intrigued but a little nervous to learn that she had won a stipend from France and might even become a duchess and her son a prince! Newspapers across the country warned that the Bonapartes intended to rule over the United States.[64] Members of Congress were alarmed enough that they passed an amendment to the United States Constitution in 1810 stripping citizenship from any American receiving titles or payments from a foreign government; not enough states ratified the proposal so it failed but many felt Bonaparte's behavior threatened American democracy. In the end, she received money but refused to take a title, largely because the agreement proposed would have required her giving up control over her son.[65]

Through all the turmoil, the love notes continued. Suitors poured their admiration and desires onto the page and often slipped the poems, signed or unsigned, under her hotel room door. They cared not whether Bonaparte was married; they could not help expressing their intense feelings. Men often used references to nature to describe her charms; they called her a "blushing Rose" or a "little tender flower."[66] A British baronet wrote that her "eyes with moon beam softness shine."[67] One described her "swan like neck, with perfect curve" and her "lips of ruby, graced with pearl," which no artist could ever reproduce. This poet, using the initials ECH, admitted not being able to believe what he saw. He wrote:

> Thy beauties, in perfections mould,
> This passing thought, above conception,
> I gazed with wonder and delight
> In doubt if mortal, or deception.[68]

The admirers praised her for more than simply her beauty. They often also appreciated her wit and her intellect. Patterson was well-read and a great conversationalist. Suitors such as a Nicholas Nemo argued she had honed skills, with the help of the Goddess of Wisdom Minerva, to control the men around her attracted to "her person, her manner, her wit." Maybe Nemo had witnessed Bonaparte put a forward companion in his place or had himself felt the sting of a comment. He certainly did not seem to admire her any less for having used her spear and even underlined the word for emphasis. He wrote,

> To guard such bright charms,
> Both by council and arms;
> <u>Minerva</u> affords her assistance.
> And bid her appear,
> With a terrible <u>Spear</u>
> That may keep hosts of Beaux at a distance.[69]

One early lover felt so hopeless after realizing he could not be with her that he did not think he could go on living. He believed he was not attractive enough for Bonaparte, otherwise he would have tried to win her. He wrote in 1802, even before she had met Jerome, "And shall then another possess thee my fair. Must envy still add to the pang of despair. Shall I live to behold the reciprocal bliss. Death, Death is a refuge, Elysium to this." He concluded with the fear that imagining Bonaparte with a lover would make him insane: "Relieve me oh! death shut the scene from my view, And save me oh! save me e'er madness ensue."[70]

Bonaparte clearly nurtured her celebrity in the early years, but in many ways it took on a life of its own in more than just love notes and wax figures traveling through the country. Gossip and speculation about whether or not she would be granted a French title, if her son would be recognized as an heir, and who, among her many admirers, she would marry (she obtained a divorce in 1813) spread on their own. Newspapers across the country retold the fairy tale romance story and sad ending every time there was a development in her life, nurturing both admiration and pity. With Napoleon's final abdication and capture in 1815, Bonaparte was able to travel in Europe and there she carefully crafted her persona to include an intellectual side so she could be invited to the great salons. She was so famous there that at least one impostor emerged to try to take financial advantage of her name and artists sold paintings and engravings of her face.[71] Bonaparte stayed in Europe as much as she could afford over the next twenty years, educated her son there, and even briefly encountered her ex-husband, who was now an ex-king, in Florence, Italy. When her in-laws resumed power in France in the 1850s, they invited Bonaparte's son to join them in Paris and her grandson rose to the rank of colonel in the French Army. When her ex-husband died in 1860, he made no mention of his first family in his will but Bonaparte tried to claim inheritance rights for her son. There was little money at stake since Jerome had always spent beyond his means. Because the in-laws were again ruling France, being declared legitimate would give Bonaparte's son a place in the line of succession.[72]

Newspapers and magazines in the United States eagerly followed her progress in Europe but truly leapt into action to cover the succession story up through the court ruling that the marriage had not been legal. Much had changed in journalism since the early mostly impersonal reports on Bonaparte's wedding. Americans experienced an explosion of celebrity in the 1850s. Bonaparte could not avoid the increasingly personal coverage and the need of the public for more intimacy with their celebrities. Bonaparte weathered the storm extremely well, partly because it was obvious she was not seeking popularity anymore. While even very sincere stars of this later period were accused of crass publicity and being overblown with the label of humbug, Bonaparte remained respected. *Harper's Weekly* for instance criticized the men in her life but not her. It blamed Bonaparte's father for not understanding French law about the age of consent and failing to receive permission from Napoleon for the marriage: "No careful father would allow his daughter to marry a foreigner and a minor without some evidence of the willingness of his parents." It also labeled Jerome Bonaparte a "man of feeble will, and not brilliant intellect" who acted as a coward by deserting her. But it declared that Bonaparte herself was "universally beloved and respected."[73]

What is very surprising is that no author grabbed the opportunity to produce a fictionalized version of her fairy tale in either novel or play form during the nineteenth century. Rida Johnson Young wrote possibly the earliest depiction with her 1908 play *Glorious Betsy*. Many though retold Bonaparte's story as an example of exactly what not to do. Newspaper editors and authors used her circumstances to point out the dangers of specifically placing their faith and reputations in the hands of foreign suitors, especially those from France.[74]

Even without novels or plays about her, Bonaparte remained a celebrity until her death though she did little to nurture that status as she aged. She stopped attending social events and while she continued to wear European fashions she no longer wore revealing dresses. As they had to Martha Washington, strangers wrote to her asking for money; Bonaparte was by her last decade a millionaire.[75] Some wrote claiming a family connection and others simply hoped for sympathy. One woman requested Bonaparte tell her how she was able to stay looking so young so that she could develop a method for selling the secrets. Fans wanted an autograph or photograph. And of course, men wanted to marry her.[76] A collection of her letters was published in 1873. Articles in the major magazines of the day but also small random notices kept her name before the public in her last decade. Far from her home in Baltimore, a newspaper in Montana reported in 1876 that she was ill but did not explain who she was since it asserted that "the history of this remarkable lady is familiar to the country." It did, however, seem to promise that the world would learn a lot more about Bonaparte after she died since her autobiography would be published then.[77] Less than a year before she did die, a newspaper in the Nevada Territory reported that her "ninety-three years are easily worn. She is said to collect her own rents, and is a very shrewd woman of business."[78]

While she was still alive, the boardinghouse where she lived (on Cathedral Street in Baltimore) became a tourist attraction. She enjoyed the attention of these fans some days and turned them away on others with the order "Tell them today is not Show Day!"[79] By the 1870s celebrity tourism was widespread. Fans of Charlotte Temple could now not only visit her grave, but buy a pint of beer at the Old Tree House, which was believed to be the remnant of the building where Charlotte Temple died. When the Walton House burned in 1853, fans traveled to see the site one last time since they believed this had been the home of a rich woman who had turned Charlotte away before she died. Bonaparte's rooms in Baltimore did not maintain any status as being important after her death. Remarkably, a fictional character had an enduring celebrity that real life amazing women could not muster. This is another fascinating and unexplainable element of celebrity in early United States history.

Select Bibliography

Berkin, Carol. *Wondrous Beauty: the Life and Adventures of Elizabeth Patterson Bonaparte.* New York: Alfred A. Knopf, 2014.

Burn, Helen Jean. *Betsy Bonaparte.* Baltimore: Maryland Historical Society, 2010.

Davidson, Cathy. *Revolution and the Word.* New York: Oxford University Press, 2004.

Davidson, Cathy, ed. *Charlotte Temple.* New York: Oxford University Press, 1986.

Homestead, Melissa, and Camryn Hansen. "Susanna Rowson's Transatlantic Career." *Early American Literature.* 45 (2010): 619–654.

Lewis, Charlene M. Boyer. *Elizabeth Patterson Bonaparte: An American Aristocrat in the Early Republic.* Philadelphia: University of Pennsylvania Press, 2012.

Rust, Marion. *Prodigal Daughters: Susanna Rowson's Early American Women.* Chapel Hill: University of North Carolina Press, 2008.

Rust, Marion, ed. *Charlotte Temple: A Norton Critical Edition.* New York: W.W. Norton, 2011.

Vail, R.W.G. *Susanna Haswell Rowson, the Author of Charlotte Temple, a Bibliographic Study.* Worcester: American Antiquarian Society, 1933.

THREE
◇◇◇◇◇◇◇◇◇◇◇◇◇

Lydia Maria Child and Frances Wright
Voices of Conscience

In the 1820s and 1830s, Frances Wright and Lydia Maria Child captivated Americans with messages of equality and social justice. This is amazing since Americans of the time, female and male, largely believed that women had no role in politics or issues of public policy. One foreign traveler observed that in the United States women were "guarded by a seven-fold shield of habitual insignificance."[1] The two crusaders pursued celebrity to break through and be heard. They believed in many of the same causes but presented their ideas and tried to persuade their audiences very differently. Wright cared little for subtlety and prompted intense reaction. Child tread lightly until she was compelled by her conscience to speak more plainly. The two women won admirers but possibly an equal number of Americans denounced them. Child and Wright did not back down and promoted equality as long as they were in the public eye.

Lydia Maria Child decided early that she was going to change the world with her writings. As she wrote to a friend, "Who can calculate how far the influence of a single story may spread throughout the community."[2] She was going to use her skills to create empathy for the underdogs in American society. Child published her first book anonymously in 1824 but sales were slow. Her story *Hobomok* about Native Americans of colonial Massachusetts received mediocre reviews but Child changed that. She heard from a friend that an influential Harvard scholar liked the book. As Phillis Wheatley had done to influential people of her time, Child wrote to the professor, George Ticknor, both flattering him and asking for his help. He arranged for a more positive notice about *Hobomok* to appear and invited the young author

42

into his Boston social circle, shattering her anonymity by making her a celebrity.[3]

Being a single woman without much money, Child needed to publish her way to financial independence. She quickly tired of being a curiosity at lavish parties in Boston. Now that many knew her name, she hoped to be able to sell additional books to support herself. She wrote to her sister that she was "American enough to prefer money to fame."[4] "Whoever seeks fame rolls the stone of Sisyphus," she wrote later, referring to the Greek king of mythology condemned for eternity to push a stone uphill, never quite reaching the top before it rolled back down.[5] She needed a reputation to be able to sell her work, but clearly she felt it folly to seek fame for its own sake. Her second novel, *The Rebels, or Boston before the Revolution*, sold well even though critics dismissed it as much inferior to her debut work. As she later put it in an essay, authors like her "hunt for pearls because we have promised to furnish them, and string glass beads because they will sell better than diamonds."[6] Child realized that writing specifically for women and their children was much more lucrative so she wrote many glass beads: biographies of prominent women; *The Frugal Housewife*; *The Mother's Book*; and a book for children, *Evenings in New England,* all with this in mind. When she was offered a job editing a new magazine for children in 1826, it was a perfect fit. The position on the *Juvenile Miscellany* proved to nicely combine her two aims: she earned a good salary while publishing stories of compassion for children (among the poems, puzzles, and other content). She edited the magazine for eight years.[7]

It is difficult to believe just how famous Child was at that time since she is little known today. Her steady output ensured her continued celebrity even though she had explained to her sister that she was writing for money and not fame. The *North American Review* declared that "few female writers, if any, [had] done more or better things for our literature, in its lighter or graver departments" and called her a genius at writing for children.[8] *The Frugal Housewife* immediately became the standard cookbook in America, more than six thousand copies were bought in its first year, and was reprinted thirty-five times before 1850.[9] Sarah Hale, editor of the widely circulated *Ladies' Magazine* (later known as *Godey's Lady's Book*), advised that all families subscribe to the *Juvenile Miscellany* since even adults would prefer it to more than half of the other publications available.[10] Other famous people praised her and longed for her company, including poets Ralph Waldo Emerson and Frances Osgood. When Revolutionary War hero Marquise de Lafayette visited Boston in 1825, the governor of Massachusetts invited Child to meet him; she enjoyed the thrill of a lifetime when the old general kissed her hand. The all-male members of the Boston Athenaeum even allowed her to use their library. She was only the second woman thusly honored.[11]

Unlike the women we have already considered, Child did not seem to foster a public persona except for her initial period of fame in Boston. When one of her suitors, Francis Alexander, painted a flattering portrait of her in 1826, she declared that Alexander had portrayed her public persona and not her true self. Child wrote that the subject of the painting held "a glow and enthusiasm about it which belongs to the author of 'Hobomok'" but not to her.[12] Soon it became clear to her that "the smiles of the public no longer have power to kindle us into enthusiastic energy."[13] And by 1833 she felt that in a few years the "opinion of the world" would no longer interest her.[14] By then, she endeavored to be authentic at all times and to let her writing take center stage.

Her fans found ways to focus on her anyway. They gave her books, pictures, jewelry, and expensive dresses. One fan sent her a comb from India, which the author had included in her description of the attire of a character in her novel *The Rebels*.[15] They sent her "admiring letters from all parts of the country."[16] She puzzled over autograph seekers and found it "amusing that *strangers* should lay by a fragment of [her] hand-writing as a choice relic."[17] Children gave her flowers and some remembered decades later how they and all of their young neighbors had waited on their front stoops for the mail carrier to deliver their copy of the *Juvenile Miscellany*.[18]

In 1833, however, everything changed. Child published *An Appeal in Favor of that Class of Americans Called Africans*. She argued that it was her duty to speak out against slavery even though she realized she would displease many with her vocal abolitionism. Child felt that "worldly considerations should never stifle the voice of conscience." She wrote in the preface that if the book was the "means of advancing, even one single hour, the inevitable progress of truth and justice" she would not have restrained from publishing it for any amount of wealth or fame.[19] It was not her first antislavery or racial equality publication. She had been writing sympathetically about enslaved people and Native Americans her whole career; in 1829 early abolitionist William Lloyd Garrison had labeled her First Woman in the Republic because of the sense of social justice in her writing and editing.[20] Mostly though, she addressed race in fiction. *An Appeal* was different. It was a straight forward persuasive argument for emancipation and the acceptance of blacks in society on an equal basis with whites; of course in the chapter where she provided examples of extraordinary blacks she told Phillis Wheatley's story.

Child's fans, reviewers, family, and friends were shocked and the affect was immediate in the North, where slavery was illegal but which lacked any strong emancipation consensus, as well as in the South where slavery was growing. People stopped buying her books and cancelled their subscriptions to the *Juvenile Miscellany*, though Child had not published the antislavery pamphlet in the magazine. She even lost some of her young fans. One boy, knowing his parents disliked *An Appeal*, nearly threw a rock at a copy on display in a shop window. Child resigned as editor of the *Juvenile Miscellany* and the once extremely popular magazine ceased publication. In addition, the members of the Boston Athenaeum rescinded her library privileges, making it harder for her to do research for her books. She married in 1828 but her husband was not an effective wage-earner; the "worldly considerations" Child experienced were quite severe. She assumed her reputation would suffer, but she was shocked by how completely *An Appeal* affected the sales of the rest of her collection of works. She depended on royalty payments to keep her household solvent since her husband was not fiscally responsible.[21]

In addition to impoverishing Child, *An Appeal* brought scathing attacks. Many northerners were outraged because she used examples of racism in the North and exposed colonizing American blacks to Africa as impractical. Connecticut Minister Leonard Bacon, for example, published a ten-page

Lydia Maria Child (1802–1880). John A. Whipple of Boston printed this photograph card in about 1865. Emily Howland included it in her Civil War era album of photographs of both friends and famous people (Library of Congress, LC-DIG-ppmsca-54178).

response in the *Quarterly Christian Spectator* that defended colonization efforts and accused Child of assigning her own racist views to others. He wrote that as "unpleasant as it is to contradict a lady," she was
just wrong in believing that there was widespread racism against blacks
in New England. He explained that he had never witnessed any actions
like the ones she described and if they had occurred they were no doubt
prompted by a backlash against abolitionist efforts such as Child herself engaged in. It was fine, he continued, if she wanted to admit her own
racism but she should not accuse the rest of New England of feeling or
acting the same way. He concluded by justifying his harsh words and
tone against her; if she was going to act like a man, he would criticize her
as if she were a man. He wrote that

> in the dusty arena of controversy, sex has no privilege. If Pallas in her armor rushes
> in where blows are given and received, to strike with the foremost, what does she
> expect, but that her sex and her divinity will be forgotten? The privilege of woman
> is, to stand aloof from such conflicts. If she goes into the battle, as doubtless she
> may, if she chooses, then she goes to quit herself like a man, and like a man, to sub-
> mit to the chances and the laws of war.[22]

Other religious leaders criticized Child for crossing the line that
separated men's and women's spheres; writing sympathetic stories about
enslaved people was proper but she went too far when she forcefully
provided her opinions on matters of law and governance.[23] Secular editors also used this argument against Child. The *North American Review*,
which had praised Child in a lengthy article just before *An Appeal* was
published, similarly criticized her for straying from her "legitimate
spheres of action" of producing "agreeable" and "useful" work. They
accused her of even trying to spark conflict since she was advocating
freeing the slaves, "a cause so dangerous to the Union, domestic peace,
and civil liberty."[24]

While Child alienated many who had adored her, she also acquired a
new found influence. The abolitionist newspaper the *Liberator* declared
that only a person with a heart "harder than the nether mill-stone" could
resist being persuaded by her work.[25] Two prominent abolitionists cred-
ited Child and *An Appeal* with having converted them to the antislavery cause: United States Senator Charles Sumner and reformer Wendell
Phillips. Since her book sold well, it is safe to assume that many more,
maybe even thousands, were also convinced by her arguments; possibly
more were convinced by this book to oppose slavery than by any other
piece of writing until Harriet Beecher Stowe published *Uncle Tom's
Cabin* in 1852. The abolitionist newspaper the *Liberator* printed some
of these conversion stories. A key supporter of colonization reported

that Child had turned his wife and daughter against his cause. He admitted her power when he refused to even read *An Appeal*. He justified his decision by saying that he did "not mean to be an abolitionist." Child even reached some southerners though the book was not widely available in their region. One woman on vacation in the North from her plantation home could not stop reading *An Appeal* once she started and afterwards pledged to free her slaves when she returned home.[26]

Scottish born Frances Wright, commonly known as Fanny, despised slavery as much as did Child but like her also waited to make her abolitionism known. She published a complimentary, sometimes effusive, book about America based on a tour of the country. Wright wrote *Views of Society and Manners in America*, virtually ignoring slavery in the book, to shame England for its lack of progress in republican government. This book made her quite famous in the United States. Americans loved the adoration but some felt that it was an exaggeration. Author James Fenimore Cooper reportedly called the book "nauseous flattery."[27] Wright, like Child, was concerned for the underdogs of society and made reform her life's work. Wright continued to publish and returned to America to travel with her friend Marquise de Lafayette in 1824. During her second trip, Wright decided to shift her attention and make the United States the focus of her reform efforts and not the example. Apparently America was not as republican as she had initially thought and hoped. Slavery of course was proof but also witnessing Lafayette being treated like royalty (his presence brought grown men to tears and people sported socks, gloves, hats, handkerchiefs, and belts with his likeness) showed that America too had room for improvement in terms of equality.[28]

Wright became a bit notorious early in the trip. One Philadelphian reported that she behaved poorly at a social event there, stretching out on the sofa and only speaking to proclaim odd thoughts such as "I believe that bears have more value than men."[29] It is doubtful that Wright actually did or said this and the claim was probably part of a smear campaign. Something, however, happened in the city to turn society and specifically the social queen of Philadelphia Eleanor Parke Custis Lewis, granddaughter of Martha Washington, against Wright. Lafayette's whole entourage worked to minimize Wright's presence on the tour after the visit to Philadelphia. Wright may have been shunned because she entertained a black dignitary from Haiti, Jonathan Granville.[30] Or, possibly reports of Wright pressuring Lafayette to either marry or adopt her fueled rumors of an affair between the thirty-year-old author and the nearly seventy-year-old general. The *United States Gazette* of Philadelphia characterized the whole tour as one in which Wright chased after Lafayette as he moved around the country.[31] When a German prince traced the path of the Lafayette tour a year after, he found that people still talked about how Wright had "tagged about after General La Fayette." He reported aspersions based on her lack of chaperones and her "masculine manners." Even the reputation of her book had suffered, especially in areas where political sentiment leaned towards traditionalism.[32]

Still, many famous Americans invited Wright, with or without Lafayette, into their homes because she was prominent and intriguing. Fans in some cities, particularly in the South, treated her as a celebrity. Wright stayed at Monticello and talked with Thomas Jefferson about slavery and other topics. The former president possessed a favorable opinion of the author since he had received a copy of Wright's book *A Few Days in Athens* from Lafayette. Jefferson copied out seven pages of quotes from it and praised the novel, which Wright used to explain her belief in the materialism philosophy of Epicureanism. Wright also stayed with James and Dolley Madison at Montpelier. In Washington, D.C., she gave readings from a play she had written and was a favorite among the Congressmen, who showered her with attention when she attended House of Representatives debates. In New Orleans, where her book on America was still highly regarded, the governor of Louisiana treated her to a personal military display and introduced her to thirty dashing officers. Newspapers of the south praised her talents and reported on her social movements.[33]

After Lafayette returned to France, Wright and her sister remained in the United States to commence their reforms. Endowed with

Frances Wright (1795–1852). Elizabeth Cady Stanton included this engraving of Wright in the first volume of *History of Woman Suffrage* (Library of Congress, LC-USZ62–39344).

family money, Wright funded an experiment in slave emancipation. She created the colony of Nashoba, located near Memphis, Tennessee. She bought thirty enslaved people and intended to both transition them to freedom as well as allow them to repay their purchase amount with five years' worth of work in the community. She hoped the experiment would serve as a viable method for ending slavery. Wright, however, also incorporated into the plan her other social reform ideas. She believed in racial and gender equality and felt that organized religion, social norms, and marriage laws of the 1820s hindered these goals. In 1827 Wright defended the colony when newspapers reported that an unmarried mixed-race couple was living together at Nashoba; her notoriety grew. She became coeditor of the *Free Enquirer* and began lecturing to spread her ideas about equality. Supporters, critics, and the simply curious crowded into halls to hear her speak and for two years at the end of the 1820s, no woman in America was more famous than was she. Wright sold out her lectures night after night, with still thousands being turned away.[34]

Wright exposed herself and her ideas to audiences in a way that was uncommon for women at the time. She used the same rational logic perceived to be the sphere of men that Child used but she went further by doing it in person and not on the printed page. Author Susannah Rowson recited lines on stage (such as her epilogue for her play *Slaves in Algiers*) and later in Boston her students read aloud lectures she had written. Graduates at other schools gave commencement speeches. In 1787, student Miss Mason both exercised and defended logically her right to speak in public with her salutatorian address at the Philadelphia Female Academy graduation ceremony. In 1819 Troy Female Seminary founder Emma Willard appeared in front of the New York State Legislature to request endowment of her school.[35]

Deborah Sampson Gannett, however, provided the best precedent for Wright. Gannett completed a lecture tour in 1802, being one of the few women to pave the way for Wright. She fought in the American Revolution, disguised as a man, and worked to obtain the pension due her for her service. She was already a bit of a celebrity, having been featured in the *American Museum* magazine in 1792 and in a biography of 1797. Gannett spoke in at least twenty towns. She convinced crowds of the truth of her story with words but also by demonstrating military skills. She first spoke to the audience dressed as a woman and then reappeared on stage in uniform. She demonstrated military maneuvers with Old Betsey, her army musket. One audience member thought she had gone through the routine "briskly and with perfection and she brought the musket butt smartly down to the floor with a Thud." The crowd broke into patriot songs when she was through. Large audiences attended her talks and some of her admirers, including Paul Revere, sent letters to Congress on her behalf. Congress awarded her thirty-four pounds in 1792 but a full monthly pension in 1802 after her lecture tour.[36]

Wright possessed equal skill as a performer. A British woman who was traveling in America attended Wright's lecture in Cincinnati, Ohio, and could not believe how effective she was as a speaker. Frances Trollope marveled at "the splendor, the brilliance, the overwhelming eloquence of this extraordinary orator." She wrote later that Wright's speaking style, her message, and her striking appearance "contributed to produce an effect, unlike any thing I had ever seen before, or ever expect to see again." Trollope felt that a woman lecturing in the United States was even more unexpected than in other parts of the world because in America "women are guarded by a seven-fold shield of habitual insignificance."[37]

Wright's convictions, intellect, and communication skills allowed her to break out of insignificance and brought her continued praise from many. Poet Walt Whitman admired her and borrowed from her writings. He read his father's copy of her newspaper and as a child attended one of her lectures. He loved her book *A Few Days in Athens* and told a friend it had been "daily food."[38] Mary Shelley, the British author of *Frankenstein*, adored her and reportedly always carried a lock of her hair.[39] The *Cincinnati Daily Gazette* expressed support for her gender equality cause, lamenting that such a talented woman would be expected to be merely "an ornament to society as a wife and a mother."[40] Geologist Henry Darwin Rogers attended all five of her lectures in Baltimore and reported to his brother that she awed the city with "matchless eloquence." He found her "a prodigy in learning, in intellect and in courage."[41] She stayed in the homes of important people and walked onto the stage flanked by well-connected community women everywhere she lectured. Fans mobbed her and subscribed to her newspaper after her lectures. Admirers gave her money and she usually deposited it with the community to be used for the creation of what she called a Hall of Science where issues could be rationally discussed. Attendees at Thomas Paine birthday celebrations often toasted her and her work.[42]

Many Americans, however, disliked her message. Surprisingly though, it was not her antislavery work or declarations of the equality of all men and women that engendered the most hostility. Americans felt most threatened by a woman's criticisms of religion, particularly at a time of a growing religious revival movement. Wright believed that organized religion enforced gender and racial inequalities and challenged the assumption that the founding fathers were devout. British author Frances Trollope heard Wright speak again in 1830, this time in Philadelphia. She noted that the audience hissed when Wright, using Thomas Jefferson as her source, declared that George Washington was not a Christian. Trollope sided with the crowd and even quoted a passage about the importance of religion from Washington's farewell address.[43] James Akin captured this animosity toward Wright on religious issues by depicting many Christian elements in a caricature of Wright that was published at the time. Akin drew Wright in a black dress with a long flowing white scarf standing behind a table that holds two lit candles and books. An attendant stands off to the side and the scene resembles a preacher going through a ritual ceremony. Except of course that Akin has drawn Wright with a goose head. He labeled his picture "A DOWNWRIGHT GABBLER, or a goose that deserves to be hissed." Not only did Americans feel Wright criticized religion, but her appearances were mocking religious sentiment in the United States.

A DOWNWRIGHT GABBLER,
or a goose that deserves to be hissed _

Frances Wright (1795–1852) caricature. James Akin published "A Downwright Gabbler, or a goose that deserves to be hissed" in 1829 to criticize Wright's lectures (Library of Congress, LC-USZC2-599).

Ada composed a poem that was published in the *Free Enquirer* in February of 1829 that both praised Wright and lamented the overreaction of people like cartoonist Akin. She titled her composition "The Panic" and nicely captured what many women surely sensed: during the lives of their grandmothers, smart women were respected but now they were feared. All it took was the emergence of a free thinking intellectual female celebrity to expose it all:

> What a panic has seized all the men!
> How scared, that we women should know
> Something more about handling a pen,
> That our grandams, some ages ago!
> They say that we authors are turning;
> (Alas! How they grieve at the times!)
> And our knowledge of housewifery spurning,
> To eke out a few paltry rhymes.
> The dear fellows have taken a fright;
> And forsooth not without a good cause;
> For the lectures of Miss Frances Wright
> Are received with unbounded applause.
> What a fuss among bigots and priests,
> What a running and groaning and praying,
> And proclaiming of fasts and of feasts,
> To disprove all that Fanny is saying.
> She tells us we women possess
> An intellect equal with them;
> But this the poor souls won't confess
> And that part of her doctrine condemn.[44]

Americans tried various ways to silence Wright and eliminate this threat to religion and to gender norms. One friend from New Orleans ominously overheard a man musing that someone might cut Wright's throat. Owners of theaters and halls refused to rent space to her and sometimes caved to public pressure by cancelling her engagements after initially allowing her to book a speech. When the gas was turned off in one hall the lights went out leaving the audience in the dark until candles were lit. A barrel of fuel was set ablaze in the entrance of the same hall on a different night. A false cry of "Fire!" caused panic in a separate incident but Wright was able to calm the crowd of two thousand. Ministers urged their congregations to stay away from her events. Oliver Oldschool, writing to the *Cincinnati Evening Chronicle*, proposed the most widely supported method for silencing her: what she needed was to get married and start a family. Newspapers refused to run ads for her lectures and would not print letters from her supporters. Merchants in Boston signed a petition urging the newspapers to give her no press, but editors knew that stories about her sold papers and wrote about her anyway.[45]

While some Americans may have been shocked by her anti-religion message, newspaper editors pointed out that many men had argued similarly; the editors took issue with the fact that she was a woman speaking about matters and in a method not suitable to one of her sex. Or, as the *Louisville Focus* put it, she had "leaped over the boundary of feminine modesty, and laid hold upon the avocations of man, claiming a participation in them for herself and her sex."[46] So they tried to marginalize her with personal attacks. Some made fun of her earnestness and perceived sense of martyrdom. Others criticized her looks. She towered over most people, being about six feet tall, wore sensible clothes (sometimes a riding habit), and kept her hair short. Even though she softened her look with ringlets on the sides of her head over her ears, a neck ruffle, and a silk scarf fastened with a brooch, many described her as lacking the attributes of a lady. She was "ungainly," of "masculine proportions," with hands "neither white nor well-turned," and a "complexion reddish and wind worn" one wrote.[47] Another actually questioned her sanity and supposed that her behavior was due to her seeking revenge for the "neglect of men to her indescribable charms."[48] Lest readers feel that the newspapers were defying decorum by attacking a woman, the *New York American* argued that she had brought it on herself. As the Reverend Bacon had explained his harsh tone about Lydia Maria Child, the newspaper argued in January of 1829 that

> when one thus shamefully obtrudes herself upon the public waiving alike modesty, gentleness, and every amiable attribute of her sex, she also waives all claim to its privileges; she ceases to be a woman, and is no long aught else than what we have taken the liberty of calling her—a female monster.[49]

If only Ada had read that insult and included it in her poem!

William Leete Stone, in his *New York Commercial Advertiser*, printed the most offensive attacks, maybe the harshest words ever in the American press to that point about a woman. One Wright biographer explains that Wright "stirred something so deep and powerful in him that he lost his self-control." He wrote numerous articles and "repeatedly he returned to the attack, with a rage and hatred so little suppressed that it seemed pathological." He wrote that "she comes among us in the character of a bold blasphemer, and a voluptuous preacher of licentiousness.... Casting off all restraint, she would break down all the barriers to virtue, and reduce the world to one grand theatre of vice and sensuality in its most loathsome form."[50] He also conducted an investigation of her finances and accused her in print of fraud. He claimed that most of the people she claimed to have freed had not even been slaves. Stone continued that she actually pocketed thousands of dollars from her gradual slave emancipation colony Nashoba and her subsequent trip to Haiti to settle in freedom those who had been living and working there. Wright defended herself, and while she was able to offset some of her expenses with donations, the charges seem largely untrue. Stone printed her item by item explanation of her expenses as well as her offer to show anyone the receipts if they stopped by the office of her newspaper. He did not retract his accusations or apologize, but he retreated from his harshest claims. Wright refused to be backed into a corner by the likes of Stone.[51]

Wright moved people, in addition to Ada, to compose verse, but these were largely satirical and critical. Breaking through the layers of insignificance had consequences. William Cullen Bryant published in his newspaper a verse from the perspective of the British Islands, imploring Wright to return to them since "as is a patron's duty, reform thy native country first."[52] An excerpt of a verse in the *Courier and Enquirer* of New York from June of 1830 summed up admiration and the main criticisms of the "petticoated politician":

> For she had gold within her purse,
> And brass upon her face;
> And talent indescribable,
> To give old thoughts new grace.
> And if you want to raise the wind,
> Or breed a moral storm
> You must have one bold lady-man
> To prate about reform.[53]

Criticism of Wright became so widespread that editors used her name to smear emerging political movements they disagreed with. Newspapers labeled members of Working Men's Parties of the late 1820s Fanny Wrightists and Wright Reasoners even though their platforms had few similarities to Wright's causes. Even on issues where they agreed, Wright often took a much more radical view. Working Men's Parties pushed for better education for their children, for example, but Wright spoke about a national educational system that would separate children from their families. Even though she had no formal connection to the parties and they differed on so much, opponents connected them together. The Working Men's call for economic opportunity was belittled as the "robbing of mails, picking pockets, shoplifting, housebreaking, and other natural modes of restoring this equilibrium of property, are in strict accordance with the rule of Wright and the eternal fitness of things."[54]

Lydia Maria Child also differed on economic issues with Wright. Child demonstrated a sympathy for working class people in America but did not see free thought or class solidarity as solutions to their problems. Child believed the existing system of economics and government were satisfactory, with the obvious exception that slavery needed to be abolished and also some additional protections for women were required. In general, Child advocated equal access to the institutions of America, which offered upward mobility, and a robust system of charity from the rich to help those who had fallen on tough times. When Wright appeared in Boston in 1829, Child contributed a letter to the *Massachusetts Daily Journal* criticizing Wright's "vague premises" and her anti-religious stance. Child wrote she was at first surprised that so many people had gone to see her but in the end she understood that people "were weary of going to the museum, and they were as thankful to Miss Wright for giving them something new to talk about, as they would have been to a Boa-Constrictor, or a caravan of monkeys."[55] It is unknown whether or not Wright read this putdown or what she might have thought of Child.

In the summer of 1830, Wright's enemies received their wish and Wright left the United States. She found herself in a situation that forced her to return to Europe and remove herself from public life. She was pregnant and could not betray all she argued for by marrying the father but also could not allow her child to be labeled a bastard. Wright faced the realities of being a free thinker at a time when thought was not at all free. She left the United States abruptly, married her daughter's father, French educator William Phiquepal d'Arusmont, and lived in seclusion in France for nearly four years. She wrote to a friend that she had retired from the spotlight because she did not want Americans, whom she felt she had "succeeded in awakening to matters of real import, diverted from these even temporarily to gossip of my private affairs."[56] She returned to America in 1834 only after her second daughter had died and she had made her first child legitimate by adopting for her the birthdate of the second child—a lie that was not discovered for decades.[57] In the meantime, Americans quickly moved on to other issues, like dropping Lydia Maria Child from the ranks of celebrity when she published *An Appeal.* Frances Trollope commented to a friend in 1831 how quickly things changed.

> How easily do the wonders of a day pass away! Last year I hardly ever looked at a paper without seeing long and repeated mention of Miss Wright. Her eloquence and her mischief, her wisdom and her folly, her strange principles and her no principles were discussed without ceasing. Now her name appears utterly forgotten.[58]

Trollope summed up the essence of Wright and of celebrity in 1831 wonderfully. A woman easily became re-cloaked in the "seven-fold shield of habitual insignificance."

When Wright returned to the United States in 1834, however, she reemerged and her name was even more divisive. In Concord, Massachusetts, George Thompson, a British abolitionist, was nearly killed for being a Fanny Wrightist. One defender of the rights of labor said, "If this is Fanny Wrightism, let them make the most of it."[59] She was blamed for worker unrest as the country sank into a depression after the Panic of 1837. Now, crowds prevented Wright from speaking. Newspapers called for her arrest and threatened that she would be harmed if she persisted in lecturing. Their attacks more often became personal than earlier in the decade. One wrote that with "a face like a Fury, and her hair cropped like a convict" she was an "awkward bungle of womanhood"; it continued that surely her husband must be pitied for having to put up with her. Another showed the grudging admiration that was typical of reports of Wright by printing that, with "a brain from Heaven and a heart from Hell," she was the cause of unrest in the country. He paid her a great compliment indeed by giving her credit for the equalizing trends let loose by Jacksonian Democracy. "She has employed all the powers of her intellect, in removing the ancient land-marks of morality and social order."[60]

Catharine Beecher agreed. The older sister of Harriet Beecher Stowe, she was one of the most prolific writers of the time and had devoted her life to women's education. She opposed, however, other types of equality for women such as the right to vote. Beecher felt compelled to announce to the world in her book of 1836 that she could not "conceive any thing in the shape of a woman, more intolerably offensive and disgusting" than Fanny Wright because she called for equality and lectured on serious topics in defiance of gender norms. To Catharine Beecher, lecturer Fanny Wright defied all proper rules of 1830s femininity:

> delicacy of appearance and manners, refinement of sentiment, gentleness of speech, modesty in feeling and action, a shrinking from notoriety and public gaze, a love of dependence, and protection, aversion to all that is coarse and rude, and an instinctive abhorrence of all that tends to indelicacy and impurity, either in principles or actions.[61]

With attacks like these, Wright ended up lecturing in warehouses or abandoned factories outside of town because in some cities she could find no normal venue willing to rent her space. She canceled one speech because the stage had been destroyed. Crowds hissed, pounded canes on the floor, and yelled out obscenities. In Wilmington, Delaware, she canceled her second lecture when she was ridiculed during her first. At one event, boys injured audience members by throwing rocks while the police, reportedly, did not intervene. In New York she needed police protection after a lecture on October 12, 1838. Wright argued that newspaper reports were exaggerated but it seems that the city experienced a riot with many people arrested as the crowd of five thousand who attended her lecture swelled to fifteen thousand with those out on the street. Wright was escorted home unscathed, but female supporters who attended her lecture were harassed and called whores.[62]

Afterwards, most venues were closed to her and the newspapers began ignoring her. By 1839, crowds at her lectures in out of the way, small halls had diminished and she retired from lecturing. She traveled many times between Europe and America in her last two decades, but always considered Tennessee her home. She died in 1852 and is buried in Cincinnati, Ohio.[63]

Although Lydia Maria Child found herself infamous because of her own beliefs in equality, she would never subject herself to the ridicule that followed Wright. Child publicized her ideas but she refused to debate with men in public, either in print or on stage. She would not defend herself against attacks the way Wright did and Child refused to become an abolitionist speaker. She did not attack Wright in the harsh manner that Catharine Beecher did, but clearly she believed a stage was not a proper place for a woman. Though many urged Child to use her skills this way, she explained to a friend in 1837 that because she was a woman, she would not do it. "Oh, if I were a man how I *would* lecture! But I am a woman, and so I sit in the corner and knit socks."[64] She of course exaggerated. In addition to her domestic duties she did much work for abolitionism. She helped protect speakers like George Thompson (who had been called a Fanny Wrightist) by shielding them from mobs. She returned to her customary methods and published a collection of fiction on abolitionism, *The Oasis*. Critics and audiences both liked the book. It did not bring back Child's celebrity status but it was widely available, and even made its way into the South against great odds. It was illegal in many areas to possess abolitionist works and in 1835 a student was whipped for possessing *The Oasis* and three other antislavery books. In addition, Child edited the *National Anti-Slavery Standard* for three years, more than doubling its circulation in the process.[65]

Her columns in the *Standard* did bring back a measure of Child's laudatory fame and were republished in a Boston newspaper. Particularly influential were pieces on women's rights, many of which she also reprinted in a two-volume collection. While Child continued to refuse to speak in front of crowds, she did perform in a way to help save the life of Amelia Norman in addition to writing about her plight. In 1843 Norman stalked and stabbed Henry Ballard, the man who had seduced her when she was sixteen with a promise of marriage and then abandoned her in a brothel after their child was born. Child recruited women to attend each day of the Norman trial with her. This show of support for a seduced woman as well as the columns Child wrote helped to acquit Norman despite overwhelming evidence against her. Child and Norman's lawyer both used sympathy aroused by seduction tales like *Charlotte Temple*, which was still extremely popular, to show how Norman was actually the victim and not the perpetrator. Child criticized *Charlotte Temple* for leading young women astray but now it became helpful to her. She was especially incensed that what laws existed about seduction did not protect the woman but actually considered a father or an employer as the wronged party. When New York made seduction a crime against a woman's body, reputation, and personhood in 1848, the legislature used Child's words and reasoning.[66] The volumes of her columns were among the best-selling books of the 1840s.[67] Child now found that publishers again accepted her work.

Child enjoyed renewed celebrity status in the 1840s. She received fan mail and gifts. An aspiring twenty-year-old author who did not know her sent her flowers and she was repeatedly invited to meet Charles Dickens when he was on tour in America in 1843.[68] Even publications in the South took note of her work; the *Southern Quarterly Review* wrote that all women should read her book *Good Wives*. "There are few living writers in the English language, of either sex, who employ a style more pure, unaffected, nervous and elegant," it argued in 1846.[69] James Russell Lowell included her in his 1848 *A Fable for Critics*:

> Yes, a great heart is hers, one that dares to go in
> To the prison, the slave-hut, the alleys of sin,
> And to bring into each, or to find there, some line
> Of the never completely out-trampled divine.[70]

And when she was again put at the center of abolitionism by the publication in 1859 of her exchange of letters with a southern woman and the Governor of Virginia, she was treated as an influential person. Northerners, now more widely in support of abolition, applauded her eloquent dismissal of the southerners' criticisms of her and defense of slavery. Child found herself in large demand, responding to between twenty and thirty letters a week from supporters, who were part of a growing mania about celebrities in the 1850s.[71] Many people asked her for personal items, such as a black man in Ohio who wrote to request a photograph. Not all the letters were positive and in fact, like any celebrity, she again had critics. Some of the letters shocked her with their vulgar language; many of their authors using skills possibly honed by writing similar letters to Harriet Beecher Stowe, author of *Uncle Tom's Cabin*, early in the decade. Southern newspapers even printed a false story alleging that she had abandoned a crippled child who was now being raised by a Mississippi slaveholding family.[72] No such rumors were spread about Stowe. Child, with her common sense appeal to equality, was in a way more dangerous to the region even than that celebrated author.

After the Civil War, Child felt that the times had passed her by. She continued to publish honest and groundbreaking works, such as a collection about aging. But when she died in 1880, her obituaries focused on her pre-war writings.[73] Like Martha Washington, Child burned her letters to prevent anyone from knowing more about her true self. She never promoted a false identity but clearly kept secrets she did not want revealed. While many celebrities to come would speak their minds strongly, meeting with both praise and censure, Child and Wright were among both the first and the most famous to attempt to raise an American conscience to the existence of injustice. They emerged at a time of spreading democratization and causes promoting more equality. This heightened their celebrity. The continuing limits on the public activities of women hindered their efforts in the 1820s and 1830s but ironically also raised awareness of their words. They subverted gender restrictions by what they said but also by simply speaking out. They broke through the shields of insignificance and celebrity helped.

Select Bibliography

Campbell, Karlyn Kohrs, ed. *Women Public Speakers in the United States, 1800–1925.* Westport, CT: Greenwood Press, 1993.

Clifford, Deborah. *Crusader for Freedom: A Life of Lydia Maria Child.* Boston: Beacon Press, 1992.

Connors, Robert. "Frances Wright: First Female Civic Rhetor in America." *Journal of College English.* 62 (Sept. 1999): 30–57.

Eckhardt, Celia Morris. *Fanny Wright: Rebel in America.* Cambridge: Harvard University Press, 1984.

Hibbard, Andrea. "Law, Seduction, and the Sentimental Heroine: The Case of Amelia Norman." *American Literature* 78 (2006): 325–355.

Karcher, Carolyn. *The First Woman in the Republic: A Cultural Biography of Lydia Maria Child.* Durham: Duke University Press, 1994.

Karcher, Carolyn, ed. *A Lydia Maria Child Reader.* Durham: Duke University Press, 1997.

Kenschaft, Lori. *Lydia Maria Child: The Quest for Racial Justice.* New York: Oxford University Press, 2002.

Meltzer, Milton, and Patricia Holland, eds. *Lydia Maria Child Selected Letters, 1817–1880*. Amherst: University of Massachusetts Press, 1982.

Osborne, William. *Lydia Maria Child.* Boston: Twayne Publishers, 1980.

Perkins, A.J.G. *Frances Wright, Free Enquirer: The Study of a Temperament.* 1939. Reprint, Philadelphia: Porcupine Press, 1972.

Waterman, William Randall. *Frances Wright.* New York: Columbia University Press, 1924.

FOUR

◇◇◇◇◇◇◇◇◇◇◇◇◇

Fanny Elssler and Jenny Lind

*Conquering America
Through Art and Humbug*

In the summer of 1840 a man walking the streets of New York with a woman's slipper around his neck proudly told any who asked that the shoe belonged to Fanny Elssler. Desperate to display his ardor, he bought the shoe from Elssler's maid.[1] Americans had never experienced anything like Austrian ballerina Franziska Elssler or the campaign to publicize her tour.[2] Helpless against her and the frenzy, they caught Elsslermania, went to extreme lengths to honor her, and mostly did not care to consider whether she was worthy of such praise. The critics among them tried to sully her name. Elssler, however, remained a popular celebrity, with help from a publicist, through her entire American tour. Ten years later, Swedish singer Jenny Lind and showman P.T. Barnum perfected the art of the created national celebrity. Both Lind and Elssler benefited from hype. They made more money because publicity stirred a longing that went beyond a desire to go to a cultural event. Attending one of their performances put people in the know, among the lucky ones, with the crowd. And people did not care that this satisfaction was fake or manufactured humbug. They felt that they were in on the joke. Even before there was a truly national media, there was this perception of belonging in a cultural sense.

Henry Wikoff convinced Elssler to embark on the tour and he was determined to make America love her. He used the newly emerging national press system to publicize Elssler and keep her in the news. Publishers were both printing cheaper papers and including more general interest information in them to tap into a grass roots audience that contained more people able to and eager to read. Editors freely reprinted stories originally published in other papers, allowing a local or regional story to gain national focus, especially since it required no postage to send a newspaper to another editor. The *New York Herald* was one of the most important newspapers in the country in 1840 and what it printed was widely disseminated.[3] When he and Elssler arrived in New York in May of 1840, Wikoff gave James Gordon Bennett, publisher of the *Herald*, complimentary dance reviews of Elssler's recent European performances and glowing articles about her life. Bennett printed the pieces in a special edition and in subsequent issues. Though Bennett had yet to meet Elssler, the first article started with "Yesterday, the beautiful, enchanting, the wonderful Fanny Elssler, the queen of the dance in

Fanny Elssler (1810–1884). This lithograph from 1841 is based on a painting by Henry Inman. Prints like this sold for five dollars in New York City (Library of Congress, LC-DIG-pga-01535).

Europe, arrived at New York."[4] Bennett accepted gifts of silver and jewelry, valued at five hundred dollars, from Elssler but argued that they did not affect his coverage of the ballerina's tour.[5]

Even without the hype, Americans understood that Elssler's arrival was a legitimate big deal. Many knew she was an established star in Europe having danced for the Paris Opera, the pinnacle of success for a ballerina, as well as on request for royalty. Some knew of her great rivalry with Swedish ballerina Marie Taglioni. They learned she was the first reigning cultural queen to travel to the United States. Other stars had visited, such as the French ballerina Celeste who was on her third tour of America, but none were considered the best in the world as was Elssler.[6]

She made a good impression from the start, as the *Herald* reported, graciously receiving important guests, buying tickets for a charity performance, and touring the warship USS *North Carolina* at the invitation of the captain. Elssler caught the attention of the sailors but also of a spectator who declared that simply watching her walk was worth a ten-dollar ticket.[7]

The rich and poor tried to buy tickets to see her dance but they sold out quickly. Desperate fans offered to pay ticket holders three times the regular price for the best seats but often settled for simply getting into the Park Theater. As a result, even high society ladies viewed the performance from back, upper tier-seats they would normally have avoided. Some went to more extreme measures. Maria Stone stole two dresses to sell them for ticket money so eager was she to attend a performance. Unfortunately for Stone, she was arrested and sent to the dreaded New York prison the Tombs. She missed her chance to see Elssler perform, though of course now that was the least of her worries.[8]

People in other cities tried to lure Elssler out of New York. Celeste traveled widely throughout the United States, dancing in small towns, during her tours and everyone expected Elssler to do the same. The Washington correspondent to the *Herald* reported that everyone was talking about Elssler in the nation's capital and hoped that she might perform there before Congress adjourned.[9] Theater managers from across the United States flocked to New York with lucrative contract offers even before she had set foot on a stage. A New Orleans poet used complimentary words in addition to offers of cash to convince Elssler to schedule a performance in Louisiana:

> Fanny, we're dying with a fever here; but not the yellow, fever, Fanny dear; We want to see your "twinkling feet" and eyes; We want to read that "poetry unwritten," with which the worthy Gothamites are smitten.... Ten thousand dollars—Fanny, here's a chance! To see you dance—we'll pay it in advance.[10]

Those lucky enough to attend performances praised her dancing enthusiastically. Crowds cheered so loudly they made the theater
shake. They threw coins and bouquets of flowers onto the stage. Fans
in the upper tiers at one performance created a beautiful scene by toss-
ing "poetical souvenirs" that were printed on colored sheets of paper.[11]
Many fans sent their poems to newspapers and magazines, such as the
New York *Spirit of the Times*. Reviewers found themselves struggling
to explain just how lovely was Elssler's dancing. A correspondent for
the *Alexandria Gazette* compared the experience to glimpsing heaven;
watching her dance, he wrote, could "lift the spirit to the most glorious
visions of Elysium."[12] The *New York Mirror* unfortunately printed only
one of the many poems and reviews it received, explaining it simply did
not have space for more. But the chosen prose piece also used metaphor
to convey the experience. It compared the performance to poetry but
argued that it was on an even higher plain: "For the first time in our lives
we *felt* what the poet meant by the 'airy gems.'"[13] Words could elevate the
spirit but Elssler's dance could bring transcendence.

Elssler accomplished this with mesmerizing performances notable for their strength and precision. Celeste introduced French ballet
to Americans but Elssler was more gifted at it and at the other styles
they both performed. Elssler demonstrated pieces from romantic bal-
lets such as La Sylphide that featured quick steps, leaps, high kicks, and
dancing on her toes. Elssler also expanded her offerings with versions
of folk dances from Spain, Italy, and Eastern Europe. When she danced
these, Elssler incorporated more upper body movement, even bowing
all the way to the floor and arching her back while spinning around as
she did in her most famous dance the Cachucha.[14] The correspondent
for the *Alexandria Gazette* reported that her steps combined "a most
miraculous rapidity and agility with the mathematical precision of an
automaton." But the effect, he argued, was magical and filled one with
"a most delicious giddiness."[15] Another reviewer could hardly believe
Elssler was capable of such dance: "The wonderful forces and precision
with which she executed movements, we should have deemed impossible, had we not seen her accomplish them."[16]

Fans were moved beyond praise to action and not all could obtain
one of Elssler's old shoes to demonstrate their love. Crowds serenaded
her when she was at her hotel and mobbed her when she appeared in
public. The curious made William Colman's book shop on Broadway the
most popular spot in the city because he had on display and for sale
plaster busts of Elssler. As the *New York Mirror* argued, "those who cannot see the first dancer in the world, at the theatre, have a curiosity to
see how so celebrated a woman *looks*."[17] Women copied her hairstyle,

Fanny Elssler (1810–1884) in the Shadow Dance. In 1846 Nathaniel Currier published this hand-colored print of Elssler doing the shadow dance. Elssler is wearing a bright red bodice and white tutu (Library of Congress, LC-DIG-pga-04817).

which was parted down the middle, swept low over her ears, and then up in a tight bun. Editor James Gordon Bennett christened for her one of his *New York Herald* boats that met incoming ships for the purpose of gathering news stories. Breeders named their race horses after her. Anyone with five dollars could buy a small poster of Elssler, that is until the printers sold out. Devotees in New York had many chances to spend their money though since Fanny Elssler champagne, candy, cough drops, bread, boots, shawls, fans, shaving soap, cigars, and other items were all available for sale.[18]

Admirers saw "poetry unwritten" with every move of Elsslers feet, hands, and torso but she became popular despite common attitudes. Americans, generally, were concerned with displays of the body, especially by women, because of a religious revival movement that had swept the country in recent decades. Ladies were expected to wear excessively modest clothing and even appearing in public showing a pregnancy was considered indecent. The empire waisted, cleavage revealing, clingy dresses of Elizabeth Patterson Bonaparte were long out of fashion. Women could shock with even much more coverage now, and

Elssler's dance costumes were shocking for the time. She may have lowered her hems in consideration of American sensibilities, but in order to perform she still needed skirts well above her ankles that would lift with her leg kicks. Ministers warned their congregations of the consequences of attending her performances; fine arts were not exempted from the rules of modesty.[19]

Many came to her defense. One indignant fan predicted that she would not be affected by "vulgar motives of a false modesty."[20] The *New York Herald*, of course, was particularly harsh about her critics. It shamed men who leered at Elssler by labeling them brutes, beasts, barbarians, and malformations. The newspaper also personally attacked entertainer Hervio Nano for arguing that "it proves the degeneracy of the public taste when they fill the theatre to overflowing to witness a woman kick her legs about." A *Herald* writer viciously responded, "What does it prove, Hervio, to see a poor wretch whose vices have brought the curse of God on his legs, so that he cant use them at all?" Harvey Leach used the stage name Hervio Nano, which translates as Harvey the Dwarf. Leach actually performed amazing acrobatics, including walking on the ceiling, even though he had malformed legs.[21]

Journalists admitted, however, the sensual attraction of Elssler's dance and seemed to revel in discussion of her body, which would normally be taboo.[22] Even the *New York Herald* admitted that Elssler's performances were more in the category of the forbidden than the divine. When previewing upcoming events in the city that included both Elssler performances and an unusually large number of religious anniversary celebrations, it encouraged "sinners and saints, make ready for the great movements of next week."[23] It left no doubt what events would attract which type of New Yorker. The *New York Mirror* lingered on her features, describing Elssler's "raven hair, her dark flashing eyes, her twinkling feet, and her figure of perfect proportions."[24] F.L. Waddell wrote a poem for the New York *Spirit of the Times* that described Elssler's "voluptuous form, with raptures, gently throbbing" and "her bosom swelling like the sea."[25] The correspondent for the *Alexandria Gazette* went even further, evaluating her body in unusually intimate detail:

> Muscular exertion has done its work upon the contour [of her body], and the limbs, when at rest, have a certain robustness, or rather hardness of outline, inconsistent with absolute beauty. The feet and ankles especially, and also the ligaments of the throat, indicated the early toil of her profession.—But in motion all defect vanishes.[26]

New York banker Samuel Ward considered her a wonderful dancer but a dangerous woman. He wrote to his friend, the writer Henry

Wadsworth Longfellow, that Elssler's "influence is sensual, her ensemble the incarnation of seductive attraction." She charmed men like a snake but was too jaded by her experiences of being "bought and sold" to be capable of true feelings. "She retains the shadow of love," he wrote, "the substance had long since departed." He believed that she no longer acted like a woman but "seeks and feeds on triumphs, revels in ambition." She desired only "to gather laurels, smiles, applause and gold." He hoped that when her beauty was gone that she would no longer attempt to dance: "We should almost pay Fanny to appear no more when wrinkles replace her smiles."[27]

Elssler's own gentle manners blunted this lewdness for many other fans, writers, and artists. After performances, she often gave little speeches of thanks, in many languages, but most commonly in English with what was considered an adorable German accent. She endeared herself to the audience with these simple and shy greetings.[28] She said after concluding her first season in New York, according to the *Ladies' Companion*, "I have been so happy along with you, that I am sorry to go away from you, but (pausing and smiling archly) I will come back again."[29] She clearly charmed the *Companion* reporter, who gushed about Elssler's naïve manner and accent. Artists drew and painted her as a lovely, feminine, young woman with no hint of lewdness in her appearance.

Entertainment rivals, however, lampooned her accent and basically her entire performance. William Mitchell built his career on a parody of Elssler. He brought English-style burlesque with him to New York and one of his first successful appearances was as dancer Low-Retta in La Mosquitoe, which he began performing about a week after Elssler's debut. Mitchell based the dance on Elssler's performance of Tarantula, or spider dance, a quick step Italian folk dance. He looked ridiculous: an overweight man in a short petticoat, tights, a wreath of flowers on his head, and brightly-colored ribbons that flowed from his shoulders. He jumped frenetically, slapping and scratching as well as leaping with the aid of ropes that often left him stranded in the air to the delight of the crowds in his Olympic Theater. When finished, he thanked the audience with an exaggerated German accent: "Tousan tank, me 'art too fool."[30] Mitchell managed the theater for eleven years, staging more than two hundred shows, but was long remembered for his Elssler parody.[31]

Many others showed how deeply Elssler had penetrated culture by including her in amusing anecdotes. The *New York Atlas* reported that an artist in the city had produced such a lifelike sculptor of Elssler's legs that "when the proper tune is played they get right up and dance the Cachuca, first rate." The *New Orleans Picayune* editor could not resist enhancing the joke. He added to his reprint that the editor of the *Atlas* knew this to be true because when he got too close "one of the legs kicked three of his front teeth down his throat."[32] One anonymous writer for the *New York Mirror* suggested to a young man that he could cure himself of love by attending the opera "when Fanny Elssler dances the Cracovienne or the Cachucha, in order that you may dream of her afterwards."[33] Some critics labeled enthusiasm for her "Elsslermaniaphobia."[34]

Not all reactions, however, were laughing matters though printers tried to make them so. Elssler and her fans unwittingly enflamed ethnic tensions. Being from Vienna, Elssler was particularly idolized by immigrants from other German-speaking areas of Europe. They often serenaded her and played German folk tunes for her when she was in her hotel room. After one of her performances in New York in late summer of 1840, anti-immigrant Bowery Boy toughs broke up one of these late-night adulation sessions. A printer portrayed the event humorously, with a lithograph titled "Fanny Ellsler's Last Serenade: Soap-Locks Disgraceful attack upon the Germans," using the nickname for the Bowery Boys that emphasized their long hair slicked down with soap. The artist showed well-coifed, hatted men using musical instruments to beat up the band. Former New York City mayor Philip Hone recorded in his diary that the attackers stabbed one musician in the neck and burned the instruments in a bonfire.[35]

The *New York Sunday Morning News* reported the episode differently. It noted that nobody had been injured in the event and editorialized that the musicians and Elssler had it coming, using both ethnic and gender arguments.

> That she is an excellent dancer we readily admit, but that she is in any degree worthy of the "ovation," which her countrymen had prepared for her, we utterly deny. It was an uncalled for and ridiculous attempt. Surely it must confound all ideas of the value of female honor, of the dignity of virtue, of the sacredness of chastity, of the merit of all those high and noble attributes which render woman truly "divine," tacitly to stand by and see such "honors extraordinary" paid to a dancer![36]

Elssler inspired this same mix of commercialism, voyeurism, appreciation, and humor (and sometimes hostility despite the publicity campaign) wherever she went on tour. She planned to stay in the United States only for a few weeks to complete one season of performances but found the venture so lucrative that she ended up staying for more than two years. After New York, Elssler performed in Philadelphia, where one writer explained that her appeal was "the agility of her legs and the nudity of her person."[37] The Franklin Institute Science Museum

FANNY ELLSLER'S LAST SERENADE.

Soap-Locks Disgraceful attack upon the Germans

Fanny Elssler's (1810–1884) Last Serenade caricature. In 1840 Henry Robinson published this cartoon of a riot in New York caused by an attack on German musicians who were playing in the street for Elssler (Library of Congress, LC-USZ62–2535).

exhibited Fanny Elssler matches that lit without Sulphur, apparently commenting on her ability to light a flame among her audiences.[38] British actor Fanny Kemble attended every Elssler performance in Philadelphia (as well as some in New York). She felt that Elssler excelled at both acting and dancing. Kemble retired from the stage when she married one of her American fans. She published a tell-all journal of her years on tour in the United States that caused a scandal, so understood that being a celebrity was both rewarding and precarious.[39]

Elssler met with much reward on her visit to Washington, D.C. She performed five separate nights and kept Congress from conducting business from lack of a quorum. Elssler also visited Capitol Hill and met President Martin Van Buren. She was "talked of by every one—applauded, caressed—admired and ran after." She was given a cross supposedly made from wood from the bier that had held George Washington's coffin.[40] A printer by the name of Robinson was selling a color portrait of her.[41] It was in this city that Elssler delivered her most endearing speech. She attempted to say that she would take with her "recollections" she would never forget but used the incorrect word "collections" instead, causing the audience to softly chuckle at her. She was embarrassed until the error was pointed out. "Sweet girl!" the reporter concluded. "May God bless her a thousand years."[42]

Elssler next moved on to Baltimore where her fans outdid all others in their enthusiasm and because of it became the object of ridicule. Tickets were in such demand that the theater put the best seats up for auction and fans paid four times their face value. Elssler decided to extend her stay in the city and on what was to be her last night her elated fans treated her to an unusual escort back to her hotel. Men unhitched the horses from her carriage and pulled it slowly through the streets. Bystanders cheered them on and waved to Elssler. Publisher John Childs of New York printed a satirical lithograph of the scene with Elssler dressed in street clothes doing a leg kick in the carriage being pulled by men with donkey heads. In the cartoon she is saying, "My friends I tank you very! I understand you! I shall remember you for long 'years!'" Newspapers across the country called the Baltimore men jackasses and the *Native American* from Washington, D.C., joked that "this

FANNY ELSSLER AND THE BALTIMOREANS

Fanny Elssler (1810–1884) and the Baltimoreans caricature. John Childs printed this humorous critique of Elsslermania in 1840 (Library of Congress, LC-USZ62-70512).

is the first time we ever heard of *jacks*, of their own will, going to work after *play*."[43]

Elssler made very different fans in Boston though many in the religiously conservative city were predisposed to dislike her. High society ladies came to love her because she performed in a benefit for the Bunker Hill Monument Association, raising more than five hundred dollars for the completion of that edifice.[44] Literary figures were inspired by her. Harvard professor Henry Wadsworth Longfellow modeled a character in *The Spanish Student* on her. Longfellow wrote of a dancer who was young and innocent though many assumed she lived an immoral life, even though his friend Samuel Ward thought such a portrayal of Elssler ridiculous. Writer Charles Newcomb believed Elssler a "vile creature" until he attended a performance and became a fan. He bought one of the many portraits for sale and nailed it to his bedroom wall right between illustrations of two Catholic saints. Margaret Fuller called Elssler's dance poetry and her companion in the audience Ralph Waldo Emerson likened it to religion. Emerson feared, however, that the Harvard boys would be distracted by her "tripping satin slippers" and unable to study.[45] Others wondered whether watching Elssler dance could actually make men commit crimes. Lawyer B.F. Emery used this argument in his defense of sailor John Anderson who was on trial for indecent exposure. The *Boston Post* reported that the court convicted Anderson anyway and could not resist getting in one more joke at the expense of the jackasses of Baltimore. Emery's summation, it argued, "would have sadly shocked the silk-tight-loving sensibilities of the asssinine admirers of that hop-skip and jump divinity."[46]

By the spring of 1841, Elssler was performing at the St. Charles Theatre in New Orleans—P.T. Barnum was managing a dancer, John Diamond, in the same city and was impressed with the success of the publicity campaign.[47] A year into Elssler's tour, she still sold out shows and inspired unusual fan behavior. Admirers threw wreaths of strawberries on stage and bid in an auction for the carriage cushion on which she had arrived to the city. Musicians serenaded Elssler with French songs and, like in New York, braved the threats of anti-foreign thugs.[48] The *Boston Post* labeled the enthusiasm "dancing mania" and joked that since Elssler's arrival in New Orleans "when people meet in the streets, instead of extending their hands they stick out their feet to be shaken!"[49] English actor Fanny Fitzwilliam performed a piece at the nearby American Theatre that included imitations of some of Elssler's dances. The manager deemed them "not bad resemblances either; a little extravagant, perhaps, but far from contemptible."[50] *New Orleans Picayune* assistant editor Matthew Field summed up nicely both the appeal and the excessiveness of Elsslermania in his poem that was widely reprinted. In the verse, Field, using the pen name Phazma, pledged his devotion: "Just be my heiress, Fanny, I implore you, my large possessions I now lay before you, I'll serve you, laud you, follow and *encore* you, if you will just permit me to adore you!"[51] His brother Joseph Field published an "Elssler-atic Romance" in verse that recounted many of her adventures in the United States.[52]

Wikoff's publicity campaign failed to prevent newspapers of other southern cities from criticizing Elssler and ridiculing her fans in a manner that showed more contempt than amusement. A newspaper in Mississippi reported that Elssler received a thousand dollars a night for her performances in New Orleans "for throwing out one foot and standing on the other." While many work for a living, it argued, "Fanny, Princess of Pironettes, glides through with a hop, skip, and a jump." The reporter also conjured a ridiculous picture of New Orleans by claiming that while she was in the city her fans imitated her dance steps everywhere they went, including when walking down the street.[53] The *Memphis Enquirer* dismissed the idea that Elssler was a fine artist and labeled her a "foreign demoralizer." It argued that it was indecent simply to describe Elssler's costume and dance but hundreds were attending to see "a half-naked woman, with bosom and limbs all exposed, putting herself into all sorts of lascivious attitudes before a mixed crowd of gloating voluptuaries."[54]

In the summer, when she was back in New York, newspapers in many parts of the country printed salacious rumors about her. Although Wikoff tried to dismiss the libels by publishing a *Memoir of Fanny Elssler* that recounted a chaste and virtuous life, most of the rumors were at least partly true. Fanny celebrated her thirtieth birthday while in the United States. She was hardly the young, naïve, girl many people thought she was and they were shocked when they read this in the newspaper, especially since most printed her age as being nearly forty. More damaging to her reputation was the fact that Elssler was not married but was the mother of two children by two different fathers, though she never had an affair with Napoleon's son as was widely reported. She gave birth to her first child when she was only seventeen; the boy's father was Prince Leopold, the brother of the King of Naples. Elssler also had a girl as a result of an affair with a fellow dancer. While newspapers only revealed the secret of the boy, the stories confirmed the worst assumptions about Elssler and her profession.[55]

Elssler trusted those who knew about her private life and relied on Wikoff to manage her public image. Both had failed her but still she did not speak out. In fact, Elssler said very little while in the United States.

She thanked her audiences but remained otherwise silent. Neither newspapers nor people who met her reported anything that she had to say about anything. She danced. She contrasted in this way with other women we have considered so far. How Elssler felt about these attacks, about fame, about Elsslermania all remain a mystery.[56]

The bad publicity continued. Peter Pindar published a pamphlet about Elssler's life of seduction and romance that would have left her no time for the practice of her profession.[57] Horace Greeley of the *New York Tribune* called Elssler "the cast-off mistress of half the titled libertines of Europe" and urged readers, especially women, to stop attending her performances. He feared that Elssler was harming the reputation of all women. "Who can fail to realize that every cheer to this fallen spirit is in truth a scoff at female virtue and an impulse to female degradation?"[58] The *Boston Times* similarly libeled Elssler as an "ignorant, low-born, and abandoned woman" well-known in Europe as a courtesan who only attracted audiences to her performances with shameful displays of her body.[59] One author seemed truly perplexed about Elssler's appeal. He wrote:

> In this wise drama shall it come to pass,
> That Fame and Dollars crown the greatest ass?
> Must York's sons, matrons, widows, glorious maids
> Court, feast, and marry Europe's renegades?[60]

Other critics thought they understood exactly what was going on: humbug. The *Baton-Rouge Gazette* called lithographs of Elssler selling for five dollars humbug. Park Benjamin labeled Elssler herself "a stupendous humbug," clearly defying most critics who considered her talent real. Louis Tasistro blamed Wikoff for the humbug surrounding Elssler, most especially the publicity about her charitable giving. The *Richmond Palladium* hoped that "neither extortion nor imposition will be suffered by any manager, and that for once, humbug will find its proper sphere" when Elssler appeared in New Orleans.[61]

Critics increased their attention to other economic aspects of Elsslermania also. The *Alexandria Gazette* called the practice of naming items for Elssler "contemptible." Since she was "any thing but a model for reputable women," the practice "should be ridiculed into disgrace."[62] One writer poured out indignation in a story that contrasted the lavishing of money on Elssler with the plight of a poor family with a sick baby. In the tale, Elssler leaves the stage with "her ingots of gold and silver" at the same time that the child dies in a hovel without heat.[63] The article clearly resonated since many newspapers reprinted it. George Dixon displayed the same sentiment with a cartoon on the cover of his newspaper the *Polyanthus* that showed Elssler with thousands of dollars while a mother mourned a starving child.[64] Others lamented for the theaters that had hoped Elssler's arrival would save them from closing because of a continuing economic depression. While they enjoyed sell-out crowds, they made modest amounts of money because of the $500 or $1,000 per night fee they paid to Elssler. William Wood reported actually losing $1,000 when Elssler performed at his Philadelphia Theatre for eleven nights.[65] The manager of the theater in Baltimore refused to pay Elssler and the other dancers because he claimed the theater had not covered its expenses.[66] N.M. Ludlow, manager of a theater in New Orleans, doubted that she had a soul, "or if she had one," he wrote years later, "it was cased in iron, and was never permitted to be brought into use. She was avaricious to an excess."[67]

Elssler earned an enormous amount of money, possibly $140,000, while in the United States but she was in fact also generous. She gave more than $5,000 to charities while she was on tour and performed for free in benefit concerts, including the one for the Bunker Hill Monument. In Baltimore, when the manager refused to pay the company of dancers, she gave them money to pay their expenses. When she left the United States, her servant wanted to stay behind and not return to France so Elssler gave him enough money to start a business. Her coachman Charles invested the money in a stable and riding school in Philadelphia.[68]

Admirers attended her performances in large numbers despite the negative publicity and associations. Former New York mayor Philip Hone speculated that audience members were not just ignoring the calls to boycott her performances, they were actually compelled to attend because of the criticism. Elssler toured for another year consistently drawing large crowds. While in the United States she performed nearly two hundred times. She sailed back to Europe in the summer of 1842.[69]

Almost immediately, P.T. Barnum named his orangutan Fannie Elssler. Barnum intended to profit from and ridicule the tour but he also learned many valuable lessons from it. Possibly the most important one was that with a cultural tour, the product you were offering needed to be unimpeachable. How much more money could Elssler and Wikoff have made without the scandals? When Barnum sent an agent to London to woo sensation Jenny Lind to the United States, it probably did not surprise him that a rival for the singer was Elssler's publicist Henry Wikoff. But Lind did her homework and found that people believed that Barnum would and could honor any agreement she made with him. She was in a strong bargaining position and she used it to ensure the trip would be profitable. Lind insisted that the entire amount owed her and her company be deposited in a London bank. Barnum agreed and sold or mortgaged nearly everything he had but still needed to borrow money to raise the nearly $200,000 in cash.[70]

Barnum knew Americans would love Lind, but they needed to get to know her first. His basic plan was similar to Wikoff's but multiplied many times over. Barnum's publicity machine left very little to chance. Before she arrived in the United States, respected writers had published three short biographies of her that provided all the material that journalists and Americans in general needed to know, all of which was of course provided by Barnum. The writers told a story of rags to riches that was sure to capture America's imagination, but in this case was largely true. Lind started out in poverty in Sweden but started to develop early as a singer. Still, her path to fame was difficult. Just when she was gaining popularity, she strained her voice by performing and practicing too hard; she was not yet twenty years old. Her only hope was to completely rest her voice for six weeks but there was no guarantee even that would be successful. After the rest, Lind was able to recover and even strengthen her voice. She began performing widely in Europe, becoming a star. The biographies reprinted ecstatic reviews and enthusiastic letters from Americans abroad attesting to her amazing performances. There was little question that Lind was considered the best singer in the world.[71]

Lind was also an amazingly generous

Jenny Lind (1820–1887). B.R. Knapp published this lithograph titled "A Cheerful Giver" around 1850. In the border around Lind are examples of her various donations. At the bottom is a small advertisement for John Genin's hat shop and details of his purchase of the first Lind concert ticket (Library of Congress, LC-DIG-pga-05446).

person and the biographies emphasized her generosity. She gave much of her money to charities and often sang in benefit concerts. She visited hospitals, orphanages, and poor neighbors. Lind readily granted favors. After telling a few stories of selflessness, one biography continued with

> The above particulars, showing the admired celebrity off her pedestal, as they do, will by no means diminish the interest of her reception in America. The qualities of character which they reveal, are appreciated, and earnestly looked for, by the largest and best class of our country people—the unostentatious and plain-hearted. Her coming among us will be that year's most noted event, in all probability, and we only trust that a prophetess, whose whole mission, with her gold-amassing powers, seems one of pure benevolence, may not be disparaged, for her humble simplicities of ordinary life.[72]

Lind presented a much better image than had Elssler. Nobody could claim that Lind was merely humbug or greedy. In reality she started giving money to charities as soon as she had enough money to live on. Lind performed in benefit concerts exclusively for long periods of time. She showed the depth of her charitable feelings in private correspondence. She wrote to a friend in 1849, "For a year I have been singing only for schools, institutions, and charities, for without some kind of beautiful goal, one cannot endure life. At least, I cannot."[73]

Barnum devised an additional aspect to his pre-arrival publicity campaign that would play on patriotism and also allow for participatory fandom. He announced that Lind was eager to sing a greeting to her audiences written by an American. Barnum offered a prize of two hundred dollars to the author of the best poem submitted, which would then be set to music. Poets from across the country sent in hundreds of poems. Bayard Taylor, established travel writer, won the contest with a poem that included this verse:

> I greet, with full heart, the Land of the West,
> Whose Banner of Stars o'er a world is unrolled;
> Whose empire o'ershadows Atlantic's wide breast,
> And opes to the sunset its gateway of gold![74]

Lind arrived in September of 1850, to an elaborate welcome orchestrated of course by Barnum but attended by genuinely interested New Yorkers. She premiered on September 11 and between that date and June 9, 1851, she performed nearly a hundred times in about twenty different cities. Lind earned $1,000 plus half of the proceeds of each show. She often donated most of the money she received above the $1,000. She and Barnum each made about $200,000 from the tour.[75] While many European performers visited the United States after Elssler's return to France, none equaled her monetary success. Lind, however, shattered the records set by Elssler. In Boston, for instance, total receipts for thir-teen Elssler performances equaled nearly $15,000.[76] Barnum sold tick-ets there worth that much for one Lind show. He used auctions to increase both enthusiasm and ticket prices. Fans and publicity seekers paid more than six hundred dollars for the first ticket of an auction in three different cities.[77] Ticket speculators followed the tour from city to city, increasing prices for admission even more by reselling tickets, but of course neither the performer nor her manager received any of the increase. When Lind ended her contract amicably with Barnum in June of 1851, she directed her new managers to not hold auctions and to try to prevent ticket profiteering by prohibiting sales of groups of more than ten tickets. She performed forty more times in seventeen different cities up through May of 1852.[78]

Americans found that Lind lived up to the hype. They loved her singing; whether she performed opera or folk tunes, in English or any number of other languages, her pitch, range, and articulation were flaw-less. Audiences heard her songs but also felt the emotions of the tunes because Lind was an accomplished actor who used expression, ges-ture, and dance to enhance her performance. Fans worshipped her even more because they felt Lind was a natural singer and this fit her assumed unassuming character. Henry Southworth wrote in his diary that Lind sang "with perfect ear and is at home, in everything she does." South-worth enjoyed the Lind concert but proved to be even more star struck. He was among the many New Yorkers on the docks to welcome Lind to New York and he also visited her hotel to try to see her as she emerged from the entrance.[79]

Critics praised Lind also. *Harper's Monthly* likened her voice to a "melody from the nightingale's throat, to light, to water which flows from a pure and inexhaustible spring."[80] They were also moved by her story and impressed by her generosity. Nathaniel Willis in his *Home Journal* summed up the reasons for Lindomania:

That God has not made her a wonderful singer *and there left her*, is the curious exception she forms to common human allotment. To give away more money in charity than any other mortal—and still be the first of prima donnas! To be an irreproachably modest girl—and still be the first of prima donnas! To be hum-ble, simple, genial and unassuming—and still be the first of prima donnas! To have begun as a beggar child and risen to receive more adulation than any queen—and still be the first of prima donnas! To be unquestionably the most admired and distinguished woman on earth, doing the most good and exercising, the most power—and still be a prima donna that can be applauded and encored! It is the combination of superiorities that makes the wonder, it is the concentrating of the stuff of half a dozen heroines in one simple girl, and that girl a candidate for applause, that so vehemently stimulates the curiosity.[81]

Fans agreed that Lind was an exceptional woman not only an accomplished singer. William Hoffman may have been her biggest fan who never had the pleasure of hearing her sing. Hoffman jostled with the crowds on the dock to greet Lind on her arrival in New York from Europe. He repeatedly tried to buy a ticket to one of her shows in Castle Garden but could not afford the high admission prices on his clerk salary. Hoffman, however, followed the newspaper reports on Lind and even transcribed some passages from them into his diary. Hoffman noted particularly information about Lind's charity. He wrote that her kindness demonstrated she possessed "the most enviable qualities of soul that any being ever could possess." Caroline White was able to hear Lind perform in Boston and she too believed Lind to be extraordinary. She wrote about the inspiring nature of the performance and asked if it was possible to listen but "not feel one's aspirations glow warmer, loftier, holier, than ever before?" Virginia Clay also experienced the lasting effect of a Lind performance. While she doubted her ability to describe the event better than others had, Clay felt confident that no one had a "clearer remembrance of that triumphant evening." She even named her favorite horse for the singer.[82]

In the midst of all this praise, Lind behaved like that simple girl Americans loved because she cherished her success and what it allowed her to accomplish. Though she had clearly worked hard on her voice, Lind attributed her talent to God. She wrote a friend in 1846 that she was beginning to get used to the applause but "I cannot conceive what it is that satisfies people. But that is God's doing."[83] She longed to retire from the stage but every new opportunity meant she could help others with the money she raised. Lind sang almost exclusively in benefit concerts for schools and charities for the year before she traveled to the United States. She explained to a friend how the offer of the American tour fit into her plans: "I have decided to go to America. The offer was very brilliant, and everything was arranged so nicely that I should have been wrong to decline it; and since I have no greater wish than to make a large amount of money in order to found schools in Sweden, I cannot help looking upon this journey to America as a gracious answer to my prayer to Heaven!"[84]

Lind disliked excessive displays of adulation because of this modesty. Before even experiencing Lindomania, she wrote to a friend in 1846 that in Vienna she was called back out on the stage so many times "that I was quite exhausted. Bah! I don't like it. Everything should be done in moderation; otherwise it is not pleasing."[85] In the United States, she preferred to travel unrecognized and requested that Barnum keep their plans secret. Crowds greeted her in every town they arrived in because, of course, Barnum could not pass up a publicity opportunity and always wired ahead against her wishes.[86] Thirteen-year-old Louisa May Alcott received from her sister Anna a photograph of Lind. Alcott, who wrote *Little Women* about twenty years later, admitted in her journal that she would like to be famous like Lind. "She must be a happy girl," she mused.[87] Lind was not particularly happy and viewed intrusions of her privacy not as signs of admiration but only of curiosity, which she did not want to satisfy.

And in the United States there was much to make her uncomfortable. Lindomania was Elsslerism on steroids. Of course, nearly every conceivable item for sale in stores was named for her and advertised in the newspapers. Merchants stocked Jenny Lind tobacco, chewing gum, singing tea kettles, fabric, cigars, poker chips, handkerchiefs, gloves, and hair combs, none of which Lind was known to use or have authorized. Lind may have been one of the first celebrities to endorse a product though, the Jenny Lind Riding Hat, which was made of black beaver, satin, and velvet and decorated with rosettes. She wore the hat on her morning rides according to *Godey's Ladies Book*. Lind received it from John Genin, a hatmaker with a shop next door to P.T. Barnum's American Museum. Genin also purchased the first ticket auctioned for Lind's debut in New York. He paid $225 for the ticket but probably did not pay Lind to wear his hat.[88] Lind may have just liked the hat or maybe Barnum suggested she wear it to show her appreciation to Genin.

Horticulturalists named varieties of muskmelon, gooseberry, and dahlia for her. There was a Jenny Lind tea cake and one that had three layers, the top and bottom being white or yellow with the center being darkened with dried fruit and spices. Residents of small towns in Arkansas and California named their communities for her, though she did not visit either. Lind even displaced the devil from part of Kentucky. She sat in Devil's Armchair on a visit through Mammoth Cave and the feature has ever since been known as Jenny Lind's Armchair. America's most celebrated artists wrote poems, songs, and dances in her honor.[89]

Everyone of course most of all wanted a ticket to a performance. A woman in Boston paid half her month's wages for a ticket.[90] More than a thousand fans bought standing tickets for a show in New York and when some of the men could not make their way inside they climbed up the side of the building to hear her through the windows.[91] At Hartford, Connecticut, those who could not buy tickets tried to listen to the concert from the roofs of adjacent buildings and rioted when the windows and blinds were closed.[92] *Holden's Magazine* irresponsibly and callously encouraged their readers to

Jenny Lind (1820–1887) Tobacco Wrapper. Boggs & Gregory marketed their Fine-Cut Cavendish Tobacco using Jenny Lind's image around the year 1850. Lind endorsed a riding hat but none of the many other products marketed with her name and likeness (Library of Congress, LC-USZ62-86770).

> sell your old clothes, dispose of your antiquated boots, hypothecate your jewelry, come on the canal, work your passage, walk, take up a collection of pay expenses, raise money on a mortgage, sell "Tom" into perpetual slavery, dispose of "Bose" to the highest bidder, stop smoking for a year, give up tea, coffee and sugar, dispense with bread, meat, garden sass and such like luxuries—whatever you must to get the needful change—and then come and hear Jenny Lind![93]

Fans also went to extraordinary lengths for a chance to meet Lind or grab a souvenir. Americans had no reservations about Lind the way that they did Elssler. Their adulation was not tinged with sensuousness and they felt that being close to her or her belongings would enrich their lives. A New York house painter offered a thousand dollars for the chance to check her back for angel wings. In Charleston, a young woman paid to take the place of the hotel servant who was to serve Lind her tea. The woman was so discreet that Lind did not even know of the deception until told of it later. Fans cheering her below her hotel balcony in Baltimore tore to shreds the shawl she inadvertently dropped, all clamoring for a piece. Souvenir seekers bought clumps of hair a hotel maid claimed she had taken from Lind's hair brush.[94]

Even though Lind was genuinely unassuming, sincere, and generous, critics complained and comics lampooned her. This would now be a permanent element of celebrity no matter how worthy of praise the star was. New York lawyer and satirist William Allen Butler anonymously published a poem that characterized Lind as a snob. She appears on stage, dressed very elegantly, and immediately retreats to Barnum to complain about the audience: "Such people I never have met, in any respectable place; to sing to this Plebian set, will be an eternal disgrace." She details her objections that include faces lacking aristocratic features, people eating fruit and nuts, and women under dressed without collars, cuffs, or diamonds. She concludes with "O show me a genuine jewel, or a yard of Valenciennes lace, ere you force me, relentless and cruel, to sing in this horrible place!" Butler wrote another piece that portrayed Lind as greedy, demanding a thousand pounds a performance (which was five times what she was getting) and lavish living arrangements.[95] George Templeton Strong, another New York lawyer, objected to the amount of praise she was receiving, which was he estimated, more than would be received by "the greatest man that had lived for the last ten centuries."[96] One journalist agreed and published a review of her performance at breakfast, which included a sneeze that was applauded and cheered three times.[97] Comedians at three New York theaters performed skits making fun of Lind and Lindomania. William Burton at the Olympic Theater staged *Jennyphobia* starting only a week after Lind's premier in New York; La Mosquitoe burlesque of Fanny Elssler was at this same theater.[98]

These critics might sneer at Lind and Barnum but everyone knew that the money they were making was substantial. Critics of Barnum's humbug tried to reason with Americans but to no avail. One Boston critic reminded readers of the importance of paying their bills and urged them not to "rush madly" to give their last dollars to Barnum. He feared Barnum was tricking people into feeling they must hear Lind sing, even if they could not afford it.[99] Of course he had a valid point but few cared to listen. Whether or not this critic realized it, a new era of celebrity had begun. Barnum and his intense publicity campaigns were only part of the story. Americans embraced celebrity wholeheartedly in the early 1850s and made stars of many notable women. The *New York Herald* argued that setting aside other pursuits in order to worship celebrities was part of "our national character—fun and frolic of 1852."[100]

There was much entertainment to distract Americans from growing regional tensions and other serious issues of the early 1850s, and women

PANORAMA OF HUMBUG.

Showman. "Walk up, Ladies & Gentlemen and see the greatest wonder of the age—the real Swedish Nightingale, the only specimen in the Country."

Jenny Lind (1820–1887) humbug. William Schaus published this print in 1850 that likened a Lind concert to all the other P.T. Barnum humbug. Come see "the Real Swedish Nightingale, the only specimen in the Country," the barker in the middle shouts (Library of Congress, LC-DIG-pga-12658).

provided much of it. Susan Warner published *The Wide, Wide World* in late 1850, at the same time that Lind was still enthralling audiences in cities on the East Coast. That sentimental novel sold an unprecedented forty thousand copies in a year. Warner immediately began receiving fan mail praising her story and asking for a sequel. With Lind and Warner both gaining popularity, another budding celebrity appeared on the scene. Sojourner Truth spoke at a women's rights convention in Akron, Ohio, at the end of May in 1851, and her common-sense Truth-isms were published in many newspapers. A week later, Harriet Beecher Stowe published the first chapter of what would become *Uncle Tom's Cabin*. The book in its entirety would not be printed until March of 1852, but by then the author had already eclipsed Warner and would acquire international acclaim never before experienced by any American author. While *Uncle Tom's Cabin* was being serialized but before it was published in a volume, two additional stars emerged. Fanny Fern published her first essay in September of 1851, setting off a frenzy of speculation about who she was that would last three years.[101] With the country already at a fever pitch of enthusiasm over these women, Lola Montez arrived from Europe and made her dancing debut in New York, December 27, 1851. Deemed less talented and more provocative than the others, Montez heightened speculation about not only her background but her effect on American audiences.

The period from 1850 to 1852 was a great time to be a fan of women celebrities. Americans could hardly read a newspaper that did not include an article about one of these stars. We will consider many of their stories in subsequent chapters. They differed widely in talent and in legacy. While Lind and Elssler were both equally talented, their long-term impact on the United States differed immensely. Elssler established romantic ballet in the country but was quickly forgotten. The *New York Herald* printed a story titled "Our Last Paragraph on Fanny Elssler" on the day she sailed back to Europe. The article was actually three long paragraphs, but it seemed to foreshadow the disappearance of Elssler from public consideration, even by a newspaper that had published something about her nearly every day while she performed in New York. When Elssler retired in the summer of 1851, American newspapers printed only brief notices of the end of her career.[102] Jenny Lind, however, has remained a celebrity through to today. Her likeness appeared in the 2017 movie *The Greatest Showman*, though portrayed inaccurately, and in season three (2019) of the TV series *Victoria*. As of this writing in 2020, more than a thousand Jenny Lind related items are for sale on eBay, including a vintage wrapper for Carleton's Jenny Lind Chewing Gum with the price tag of $525. Lind did no more than Elssler to keep her celebrity alive but she somehow touched Americans in a way Elssler had not. Lind neglected her celebrity but her fans did not. Other celebrities of the 1850s would also experience the power of the public to shape their fame.

Select Bibliography

Cavicchi, Daniel. "Loving Music: Listeners, Entertainers, and the Origins of Music Fandom in Nineteenth Century America." In *Fandom: Identities and Communities in a Mediated World*, edited by Jonathan Gray, Cornel Sandvoss, and C. Lee Harrington, 235–249. New York: New York University Press, 2007.

Costonis, Maureen Needham. "The Personification of Desire: Fanny Elssler and American Audiences." *Dance Chronicle* 13 (1990) 47–67.

Delarue, Allison. *Fanny Elssler in America: Comprising Seven Facsimiles of Rare Americana*. New York: Dance Horizons, 1976.

Guest, Ivor. *Fanny Elssler*. Middleton, CT: Wesleyan Press, 1970.

Lampert, Sara E. *Starring Women: Celebrity, Patriarchy, and American Theater, 1790-1850*. Urbana: University of Illinois Press, 2020.

Linkon, Sherry Lee. "Reading Lind Mania: Print Culture and the Construction of Nineteenth-Century Audiences." *Book History* 1 (1998): 94–106.

Samples, Mark C. "The Humbug and the Nightingale: P.T. Barnum, Jenny Lind, and the Branding of a Star Singer for American Reception." *Musical Quarterly* (2017): 1–35.

Shultz, Gladys Denny. *Jenny Lind: The Swedish Nightingale.* Philadelphia: J.B. Lippincott Company, 1962.

Swift, Mary Grace. *Belles and Beaux on Their Toes: Dancing Stars in Young America.* Washington, D.C.: University Press of America, 1980.

Waksman, Steve. "Selling the Nightingale: P.T. Barnum, Jenny Lind, and the Management of the American Crowd." *Arts Marketing: An International Journal* 1 (2011): 108–120.

Ware, W. Porter, and Thaddeus C. Lockard, Jr. *The Lost Letters of Jenny Lind.* London: Victor Gollancz, LTD, 1966.

Ware, W. Porter, and Thaddeus C. Lockard, Jr. *P.T. Barnum Presents Jenny Lind: The American Tour of the Swedish Nightingale.* Baton Rouge: Louisiana State University Press, 1980.

FIVE

◇◇◇◇◇◇◇◇◇◇◇◇◇

Lola Montez, Fanny Fern and Adah Menken

Performing On and Off the Stage

Americans heard many things about Lola Montez: she started a revolution against a despotic regime in Bavaria; she was so beautiful that men dueled over her; she smoked cigars and horsewhipped men who insulted her; she was a duchess who was kind to her servants; she mesmerized audiences with her dark eyes and hypnotic dancing; she was a bigamist who also had many lovers. Could all of these be true and could such a woman be worthy of celebrity status they wondered? Americans needed to know the true story of Montez, especially because she tried so hard to conceal her past. Everyone was curious about the lives of celebrities in the 1850s but they became obsessed with knowing only when the women tried to hide their identities and their backgrounds. While Montez seemed to always be reacting to developments, hanging on to fame and her identity re-creations by a thread, Fanny Fern purposefully hid herself behind that chosen pen name and then became the persona she had created. Adah Isaacs Menken learned from both Montez and Fern; she was such an enigma while alive that many had given up trying to know the poet and actor.

James Gordon Bennet wrote to his newspaper, the *New York Herald*, from Paris in 1847 that Lola Montez had "acquired so much notoriety of late, that many may want to know her history."[1] He was certainly correct. Bennet proceeded with a biography of Montez that was mostly untrue but which his newspaper published anyway. He, like all newspaper correspondents, found it impossible to accurately explain the background of the woman who had managed to trade her dancing career for a nobility title and influence in the kingdom of Bavaria. Where did she come from? By 1847 few believed her initial stories of having been born in Seville, Spain, and widowed by the execution of revolutionary Don Diego Leon. Most reported, however, that she was at least partially Spanish, either on her mother's or her father's side. Few knew, however, just how far she had gone to reimagine herself. By becoming Lola Montez, she left behind Eliza Gilbert James, who was born in Ireland, eloped at the age of sixteen, and divorced within five years due to her adultery. She turned to the stage to make a living and as Lola Montez she could claim an exoticism that matched her ability to capture an audience.[2]

One member of that audience changed her life, bringing the notoriety of which Bennett wrote. King Ludwig of Bavaria attended an 1846 performance in Munich and was smitten. He fell in love with Montez, built her a palace, sought her advice on state matters, and granted her the title of Countess of Landsfeld. Reporters accused her of wielding tyrannical powers; one wrote from Geneva that Montez "assumed the management of the affairs of State, and made and unmade cabinets at pleasure—disposing of the patronage attached to the Crown as her fancy dictated, and without respect to merit or qualification." Others wrote of outrageous personal behavior in Munich such as "spitting in the face of a bishop, thrashing a coalheaver, smashing shop-windows, or breaking her parasol over the head and shoulders of some nobleman adverse to her party." Readers of these accounts could not have been surprised in 1848 to learn that Montez had been exiled from Bavaria and King Ludwig forced to abdicate his throne. Montez contributed to the fall of the king but was not solely at fault as most Americans must have assumed.[3]

Americans continued to read juicy gossip about Montez and her personal life and in late 1851 learned that the notorious woman herself was planning a visit to the United States. By this time, many reporters knew much more about Montez's background due to a bigamy trial in London. The relatives of Montez's wealthy new husband surprisingly discovered that not only had Montez been married before but that the divorce granted by the court did not allow for her to remarry. When the family attempted to have her arrested for bigamy, she fled to France, but American newspapers and a New York magazine printed fairly accurate biographical details based on court records.[4] Americans could piece together what this all meant: Montez could only legally be married to her first husband but had clearly had sexual relations with two additional men and probably others. Shocking indeed.

Immediately editors and contributors denounced Montez and urged Americans to make the tour a failure by staying away from her performances. The *New York Times* labeled Montez a "shameless and abandoned woman" without a solid dance reputation.[5] One

LOLA COMING!

EUROPE FAREWELL! AMERICA I COME.

Lola Montez (1821–1861) caricature. David Claypoole Johnston created this lithograph of Montez leaving Europe and on her way to the United States in 1851 (Library of Congress, LC-DIG-pga-11158).

correspondent anticipated that Montez would try to hide her past and "hang out the banner of virtue."[6] Samuel Griswold Goodrich, an American diplomat in Paris, sent home a widely reprinted letter that was uncharacteristically blunt for the time, but that also revealed a bit of admiration. He called Montez "the most shameless, reckless, brilliant and successful prostitute of Europe" and the tour an insult to the United States. Goodrich hoped that Americans would shun Montez, but feared instead that "morbid curiosity" would compel "thousands of American ladies" to attend her weak performances.[7]

Editors realized that even before Montez arrived, this curiosity would sell papers, so they printed even more articles about her. The *Southern Press* published a glowing report from a correspondent, possibly her American agent Edward Payson Willis. The writer portrayed Montez as a completely respectable and nice person: "those who know her declare her to be noble, generous, and unselfish, even to a degree of romance."[8] Bennett, of the *New York Herald*, reported on her European tour and tried to give readers an appreciation of Montez's personality. He interviewed her in Paris in the summer of 1851 and used a story to convey both her wit and her courage. Bennett recounted that because of the events in Bavaria, some heads of governments banned her from performing in their countries, most notably Prince Wilhelm of Prussia. Bennett explained that Montez received a letter from the King of Holland that informed her of a ban on her appearance there also. Montez, Bennet joked, replied to the king saying that she had no intention of staging a performance there anyway. But Bennet also tried to temper Americans' expectations by admitting that Montez was not an artistic dancer like Fanny Elssler, who had toured the United States ten years earlier.[9]

American diplomat Goodrich also compared Montez to Elssler, and in this way contributed to a debate about what type of person should be afforded celebrity status. Goodrich argued that Elssler was different than Montez, not because she was more virtuous; he admitted that Elssler possessed a rather suspect past. He reminded Americans that "Fanny, however immoral, was not notorious for her immorality—was not solely famous for it; she was in her line the first *artiste* of her day, and in the character was worthy to be seen."[10] The *New York Herald* added that when Elssler toured, European dancers were still quite novel for the United States so they understandably drew large crowds. It also used morality as a determiner though, contrasting Montez with Jenny Lind: "there being a wide difference between a devil of a woman and a veritable angel." Still, the article continued, Montez would probably be successful because of her supposed actions since "the young men about town will go to see the lioness who has tamed kings, and kicked up revolutions with her heels in Europe."[11] The *Alexandria Gazette* agreed, reducing celebrity to physical appearance by printing that "a pretty woman will carry the day against all scruples."[12]

An editor in Richmond, Virginia, started a debate about celebrity in his city by objecting to the hypocrisy he detected in a boycott of Montez. Hugh Pleasants of the *Daily Dispatch* gave the example of Anna Bishop, an English singer who abandoned her husband and children for a lover and who Richmond citizens embraced in the late 1840s. Pleasants argued that Montez harmed no one with her immoralities, but in contrast, Bishop destroyed the lives of her children forever. He explained that he was not criticizing Richmond citizens for attending the Bishop concerts, at which her lover accompanied her, since he felt that a celebrity's art could be separate from her personal vices. He was just pointing out, he argued, the hypocrisy or what he labeled cant. One reader wrote in objecting to this characterization. She explained that patrons of the arts like her had chosen to boycott because of their repugnance to ballet and not specifically because of Montez's "unenviable notoriety." Pleasants reminded the woman that Fanny Elssler, who danced with much less modesty than Montez, drew the second largest audience ever to the Richmond theater. Another reader weighed in, explaining that she did object to Montez because of her lack of morals and her effect on the virtue of audience members.[13] The poet XYZ agreed rhyming in a Richmond magazine:

> Be Lola then unseen, unknown!
> She must, or we shall rue it:
> We have some modesty, we own;
> Ah! why should we undo it?
> The virtue prized of times long past
> We'd keep for a consoler,
> Nor cry for this, that we should miss
> The graceful step of Lola.[14]

Others argued that Montez was simply a product of publicity, but one even more created than previous celebrities. P.T. Barnum did not manage Montez's tour; he said he refused her and she said she had enough humbug in her life without him.[15] But because there was so much drama surrounding Montez, it was easy for many to see a connection. By 1852, the *New York Herald* seemed to tire of Montez, calling her the "meteor of humbug" and the "most notorious notoriety that ever passed over our horizon." The writer proclaimed her possibly the worst dancer ever to perform in New York and expressed utter amazement that puritanical Boston had embraced her. He called that occurrence

one of the miracles of the present day, in the science of humbug.... We are afraid, however if the Countess of Landsfeld remains much longer in Boston, or that neighborhood, either she will explode, or the Puritans will explode, or the Bunker Hill Monument will explode, or Boston itself will explode, or there will be a volcanic eruption of some kind.[16]

A month later, another writer for the *Herald* conceded that this type of contradiction set the United States apart from Europe, and confused Europeans to no end.

They cannot, by any exercise of their reasoning powers, comprehend the *furore* with which we enter into the most opposite pursuits of money making, politics, religion, socialism, fanaticism, hero worship, theatricals, fun, and drollery.[17]

Whether because of humbug, notoriety, or curiosity, Americans flocked to see Montez when she arrived. She debuted in New York on December 27, 1851, and toured eastern cities for more than a year before traveling to California and then Australia in the summer of 1855. She was not able to attract repeat audiences the way Jenny Lind, for example could, so she varied her offerings to give fans a clear reason to attend multiple times. Crowds became bored with her dances, which were not particularly scandalous and, most realized, fairly amateur in execution. She added dramas to her performances, including a play written for her about her own life, that enabled her to sell tickets when she returned to cities in which she had already appeared. Boycotts and all, she did very well in most places where she performed. When it became clear that her shows were tame, more women attended as well.[18]

Critics largely dismissed her dancing but pointed to a magnetic presence as the reason why audiences applauded Montez so enthusiastically and paid double the regular ticket prices. When she began performing plays, she received good reviews. Critics appreciated her natural style of acting that contrasted with the more stiff and formulaic delivery that was common. The *Boston Daily Mail* called her "an original character, strongly mental, nervous and vivid as the lightning." When she began starring in a play about her own life, possibly the first woman to do so, she seemed faultless. As the San Francisco *Daily Evening Bulletin* put it, "Who can say that anybody can act like Lola Montez better than that lady herself?" The critic called her acting "very lively and animated."[19]

No matter what critics wrote, fans and anti-fans treated Montez to what had become typical for a celebrity. In addition to attending her performances, they bought photographs of her that were for sale in many of the cities where she appeared. Many tried to meet or at least see her at train stations, on the street, and at her hotel. A former governor of New York disguised himself as a coach driver to get a glimpse. In Washington, D.C., so many prominent Americans and foreign diplomats called at her hotel

Lola Montez (1821–1861). Montez posed for many photographs that she used for publicity. This one is undated (Library of Congress, LC-DIG-ggbain-31646).

that most were unable to meet her. Even famed General Sam Houston, who was representing Texas in the Senate and seeking a party nomination for president of the United States, was turned away both times he visited. The Eagle Theatre in Buffalo burned down the night after Montez first appeared there, though it is not clear whether or not the fire was set as protest against her. Burlesque actors found, however, much about Montez to lampoon. They seized on both her acting and her dancing in bits such as "Who's Got the Countess?" that played at the San Francisco Theatre through the summer and fall of 1853. While Caroline Chapman impersonated a flustered and sensuous dramatic Montez, her brother William later in the show danced a vulgar version of Montez's most popular dance, the spider dance that Elssler had popularized in the United States.[20]

Montez, unlike many of the celebrities we have considered so far, was rarely willing to let criticism go unchallenged. The men around her often came to her defense, often at her urging. Patrick Hull, editor of the San Francisco *Herald* and later her husband (though not legally because her first husband still lived) took issue with the burlesque, especially with Chapman's dance costume, which apparently did not cover all that should have been covered. Hull also published a poetic defense of Montez's virtue written by an admirer on the back of a program from one of her shows that began

> Fair Lola:
> I cannot believe as I gaze on thy face
> And into those soul-sparkling eyes
> There rest in thy bosom one lingering trace
> Of a spirit the world should decry.[21]

Occasionally men physically defended her honor, though Montez was able and probably a bit too willing to do this herself. In New Orleans, she tried to watch a friend's performance from backstage but the theater manager barred all but stage hands from the area Montez had selected. When she was told she had to leave, she called her manager to deal with the offending stage hand but proceeded to kick him herself. Both she and her manager were accused of assault and battery. Montez reportedly used a horsewhip when it was handy (on a Bavarian soldier and against a California newspaper editor).[22]

Montez most often defended herself by writing letters to newspapers. She understood that her public was insatiably curious about her past and used these letters also to confuse the facts and to introduce lies into the narrative. Montez first used this method in London in 1843 when she tried to counter reports about her true identity by repeating her claims to Spanish heritage. Nearly ten years later, when an editor took issue with her visit to a Boston public school, Montez responded to the editorial with a lengthy letter that the *New York Times* printed on its front page. She challenged the editor in Boston to back up his claims of her lack of virtue with proof. The editor of the *New York Times* prompted his own scathing letter from Montez, who he labeled a "brazen prostitute," when he pointed out that demanding proof of an act that everyone involved with wants to cover up is an easy way to claim innocence. In her letter, Montez threatened to sue the *New York Times* for libel. She admitted that her life had been "wild, eccentric, and unfortunate" but always honorable. She falsely claimed that her first husband died, that she was granted a divorce from her second, and that the King of Bavaria had wanted only her friendship.[23] Americans who had been reading about her for years would have wondered why she left her other lovers, such as famous composer Franz List, out of her short autobiography.

With her play *Lola Montez in Bavaria*, she was able to even more effectively craft the story of her life. She hired Charles Ware to write the play and it debuted May 25, 1853, in New York. Montez performed the play in about a dozen cities in the United States. It was a major production with elaborate sets and costumes, thirty-four parts, and four acts that covered the different roles for Montez: dancer, politician, countess, and revolutionary/exile. She received fairly good reviews for her acting, but many found the play poorly written. Others identified clearly that the play was specifically designed to enhance Montez's career and reputation as a fighter for justice. One bored Californian complained that he nearly took a nap and that "Lola takes the lion's share of the dialogue, and gives the Bavarians precious little to say for themselves, reserving all the wit and repartee for herself." A reviewer in the *San Francisco Daily Evening Bulletin* called the play a "farce" and marveled that Montez announced afterwards that she thought her performances in Australia had furthered there the cause of republicanism.[24]

By 1858, Montez was back in New York, having concluded her trips to California and Australia. Though she declared in an interview early in the year that she was content to "leave the events of my life to history," she was not done shaping how she would be remembered, or rather confusing the matter to the degree that her true history could never be known.[25] She became entangled in a lawsuit when she was asked to serve as a witness to the bad character of David Wemyss Jobson, the claimant. Jobson's lawyer tried to prejudice the court against Montez by asking about her own background. The newspapers summarized the proceedings but recorded Montez's testimony verbatim, demonstrating how years after her first arrival in the United States, the public was still fascinated with Montez's history. Even though she was under oath, she denied affairs in which she probably engaged.[26] On the second day of her testimony the courtroom was packed and Montez played to the crowd, alternating cracking jokes with being indignant. She denied having been a chambermaid in Scotland but argued that it was not a dishonest job anyway. When the lawyer called her a woman and then corrected himself by saying, "this lady, I will call her," Montez received laughter by replying, "Pray call me a woman—I am proud to be a woman. Your mother was a woman!" The proceedings only became more contentious from there, ending with the lawyer of the defendant actually punching Jobson.[27]

Montez published three books in 1858 and lectured all across the country in 1860 to capitalize on her continuing popularity. She began with an autobiography that she possibly hired an author to write (it does not use the first person), that lays out a family line of nobility, and that restates many of the false claims of her personal history. Montez felt encouraged by good sales numbers to also produce a book of beauty secrets and an anthology of love stories. On her lecture tour, she spoke about her past, about love, about gallantry, and about strong-minded women; all except the first were quite illuminating.[28]

Fanny Fern addressed these same topics in her newspaper articles. Fern probably never met Montez even though Fern's brother, Edward Payson Willis, was Montez's manager when she first arrived in the United States. Fern did not write

Fanny Fern (1811–1872). This is a real photograph of Fanny Fern and not one of the fakes that circulated. It was taken probably in the 1860s (Library of Congress, LC-USZ62-113065).

about her and was estranged from Edward Willis at the time. She wrote a short piece after her brother died in 1853 blaming his downfall partly on the attractions of the theater. Fern and Montez had much in common but came from different worlds and varied in their views of proper behavior. Both headstrong and intelligent, they would probably not have liked each other very much.[29]

Both women sought and used fame, but only Fern seemed to consider its implications deeply. She often compared fame, especially for women, to the "apples of the Dead Sea" mentioned in the Bible, "fair to the sight, ashes to the touch!"[30] The Second Book of Peter likens indulging in sin to eating the apples, which are beautiful but chalky on the inside. Fern appreciated the ability to make money by her fame, large amounts of money that brought her security and independence, not the pittance she could make teaching or sewing. But fame also brought unwelcome scrutiny and abuse. Montez embraced these; Fern was uncomfortable with them. Fern also hated the different gender standards. Famous men could indulge in discussion of their celebrity but she was labeled egotistic when she wrote "Nobody could be more astonished than I to find myself famous." She responded to the backlash by saying that it was only fair that

> when a lady has had a mud-scow and a hand-cart, a steamboat and a hotel, a perfume and a score of babies, not to mention tobacco and music, named for her; and when she is told what her name is, wherever she goes, till she is sick of the sound of it, that she does not earn for herself a boxed ear when she couples with it the word "famous."[31]

Fern tried to shield herself from the scrutiny by using a pen name, and she had many good reasons to try to keep her identity secret. It was common for women of the 1840s to use pen names since it was considered rather indecent for a lady to be active in public, whether in action or just by words. Widowed without wealth but with two small children in 1845, Sara Willis Eldredge remarried quickly at the urging of her father. She supported herself and daughters after she left that husband because of his cruelty. She started selling her writing but wanted to shield her religious family from being connected with her blunt ideas and also hide her activities from her second husband who was ruining her reputation by starting infidelity rumors.[32] So she did not want to write under Sara Willis, Sara Eldredge, or Sara Farrington. She chose Fanny Fern.

Fern sold her work to a pair of weekly Boston newspapers, but her pieces were soon copied by editors throughout the country. She published both sentimental stories that were typical of what female (and some male) authors wrote at the time and humorous commentary pieces that were anything but typical. Her first piece signed Fanny Fern was "The Little Sunbeam" printed in the *Olive Branch* in the fall of 1851. She filled it with vivid images of tiny flowers, rippling brooks, and a child's "dark, soul-lit eyes."[33] In contrast, she published "Hungry Husbands" in the *True Flag*. In it she coined the phrase "the straightest road to a man's heart is through his palate," which quickly and enduringly became misquoted as "stomach." In this piece she poked fun at both men and women, advising wives to take advantage of a satiated husband:

> Then's your time, "Esther," for "half his kingdom," in the shape of a new bonnet, cap, shawl, or dress. He's too complacent to dispute the matter. Strike while the iron is hot; petition for a trip to Niagara, Saratoga, the Mammoth Cave, the White Mountains, or to London, Rome, or Paris. Should he demure about it, the next day cook him another turkey, and pack your trunk while he is eating it.[34]

By the fall of 1852, Fern was the first female weekly columnist in the United States and was earning enough to escape poverty. Fern moved to New York City in 1853 to pursue even more literary opportunities.[35]

Readers loved Fern's direct writing style and amusing observations on family life. They felt she was saying exactly what she wanted to say and what many of them would have liked to say. An editor in Louisiana called her one of the "most facetious and humorous writers of the day."[36] An anonymous writer in the *Daily Dispatch* praised Fern for her "practical tendency."[37] An editor in Maryland introduced one of her articles by saluting her: "Long live Fanny Fern! and long may she maintain that glorious independence of spirit."[38] Fanny Dade of Salem, Massachusetts, treasured Fern's columns and considered her "a kind, loving sister, with a flashing smile that breaks through the drolleries."[39]

The Salem woman declared that she did not care who Fanny Fern was, but she was distinctly in the minority. Most readers needed to know and went to great lengths to figure it out. One offered to bribe one of her editors by signing up new subscribers if he would tell the real name and another said that he needed her real name to add her to his newspaper staff as Assistant Editress.[40] Most asked in letters they sent to the newspaper offices; while Fern destroyed nearly all of these letters, some were published in newspapers. Jack Plane of Groton, Massachusetts, begged to know. "I almost tear the *Olive Branch* in pieces in my eager haste to read the production of her magic pen" he wrote.[41] One reader, signed Jenny Jessamine, wanted Fern's identity so she could make money from the knowledge.[42] Many scrutinized Fern's writings for clues. The editor of the *Weekly National Intelligencer* argued that Fern must be the wife or daughter of a clergyman because she wrote so knowledgeably about life in such a family.[43] Dorcas Dandelion guessed that Fern was married because she surmised that the author could not possibly know so much about husbands simply from *observation*; it must come from *experience*.[44]

Like Lola Montez, Fern used her writings to actually confuse readers about her past more than to reveal. She did not tell lies the way Montez did; Fern simply avoided the topic of her personal history. Until she published her autobiographical novel *Ruth Hall* in 1855, Fern rarely wrote about her past, even in guarded language. Her subterfuge was on a whole new level. Fern wrote with such fluidity of style, in a time when language was still fairly gendered, that her readers were not sure that she was actually a woman or even real. Francisca Lowell admitted imagining Fern as a mystical creature like one of P.T. Barnum's mermaids even though she and her husband often discussed who she might be. Men and women both fell in love with her. Albert from Alabama proposed marriage in a desperate attempt to maintain his sanity; he despaired however that he might be "worshipping at the shrine of some imaginary divinity, of whom I shall never know aught save the weekly pencillings that have so maddened my fiery brain."[45] Eliza wondered in the poem she wrote whether Fern was a "Jack or a Gill." After three stanzas of musing, she concluded:

> The ideal picture I have sketched,
> Is a being kind and true,
> And all that's good in womankind
> I've credited to you.
> Oh mirth provoking Fanny,
> If the genius of your pen
> Can stir the heart of woman thus,
> How is it with the men?[46]

Fern answered Eliza with a clear declaration that she was a "female woman" but the questions continued, largely because many could not believe a woman was capable of producing the clear, blunt prose (considered vulgar by some) they read each week.[47] In 1852, at the same time that Montez was generating talk, speculation about Fern's identity was reaching a peak. Editors offered male possibilities. Many printed that Tom Norris, the editor of the *Olive Branch* was actually Fanny Fern and had created her to bring publicity to his newspaper—another example of humbug. Others assumed that it was some other literary fellow, such as N.P. Willis, editor of the *Home Journal*, or Richard Storrs Willis, editor of the *Musical World and Times*, both of whom were actually Fern's brothers.[48]

Fern declared herself a woman but the confusion about her sex, and Fern's articles themselves, encouraged Americans to discuss gender issues. Fern avoided direct connection to the small women's rights movement of the 1850s, but she argued, from personal experience, for women to have more opportunities and for men to be prevented from holding so much power, economic and otherwise, over women. Some condemned her for these views. Harry from Alabama believed that Fanny was a threat to masculinity and to the institution of marriage. He wrote to the *Olive Branch* threatening to start a petition against her and assumed that she was a bitter woman who had never had an opportunity to marry.[49]

Many editors contributed to the debate in a more light hearted way. Some poked fun at Fern. An editor in Indiana countered Fern's pronouncement that a woman's heart was as valuable as the hearts of twelve men with "Old bachelors, don't be discouraged by Fanny Fern, as it is only her way of trying to get a dozen husbands."[50] Others clearly showed an appreciation for her with their humor. The author of a story that originated in a newspaper from Ulster, New York, predicted that the sleepwalker profiled in the tale would never again have problems if he were to "wed an experienced widow of the Fanny Fern stamp."[51] The *Grand River Times* and many other newspapers published the joke "The fragments of the bachelor who bust into tears, on reading Fanny Fern's description of the happiness of married life, have been found."[52] Hugh Pleasants caught readers' attention with the headline Woman's Rights and proceeded to discuss Fern's success. He started the article with "there is one right which one woman is certainly entitled to, and that woman is Fanny Fern; she has a right to be proud of her writings."[53]

Others engaged in debate in a more serious way even if Fern did not. Medical student W.W.K. wrote a letter in support of female doctors, an idea that Fern had addressed in a widely circulated article. Fern joked that clearly the presence of a member of the other sex would help make a patient feel better. She painted a picture of a deathly sick bachelor miraculously improved but vowing to remain ill just so that his new pretty doctoress would visit him again.[54] W.W.K. did not dispute this effect on patients but wanted to more seriously present an argument for women as doctors (and all other professions). He explained that he and his classmates held women in even higher esteem after having shared the educational experience with them. In the lecture hall, the dissecting room, and the sickroom, the male and female students displayed "mutual defference and respect for each others thoughts and feelings."[55] Others were clearly not in favor of an expanded role for women and argued that if Fanny Fern were female, her views and language were inappropriate and much too manly for a lady.[56]

As early as fall of 1852 some of the mystery seemed gone. Many editors were printing that they believed that Fanny Fern was a Willis sister and by early spring, her real name appeared linked to her pseudonym in many newspapers.[57] In February of 1853, the *Boston Bee* published a widely reprinted fairly accurate description of Fern's appearance and family life details.[58] When one of her Boston editors outed her in his newspaper December 30, 1854, that should have ended the speculation about her true identity.[59] By this time Fern was living in New York as an extremely successful writer. She was the highest paid newspaper columnist in the United States and had published two collections of articles and a novel, with a combined sales of nearly 200,000 copies.[60]

Finally knowing that Fanny Fern was indeed a female gave women writers all across the country inspiration. Many took alliterative pen names with a nod to nature, such as Winnie Woodfern and Ruth Rustic. Although Fern made fun of the practice by giving ridiculous examples like Lily Liburnum, the women truly admired Fern.[61] Mary Gibson lived a life that mirrored Fern's in many ways. Gibson pursued a writing career in Boston, under the pen name Winnie Woodfern. She eventually left an unhappy marriage and moved to New York in 1855, ending up employed by the same newspaper at which Fern worked. She wrote sentimental fiction and satirical short pieces that clearly used Fern as their inspiration, though she wrote in other styles as well. Gibson was fairly well known but never a celebrity like Fern, though it seems she did yearn for that level of recognition. Her fiction often featured a young, ambitious girl who desired fame and fortune. Her character Hero Strong tells her friends that she "must be wealthy and famous—then famous and wealthy—and then both together. This is the burden of my song—fame and riches. And both must be won by this good right hand."[62]

Cornelia Orme, writing under the pen name Ruth Rustic, was more modest in her aims. In 1855 she published a book of her poems that had appeared in newspapers. In her preface, she acknowledged that the volume could very well be her first and last such publication. Among her collection of musings on death, travel, religion, and nature, she included a piece written for Fanny Fern. Orme honored Fern for surviving difficult times and winning a "beautiful wreath of fame." She also praised the author's satire, which Fern could

> wield with graceful hand,
> And we smile e'en while we're lashed, Fanny,
> Such skill is in thy wand.[63]

Others imitated Fern's blunt writing style and even copied her habit of misspelling and italicizing specific words for emphasis. Marian H.

Stevens responded to criticism that she was stealing Fern's style with the complaint that Fern's fans were "swelling her up a *leetle* too big for her *breeches*."[64] A woman in California wrote a toast for a celebration of the founding of Plymouth Colony that honored the women, who were, she felt, often forgotten at such events. She argued that they had to endure everything that the males did as well as put up with the Pilgrim Fathers. She concluded with the comedic logic of "how *could* they have been *fathers* if there had been no *mothers?*"[65]

Other women used Fern's ideas but ended up misquoting her. Virginia Clay, wife of a United States senator from Alabama, wrote to her father-in-law in 1856 that southerners in Washington, D.C., felt "a little as Fanny Fern says Eugenie felt when she espoused Louis Napoleon, as if we are 'dancing over a powder magazine!'" If Clay had consulted Fern's "To the Empress Eugenia," she would have realized that Fern attributed the danger to something more naturally occurring; "Well, dance away, little Empress; but I tell you that you are dancing over a volcano."[66] A Farmer's Wife, disgusted that her husband would not put up a decent clothes line for her, nearly resorted to the Fanny Fern trick of getting "right into his affections through his stomach." Fern, by using the word "palate" in her original article argued that it was not just any satisfying meal that would be effective but a particularly tasty one that would do the trick.[67]

Misquotations did not diminish the reality that Fern's writings made people think and debate. Even newspaper editors who rarely published her pieces found at least one among them they endorsed to their readers. When Fern wrote in 1857 about the absurdities of women's clothes, an editor in Eaton, Ohio, reprinted the piece, saying that he did not "like Fanny Fern's writings generally, but sometimes she makes a decidedly palpable hit."[68] The editor of the *Indiana American* reprinted the same piece with an even harsher general assessment of Fern, saying that though she possessed "an unbalanced and diseased mind, gets off some very appropriate and sensible things."[69]

In 1857, Fern again stirred a reaction on the topic of lady doctors. She started this second piece by pointing out the many reasons she was glad that women physicians were gaining acceptance, but quickly fell into satirical reflections on why she preferred a male doctor. Fern emphasized the problem of jealousy or competition between women: "Before swallowing her pills (of which she would be the first), I should want to make sure that I had never come between her and a lover, or a new bonnet, or been the innocent recipient of a gracious smile from her husband."[70] Fern's piece was reprinted in journals such as the *Family Herald* and Dr. Lydia Sayer Hasbrouck was not amused. She wrote that the article "should brand [Fern] forever as one to be scorned."[71]

Hattie, who wrote to the *Southern Enterprise*, also disagreed with Fern, but on a much lighter topic: male facial hair. She started with a Fernesque beginning: after a quote from Fern praising the "moss rosy" look of mustaches, she wrote "Indeed, Fanny, do you think so?" Hattie's humorous piece mostly focused on the impossibility of keeping food out of the whiskers. She suggested that after watching in profile a musta-chioed man eat soup, "turn to your bearded terrier, as he pitches into his mush and milk. Is not the resemblance striking?"[72]

Readers often wrote to Fern to request her help, her advice, or that she address an issue on which they wanted to hear her opinion. An annoyed woman asked Fern to chastise men for filling the seats in the ladies' cabin on ferry boats: "Give them a dig, Fanny, won't you?"[73] A woman requested a sympathetic piece about how hard it was to be a stepmother.[74] Mary M. asked for a frank answer to her question about marrying an "old bachelor" and Fern certainly gave it. "Don't do it," she advised; when a man has for years indulged in every "little selfish incli-nation unchecked" he will be very hard to please.

> He will be as unbending as a church-steeple—as exacting as a Grand Turk, and as impossible to please as a teething baby. Take my advice, Mary; give the old fossil the mitten, and choose a male specimen who is in the transition state, and capable of receiving impressions.[75]

Always eager to give advice, Fern found other attention from her fans much more annoying, especially if they were of a personal nature. She reported ignoring requests for money (to start a busi-ness, buy a dress, for cigars), for handmade items (pincushions), and for written pieces (love letters, school papers, family histories, ele-gies to deceased pets).[76] Fern wanted to provide help to other writers but she received so many manuscripts, many with spelling errors, that she found she just could not. What she hated most of all were auto-graph collectors and celebrity watchers, who often commented on her appearance.[77]

Fern remained a mystery to many even after her identity was revealed and her autobiographical novel published. Fans wrote to her asking for descriptions, fake photographs circulated, and people expressed surprise when meeting her for the first time. Impostors took advantage of the ambiguity, earning money on the lecture circuit. Fern did not pursue legal action against them but in 1856 successfully sued to prevent publication of a cookbook under Fanny Fern authorship. She won through this verdict the exclusive use of her pen name and after that it became more and more her real name; friends called her Fanny and for all but legal matters, she signed her name Fanny Fern.[78] She became then, like Lola Montez, fully a creature of her own making not of someone else's. Unlike for Montez, though, there was no debate about whether or not Fern deserved her fame. Fern possessed real talent for writing that was appreciated for its unique contribution to a discussion of social topics of the day even though it was not liked by all.

Adah Isaacs Menken may never have met Fanny Fern but she visited Lola Montez in early January 1861. Montez lived in New York City and was tended by a nurse and an old friend after suffering a stroke June 30, 1860.[79] Menken wrote to a friend that she felt a "strange, irresistible attraction" to Montez. By this time Menken was an actor in addition to a poet and had already moved on to her second private self. She first attracted attention for her poetry as a devout Jewish wife in Cincinnati, but performing male roles on stage and partying with the members of the pseudo-military Light Guard of Dayton, Ohio, undermined her claim to that identity. In New York City she became the discarded wife of famous boxer John Heenan, garnering sympathy with letters to the editor. Menken was not yet as famous as Montez but wanted to be. She clearly realized the consequences of such desires when she wrote to a friend that she thought Montez was "happier than I am. She asks nothing more of the world, while I ask much. You know wherein dwells the better philosophy."[80] We do not know much about the visit. Montez died shortly after, January 17, 1861, and while newspapers debated whether Montez's life had been important, Menken planned her next step in her own bid for contested celebrity.[81]

Menken next became an intellectual and frequented Pfaff's Tavern off of Bleeker Street while she played the daring part of Mazeppa on stage. She prepared for this transition by publishing poems that convinced many that she had depth. Critics must have been surprised how quickly and easily Menken discarded her identity as the sympathetic victim of a cad who would use a young woman and leave her. She published "Now and Then" in February of 1861, signaling that she was very much aware of the complexities of celebrity. She began the poem "A way down into the shadowy depths of the Real I once lived. I thought that to seem was to be." Later in the poem she made even more clear her ideas about the link between her real life and performance: "After all, living is but to play a part!"[82]

In June of 1861 she began playing the role that would make her an international star. She performed the lead part in "Mazeppa; or, The Wild Horse of Tartary." Men, and a few women, had enjoyed success with the exciting play for decades, bringing sword fights, war scenes, and horse tricks to the stage. Most however refused to perform the play's most dangerous stunt of being tied to a horse that gallops up a steep slope, made with scaffolding at the back of the stage. Most actors opted for a dummy to ride away in their stead, but not Menken. She performed the feat dressed similar to how the men would have been dressed, stripped of her clothes except for a thigh length shirt cinched at her waist and skin colored tights.[83] This was a shocking display of nudity at a time when a glimpse in public of a lady's ankle was rare. Of course as we have seen, the public accepted a degree of relaxed propriety for art; Menken aimed to test the limits of that principle. Her intellectual Bohemian identity allowed her to more convincingly make the argument.

When she toured California in 1864, she wore her hair short and dressed in men's clothes when she appeared on the street. Her off-stage performance extended her intellectual identity by also incorporating tragic elements. She portrayed herself as a Bohemian who made her own rules but who was haunted by the consequences of her unconventional life. She published a poem in the popular San Francisco literary magazine *Golden Era* that described a quest for celebrity as an illness and expressed regret from a life of failure, though she was still not even thirty years old. She also seemed to be responding to Lola Montez's challenge to "dare to meet one's self—to sit down face to face with one's own life, and confront all those deeds which may have influenced the mind or manners of society, for good or evil."[84] The last two stanzas of the Menken five-stanza poem are

> I can but own my life is vain
> A desert void of peace;
> I missed the goal I sought to gain,
> I missed the measure of the strain
> That lulls Fame's fever in the brain,
> And bids Earth's tumult cease.
> Myself! alas for theme so poor
> A theme but rich in Fear;
> I stand a wreck on Error's shore,
> A spectre not within the door,
> A houseless shadow evermore,
> An exile lingering here.[85]

Admirers easily believed these were the laments of the real Adah Menken and not simply another performance of the celebrity everyone called the Menken. They had given up hope of knowing the true biographical facts about Menken; so many versions of her youth had been published that still today we know little for certain of her origins. But fans thought that through her poetry they were privileged with something even more valuable: glimpses into her true nature. Few actually knew her real thoughts, but she had written to a friend in 1861 that writing her seemingly confessional poetry was another form of acting. "I do not give all my heart out in my writings—I mean for publication," she explained. "Let me confess that I sometimes affect to do so when writing of something I know nothing about. But public writing is like acting—to reach the hearts of others we must appear in earnest ourselves." In another letter, she admitted that this layering of her life was confusing and that she could not always determine what was real due to her "imaginative nature."[86] No wonder her fans did not know the real her; she probably did not either.

Menken was far from done recreating herself though. She took her performance to Europe, only returning to New York for a brief but very profitable run in 1866 on Broadway, where she earned five hundred dollars for each appearance—as much as most women who were working made in a year. During this time she readopted an off-stage type of femininity, leaving the male attire behind, to become as one author put it, a "faltering sex goddess." Menken continued to be accepted into intellectual circles because of her poetry, but now exhibited self-destructive behaviors; she smoked, drank in public, exuded overt sexuality, and gained weight that hid the boyish figure that had made playing male roles on stage so easy. She flaunted her affairs by circulating photographs of herself in intimate poses with two of the most famous authors of the day: Alexander Dumas and Algernon Charles Swinburne.[87]

This would be her final performance. Menken died in Paris on August 10, 1868; she was only thirty-three years old but had lived multiple lives. She performed many roles, both on stage and off, as well as wrote essays and more than one hundred poems. Like so much of her life, how she died is a mystery. She may have had peritonitis, tuberculosis, or cancer. One thing is certain: her early death allowed for others to craft her enduring identity. Menken left her poems, the more sentimental of which appeared in a collection, as well as fragments of an autobiography that the *New York Times* published the month after her death. Critics dismissed her life as meaningless but fans interpreted these pieces as they wished; many women celebrated her as a martyr whose treatment during life exposed the challenges women faced. Elizabeth Cady Stanton, famous suffragist, wrote that Menken's poetry collection

> reveals an inner life of love for the true, the pure, the beautiful, that none could have imagined in the actress whose public and private life were alike sensual and scandalous. Who can read the following verses from her pen, without feeling that this unfortunate girl, a victim of society, was full of genius and tenderness.[88]

Fan Millie Carpenter wrote a poem to her that also reveled in finally being able to appreciate Menken. She published it in the same weekly newspaper that had printed many of Menken's poems. Carpenter concluded with

> The sacred fire upon the hearth
> By which we now with clearer eyes,
> See her in her poet worth
> And grow through charity, more wise.[89]

Fans needed at least the illusion of knowing their celebrities. Menken is not the only woman who understood this. Many of the women we have considered provided a persona for public consumption. The extent that Montez, Fanny Fern, and Menken went to craft an ever-changing private self was much more extreme than any had attempted.

Select Bibliography

Foley, Doris. *The Divine Eccentric; Lola Montez and the Newspapers.* Los Angeles: Westernlore Press, 1969.

Laffrado, Laura. "I Thought from the Way you *Writ,* that you were a Great Six Footer of a Woman: Gender and Public Voice in Fanny Fern's Newspaper Essays." In *Her Own Voice: Nineteenth-Century American Women Essayists,* edited by Sherry Lee Linkon, 81–96. New York: Garland Publishing, 1997.

Montez, Lola. *Lectures of Lola Montez, including her Autobiography.* New York: Rudd & Carleton, 1859.

O'Neill, Bonnie Carr. *Literary Celebrity and Public Life in the Nineteenth-Century United States.* Athens: University of Georgia Press, 2017.

Sentilles, Renee M. *Performing Menken: Adah Isaacs Menken and the Birth of American Celebrity.* Cambridge: Cambridge University Press, 2003.

Seymour, Bruce. *Lola Montez: A Life.* New Haven: Yale University Press, 1996.

Varley, James. *Lola Montez: The California Adventures of Europe's Notorious Courtesan.* AH Clark, 1996.

Walker, Nancy A. *Fanny Fern.* New York: Maxwell Macmillan International, 1993.

Warren, Joyce W. *Fanny Fern: an Independent Woman.* New Brunswick: Rutgers University Press, 1992.

Warren, Joyce W., ed. *Ruth Hall and Other Writings.* New Brunswick: Rutgers University Press, 1986.

Six

◇◇◇◇◇◇◇◇◇◇◇◇◇◇

Harriet Beecher Stowe
and Victoria Woodhull

Obscenity and Censorship

The influence of celebrities grew after the 1850s but it was in no way unchecked. Many Americans of the late nineteenth century insisted on eliminating obscenity in society, and celebrities too faced the censorship that developed. In fact two of America's most famous women faced criticism for involvement in sex scandals even though they were not implicated as participants. Harriet Beecher Stowe and Victoria Woodhull simply reported in print what everyone already suspected, but in an age when it was improper to talk about sex, these women risked their reputations by speaking the truth as they saw it. Their cases emphasize one of the complications of labeling speech obscene: interpretations vary widely. Mart Brown, the editor of the *State Rights Democrat* of Albany, Oregon, demonstrated this with his criticism of Abigail Duniway, editor of the *New Northwest*. Duniway had recently returned from the East and had endorsed Victoria Woodhull with enthusiasm: "I rejoice in her mission and bid her good speed in her labors!" Brown complained that "if there is a more obscene or filthy publication extant than that of the Woodhull's we have yet to see it" and pointed out the inconsistency of Duniway printing approval of Woodhull while in the same issue condemning obscene literature.[1]

Harriet Beecher Stowe became a star by publishing an antislavery novel. When she learned in 1850 that the United States Congress had passed the Fugitive Slave Act, which among other things made it illegal to assist escaping enslaved people, she was determined to protest no matter what happened to her reputation. She wrote to her sister Catharine Beecher that when a fugitive arrived at her door in Brunswick, everyone in the house worked to find him a bed even though she might

105

have sent him on his way before the passage of the law.[2] Her anger continued to increase, partly because her sister-in-law, Isabella Beecher Hooker, described for her scenes of fugitive captures in Boston. Stowe's children remembered their mother's reaction to one letter from their aunt. Stowe read the letter aloud and after the phrase "If I could use a pen as you can, I would write something that would make this whole nation feel what an accursed thing slavery is," she stood up from her chair, crumpled the note in her hand, and declared that she would do it.[3] But in the fall of 1850, Stowe was raising an infant as well as educating at home her five older children. They had recently moved from Ohio to Maine and her preacher husband was in between jobs, neither of which paid very well. Stowe, in addition to running the household, sold religious and sentimental stories to magazines to keep her family fed. She published one response to the Fugitive Slave Law in August of 1850, but a longer antislavery piece would have to wait.[4]

Stowe argued years later that she did not actually write *Uncle Tom's Cabin* but had only put down on paper what had been revealed to her by God. In this story her first vision occurred in early 1851 while she was attending church services.[5] Stowe walked home with what would become Uncle Tom's death scene on her mind. In her room she wrote out her vision, adding the conversion to Christianity of the two enslaved men who caused Tom's death; the story centers as much on evangelical religion as on abolition. In March, Stowe told Gamaliel Bailey, abolitionist editor of the *National Era*, that she was writing an antislavery story she thought she could finish in three or four parts. He agreed to print it in weekly installments and pay her three hundred dollars. The first chapter appeared in June of 1851, and Stowe delivered forty installments, ten times what she had projected. Bailey printed them all but still only paid her the three hundred dollars.[6] While Stowe was writing for money, clearly she felt compelled to extend this story well beyond what she had promised. She could have wrapped up the tale at many earlier points. Even before Bailey printed the final chapter, *Uncle Tom's Cabin; or, Life Among the Lowly* appeared in book form.

Stowe had no reason to expect that her visions would make her rich and famous; she hoped to make enough from the sale of the book to buy a silk dress. While few Americans subscribed to the Washington, D.C., based *National Era*, many more were aware of the story. Eager readers purchased three thousand copies of the book on the first day it was available, March 20, 1852. By early the next year, they had bought two hundred thousand copies. Within a year, publishers produced more than one hundred editions. *Uncle Tom's Cabin* was well on its way to becoming the best-selling novel of the nineteenth century. Stowe's first royalty check was more than ten thousand dollars. She could buy a closet full of silk dresses with that but she renovated her home instead.[7]

As we have seen, readers of sentimental fiction felt compelled to act on their induced emotions. Stowe wrote a sentimental piece that was, however, so much more. Like Susannah Rowson's *Charlotte Temple*, *Uncle Tom's Cabin* grew out of anger about the status quo. Rowson hated the double standard that rewarded men for sexual behavior but doomed women for the same and when she combined that anger with a sentimental story, it could not fail to deeply affect the reader. Similarly, Stowe channeled her indignation about the Fugitive Slave Law into a sentimental story told with images worthy of any pulpit. Though a woman, Stowe was a Beecher and destined to be a preacher—her father, husband, and seven brothers were all ministers. She too knew how to sermonize with a parable. It is no surprise that a country under the spell of *Uncle Tom's Cabin* would rediscover *Charlotte Temple*.[8]

Readers of the 1850s emoted in many ways. Grown men foolish enough to read *Uncle Tom's Cabin* in public found themselves unable to control their weeping; former United States congressman and *New York Tribune* editor Horace Greeley unexpectedly shortened a train trip so he could find a quiet place to finish reading the book.[9] Though Stowe's story is grim and at times horrific, Americans celebrated it more often with lightheartedness than with somber reflection. The Tomism craze surpassed all others that came before. Elsslerism and Lindomania swept through cities where the women performed, maybe lingering for a time. Americans experienced Tomism every time they read the book,

Harriet Beecher Stowe (1811–1896). Stowe posed for this photograph late in life, around 1880 (Library of Congress, LC-USZ62-11212).

attended any of the play versions, or were reminded of the story from a newspaper article or even conversation with friends. Fans sang songs written for their favorite characters, viewed painted story panoramas, and of course bought merchandise. They purchased, commemorative plates, gold and silver spoons, hats, scarves, dresses, card games, figurines, and wallpaper for the rooms of their home.[10]

Uncle Tom's Cabin sheet music. Harriet Beecher Stowe's book inspired many works of popular culture, including this song "I Am Going There, or the Death of Little Eva" from 1852 (Library of Congress, LC-USZ62-7499).

Critics in the North largely reviewed the book well though they were not as enthusiastic as the public. Stowe feared the abolitionist reaction to her ending.[11] She concluded with some of her surviving characters moving to Liberia, seemingly siding with the proponents of colonization or also known by this time as the back to Africa movement. Support in the North for the movement had dwindled since Lydia Maria Child faced rebuke for criticizing colonization. By 1852, many abolitionists opposed this plan of sending newly freed people to a continent on which they or even their parents and grandparents had never lived. They overlooked even this undesirable element of the book, however, in favor of what they felt would be the overall effect: a direct blow to the perceived legitimacy of slavery and a swelling of the ranks of abolitionists.

Some in the North tried to suppress the book precisely because of its possible impact. The first publisher Stowe considered rejected the book because it had many customers in the South and did not want to jeopardize that business. (Ironically, that printer bought the copyright from the original publisher in 1854, which shows that reluctance to be short lived compared with the profits they could make.)[12] The Rev. Joel Parker sued Stowe in Philadelphia for twenty thousand dollars, possibly in an attempt to discredit the book and reduce its popularity. He claimed Stowe attacked his character by misquoting him and naming him in a footnote in the novel. Stowe used Parker as an example of a minister who objected to the owning of enslaved people being characterized as a particularly heinous sin. While she invented or misremembered the quote she attributed to him, it certainly matched the sentiment he had expressed numerous times. Stowe intended to remove the footnote, the only one in the book, but simply forgot to advise the printer of that decision. Newspapers published the nasty letters exchanged in the feud, which had the opposite effect of Parker's intentions. The public was enthralled by this bitter argument between prominent people, including a woman who was becoming more famous each day. Rather than hurt sales, the lawsuit, which was dropped, probably actually helped them.[13]

Of course, white southerners criticized the book and Stowe most harshly. *Southern Ladies Book* called the author both a liar and unfeminine. It argued that Stowe had "unsexed herself,--as an advocate she has stooped to falsehood,--as a witness she has perjured herself." It claimed her "treachery" was worse than the treasonous acts of General Benedict Arnold, who betrayed the patriot cause in the American Revolution. He acted out of "revenge of a defeated ambition" but she spewed the "cold venom of a nature naturally and irremediably vile."[14]

Judge John Bragg, United States congressman from Alabama, also criticized Stowe's integrity and femininity in harsh terms. Newspapers widely reported that Bragg called *Uncle Tom's Cabin* a "most gross and exaggerated caricature" of the South and that he wondered how Stowe could "so completely unfrock herself as to indulge in the obscene reflections with which this book is everywhere replete. Every southern plantation is represented as a harem, and every female slave as a victim of her master's lusts." He argued that the South had never produced women like Stowe, "such monstrosities, such men-women, such moral hermaphrodites." He concluded with a quote from the British poet Lord Byron: "There is a tide in the affairs of women. Which, taken at the flood, leads—God knows where!"[15] Clearly Bragg saw ominous signs in the future.

Overall, however, white southern reaction to *Uncle Tom's Cabin*, was mixed. Some wrote Stowe threatening letters. Dozens of authors penned Anti-Tom novels that attempted to refute Stowe's characterization of their region. Mary Henderson Eastman, noted author of books about Native Americans, published the popular though unimaginatively titled *Aunt Phillis's Cabin; or, Southern Life as It Is.* Some, on the other hand, found truth and merit in Stowe's book, though they would not have considered themselves fans of the author. A few embraced the book warmly, like a slave owner in Alabama who read *Uncle Tom's Cabin* out loud to his wife. They both shouted for joy when George and Eliza reached Canada and thought that the story would do more good than any book since the Bible.[16]

Most surprising, however, was how readily available it was in the South. Most state legislatures in the region outlawed antislavery speech and material (often vaguely labeled incendiary or inflammatory) starting in the 1830s. Maryland legislators in 1836, for example, declared it to be a "high offence" against the state to write or distribute material that challenged slavery. Violators could be punished with imprisonment for ten to twenty years.[17] Authorities whipped people found with books such as Lydia Maria Child's *Appeal*.[18] Stowe believed that her book was banned in the region; many believed it to be incendiary.[19] But Gresham's Book Seller on Broad Street in Richmond, Virginia, advertised in the *Daily Dispatch* that they had copies of the book for sale.[20] Mary Chestnut possibly bought her copy there. She recorded in her diary that she read it numerous times and that she heard many people of Richmond discussing the faults and merits of the book. Frederick Law Olmstead, who traveled in the South in the 1850s, wrote about seeing the book openly for sale. Book sellers complained they could not keep enough copies in stock and many readers ordered theirs directly from New York City.[21] A man from North Carolina returned from a trip to New

York with presents of both *Uncle Tom's Cabin* and *Aunt Phillis's Cabin*. Stowe's book generated much discussion on the plantation according to the New Englander who served as the tutor where the presents were received.[22] Nobody mentioned that they were breaking the law or that it was dangerous to have a copy of the book. Clearly the ban in this case was not being enforced often.

Some newspapers in the South, however, immediately called for a suppression of *Uncle Tom's Cabin*. The editors of the Richmond *Daily Dispatch*, at the same time that they were running advertisements for the book, expressed shock that southerners would wish to read it and predicted that the "wide dissemination of such dangerous volumes" would bring about an end to southern society. They printed a letter from *Fiat Justitia* (Let Justice Be Done) that asked how a book filled with lies and that advocated the murder of masters by slaves could be allowed to be available for sale.[23] The *Kentucky Watchman* urged its readers "not to buy, sell or cause to be distributed, a work, represented to be a novel" but that was really an abolitionist piece "intended to cast an incendiary fire-brand into the very heart of the South."[24] Thomas Warren, of the *Camden Journal*, admitted that he had not read *Uncle Tom's Cabin* and probably never would, but called it a lie and argued that "such publications should be prohibited in the Southern States, and it ought to be an indictable offence for any Southern bookseller to vend abolition and incendiary publications like this, which manifestly endangers the peace and safety of our homes and firesides."[25]

Residents, encouraged by such writings, enforced the laws even if the authorities seemed not to. Northern businessman Charles Grandison Parsons noted in his travelogue that slave owners in Athens, Georgia, burned several boxes of *Uncle Tom's Cabin* that were bound for Atlanta.[26] Charleston, South Carolina, ran out of town a visitor from England for providing a young lady with a copy of the book. Visiting Henry Pellew, heir to the Earl of Exmouth, argued that the woman had requested a copy but friends advised he leave the city anyway.[27] Lawyer, journalist, and eventual mayor of New York City Abraham Oakey Hall, burned his copy in 1852. Writing under the pen name Hans Yorkel for the *New Orleans Bulletin*, he called the book not only false, but also trashy and crude in style.[28]

The Rev. Sam Green suffered the consequences of having a copy and is a glaring exception to the tolerance surrounding the distribution of *Uncle Tom's Cabin*. Green was a Dorchester County, Maryland, black Methodist preacher who had purchased his freedom. Green found himself in jail for possessing abolitionist material after he returned from a trip to Canada in 1856 to visit his twenty-five-year-old son who had escaped from slavery. The proof used against him was a map of Canada, railroad schedules north, letters from his son, and a copy of *Uncle Tom's Cabin*, which he had borrowed. The lawyers in the two-week trial mostly debated whether or not the novel could be considered abolitionist and inflammatory. The judge ruled that it could and that possession of it broke the law. He sentenced Green to serve ten years in prison although Stowe's book was freely available for sale and was advertised in the newspapers of Maryland. Green served five years and was released during the Civil War.[29]

Censorship, real or imagined, did not hurt the popularity of *Uncle Tom's Cabin*. Stowe was the most famous woman in America in the mid–1850s even though the characters in the book, like Charlotte Temple had, surpassed their creator in popularity. Stowe had not set out to be a celebrity. She wrote not for fame but because her family needed money and in the words of her sister Catharine Beecher, a woman should shrink from "public gaze." Yet, Stowe signed her stories as a "way of getting a reputation" and did not shield herself behind a pen name.[30] She certainly relished the opportunities that fame brought. She immediately started to travel, first to the cities of the East Coast and then repeatedly to Europe. Everywhere doors opened for the novelist. Stowe wrote from New York to her husband, in the summer of 1852, that neither "fame nor praise" contented her but also that the best thing that happened to her occurred because of her celebrity status. Stowe was able to attend a sold-out Jenny Lind concert from a seat given to her personally by the singer. Stowe described the event as a "bewildering dream of sweetness and beauty."[31]

Fanny Fern noted Stowe's celebrity in one of her columns of 1853. Fern knew Stowe from their school days at Catharine Beecher's Hartford Female Seminary. Fern stole pies and used her geometry homework for hair curling papers, but was rarely punished because she was everybody's favorite; her father did, however have to pay for a desk on which Fern carved the initials of her name. Stowe, as the head mistress's younger sister, was both a teacher and a student who longed to be friends with popular Fern but was too shy to approach her.[32] Fern now thirty years later took notice of Stowe since she had finally surpassed Fern's own popularity. In true Fern fashion, she humorously praised and criticized all at once. Fern dismissed the claims that *Uncle Tom's Cabin* was not genius and argued that if Stowe did not like the trouble that fame brought, as a woman she could have easily avoided it by keeping silent; nobody could miss the connection of these arguments to Fern's own reception by critics. But behind the humor lingers a bit of envy. Fern and her brothers all worked hard for the recognition they received.

They must have been a bit infuriated with how easily the Beechers could use their name to catapult to fame.

> It is perfectly insufferable—*one* genius in a family is enough. There's your old patriarch father—God bless him!—there's material enough in him to make a dozen ordinary men, to say nothing of "Henry Ward" who's not so great an idiot as he might be! You see you had no "call," Mrs. Tom Cabin, to drop your babies and darning-needle to immortalize your name.[33]

Stowe must not have taken offense since the two authors renewed their acquaintance and seemed to become friends.

Stowe continued to write and remained a celebrity right through the Civil War—President Abraham Lincoln reportedly called her the "little lady who started this big war" when he met her and Susan B. Anthony called her the Queen Bee of literary women in 1869—but changing times and a scandal of her own making reduced her stature.[34] Stowe again spoke her mind, but this time, condemnation was swift and sustained. In 1869 she wrote an article for the *Atlantic Monthly* in which she besmirched the memory of the poet Lord Byron by revealing that he had committed incest.[35] (We do not know if Stowe ever saw the piece written about her by Judge John Bragg, but if the label of obscene did not rankle her possibly the quote from Byron did!) She refrained from naming the object of his affections, but many had long suspected that his married half-sister Augusta Leigh had been his unnaturally close friend. Stowe learned of this scandal from the wife of the poet in 1856 but did nothing for more than a decade. She even counseled Lady Byron to remain silent at the time of their first discussion of the affair. Stowe decided to reveal the information in an article in 1869, after the three people involved were dead, because the persistent story that Lady Byron had coldly forced her husband away, leading to untrue scandalous rumors, had again appeared in print; this time in the memoir of Lord Byron's mistress, Countess Teresa Guiccioli.[36]

By 1869, Stowe was tired of the abuse women writers were receiving at the hands of male reviewers, especially Henry James who wrote for the *Nation*. Stowe wrote to Fanny Fern in 1868 that James was an "insolent man" after he wrote disparaging remarks about famous lecturer Anna Dickinson and her first novel because he admitted that he had not even read it. He argued that he did not have to read it to know that because it was written by a woman, it was earnest but ultimately bad art. He seemed even more convinced of this since the novel was endorsed by Harriet Beecher Stowe and other women authors. It must have felt satisfying to Stowe to strike a blow against a male writer like Byron and his reputation on behalf of women under such circumstances.[37]

Stowe expected to be criticized for vindicating her friend but she also assumed that she would be believed. She was ill prepared for the attack on her character that ensued. Satirical publications printed a cartoon of a decidedly undignified Stowe climbing up a statue of Byron, leaving dirty hand and footprints. One editor called her a "venal scandalizer of the innocent dead" who was just trying to make money with her lies. He also called her article obscene.[38] The *Independent*, which published her work, printed a letter to the editor that described her action as "an authoress of reputation gets hold of a disgusting story about Byron—a story which true or false, is revolting and obscene" and publishes it for money.[39]

Coincidentally (or maybe not), obscene is exactly the word that Stowe used in 1872 to describe Victoria Woodhull when Woodhull accused Stowe's brother Henry Ward Beecher of adultery.[40] But this was not the first time that the Beecher family attacked Woodhull. While Isabella Beecher Hooker supported Woodhull and her efforts, her half-sisters definitely did not. Catharine Beecher sent anonymous letters to a Hartford, Connecticut, newspaper questioning Woodhull's character and motives, but surprisingly in more muted tones than she had used against lecturer Fanny Wright three decades earlier.[41] Stowe contributed a piece to the *Christian Union*, a newspaper edited by her brother; Woodhull considered the article libelous.[42] Stowe also created a character based on Woodhull for her 1871 novel *My Wife and I*, one of two novels Stowe published that year in hopes of regaining her popularity and the royalties that came with it. In the story, Audacia Dangyereyes was a pushy women's rights advocate who behaved like a man in public, smoking and drinking as she wished. She published a newspaper, *Emancipated Woman*, characterized by its "coarseness and grossness" and badgered men into subscribing. Nobody familiar with New York personalities could mistake Dangyereyes for anyone but Woodhull.[43] In addition to recovering her reputation, Stowe intended to use fiction to stem the tide of popularity for radical women's rights, which included free love. She had no idea that Woodhull would respond by attacking Henry Ward Beecher the next year.

Victoria Woodhull certainly experienced an America that the well-heeled Beechers never knew existed. She used her cunning to survive but could not prevent her life from becoming a rollercoaster ride; or as Horatio Alger might have put it: rags to riches to rags and back to riches. Born in Ohio in 1838, she was named for the new queen of England and determined early she was going to be famous. She tried to escape her large con-artist family at the age of fifteen by marrying a doctor. Her new husband, Canning Woodhull, however, was an alcoholic and she supported him and their two children using some of the nefarious skills she learned from her parents. She reunited with her younger sister Tennessee Claflin, and they moved east in 1869. Woodhull continued to support her first husband and use his name, though she obtained a divorce and remarried by the time they reached New York City.[44]

Woodhull and Claflin quickly became celebrities in the city. They convinced Cornelius Vanderbilt to help them start a stock market firm on Wall Street, the first such company to be owned by women. The sisters gave interviews and turned their first day of business in January of 1870 into a huge publicity event. Newspapers across the country covered the opening but the post–Civil War New York weeklies with their numerous illustrations particularly found the sisters irresistible. Frank Leslie published the respected *Illustrated Newspaper,* but also much more daring periodicals such as the *Days' Doings,* which promised readers to provide visuals of "Romance, Police Reports, Important Trials, and Sporting News." For the three years after the opening of their firm, Woodhull and Claflin were featured in the pages of the *Days' Doings* more than any other celebrities or events. This coverage turned them into celebrities although it often depicted the sisters as less than respectable.[45] Writers referred to her as "the Woodhull," showing she was not just famous but a brand and an entity like no other.

Woodhull knew she needed to continue to provide material for the army of illustrators who worked for the weeklies. She orchestrated an impressively diverse number of opportunities for them. She announced she was running for president of the United States in a letter to the *New York Herald* published April 2, 1870. Woodhull presented a women's suffrage speech in January of 1871, before the United States House Judiciary Committee. In the summer of 1871, she spoke before the National Woman Suffrage Association and in the fall both sisters attempted to vote but were denied. Woodhull was elected president of the American Association of Spiritualists in September of 1871. And to cap off a publicity laden two years, she and Claflin marched with socialists through the streets of New York later that winter in honor of those killed in the overthrow of the Paris Commune.[46]

Woodhull was not simply a publicity hound and many took her seriously in these early years even though the press largely did not. In her speech to the Judiciary Committee she accomplished what no other suffragist had by bringing national attention to the argument that women in 1871 already had the right to vote. She argued, though she was not the first, that the Fourteenth Amendment declared anyone born in the United States a citizen and while states could regulate voting, they could not withhold the vote from half of its citizens. She urged the

Victoria Woodhull (1838–1927). *Frank Leslie's Illustrated Newspaper* printed this image of Woodhull appearing before the U.S. House of Representatives Judiciary Committee in 1871. The caption did not identify her by name but only as a lady delegate (Library of Congress, LC-DIG-ppmsca-58145).

Judiciary Committee to acknowledge this fact and enfranchise millions of women. Suffragists Elizabeth Cady Stanton, Susan B. Anthony, and Isabella Beecher Hooker praised her effort although the Judiciary Committee rejected the idea. Woodhull too courted the support of spiritualists (many people, such as Cornelius Vanderbilt and Harriet Beecher Stowe, believed it possible to communicate with the dead) and socialists not only for publicity but to reach those with whom she shared important values.[47]

Woodhull contributed to her growing fame by lecturing and publishing her own newspaper; this, however, is how she got herself into trouble. She spoke eloquently about the inequalities of the world and could move a crowd like few others of her time; women lecturers were much more common than in Fanny Wright's day, though Woodhull's topics still made her events controversial. *Woodhull and Claflin's Weekly* printed groundbreaking pieces on suffrage and socialism; an English translation of Karl Marx's *Communist Manifesto* appeared first in the United States within its pages. She truly wanted to bring about change in America. Woodhull lost the support of Vanderbilt because of these views but her reputation suffered for other reasons also. Woodhull believed in sexual equality and her efforts to dismantle the gender double standard were too radical for many and easily misunderstood by nearly all. She held to the principle that no woman should have to explain her sexual choices in a world where men could continue living unquestioned. Woodhull announced to a large crowd November 20, 1871, that she was a free lover who could change her partner every day if she wished. There is no evidence that Woodhull had lovers. She was apparently happy for a long time in her second marriage. For her that

Victoria Woodhull (1838–1927) caricature. *Harper's Weekly* published this Thomas Nast cartoon in 1872. It portrays Woodhull as the devil because of her free love beliefs. It also casts Woodhull as out of touch with the real burdens of women (Library of Congress, LC-USZ62-74994).

was not the point. She did not need to exercise her right to declare it was hers and every woman's right. Victoria Woodhull would forever after be branded a free lover with all of the negative overtones the phrase implied being fully intended. Thomas Nast produced a cartoon of Woodhull as Mrs. Satan trying to lure an overburdened wife to her path.[48]

Many suffragists were particularly sensitive to being associated with the free love movement, which in general advocated for eliminating laws concerning marriage, birth control, and adultery to leave those matters up to the conscience of each individual. They believed they needed to campaign for the vote as respectable women who were not advocating social changes but simply asking for a say in government. Woodhull, however, remained popular with many reformers; more than six hundred delegates from twenty-two states nominated her to run for president in 1872 under their Equal Rights Party banner.[49] Many influential suffragists reconsidered their connection with Woodhull, especially after she tried to maintain their support for her presidential bid with blackmail and threatening to print damaging information in her newspaper. Susan B. Anthony was so disgusted with some of her views and methods that she censored her at the 1872 National Woman Suffrage Association convention by having the janitor extinguish the gas lights when Woodhull tried to speak after the official program was over.[50]

Woodhull learned damaging information about others besides suffragists and patiently waited to use it. She knew by the fall of 1871 that superstar minister Henry Ward Beecher, brother of Harriet Beecher Stowe and Catharine Beecher, probably had an affair with Elizabeth Tilton, the wife of his protégé and editor of a reform-minded newspaper. Theodore Tilton did not want the secret exposed so among other things, agreed to write a biography of Woodhull to allow her to explain her background and ideas, especially about spiritualism. The result was a piece of subterfuge that would have made Lola Montez envious. Rather than truly reveal much about Woodhull, the biography attributed Woodhull's success to "heavenly spirits" and claimed that she was actually unconscious while making her speeches. Every decision and every utterance was actually a "celestial mandate."[51]

Henry Ward Beecher was less pliant than Tilton and refused to do Woodhull's bidding, such as introduce her at one of her lectures. So, Woodhull exposed Beecher in September of 1872, in front of delegates of the American Association of Spiritualists. She revealed the affair for many reasons. Beecher's sisters were harassing her. She had lost considerable influence with suffragists and socialists so needed a new cause. She lacked money since her stockbroker firm closed and she could no longer afford to print *Woodhull and Claflin's Weekly*; she was desperate to generate publicity, which always resulted in money-making opportunities. And most importantly, she wished to use Beecher as an example of corruption in America's social system. She cared little that Beecher had affairs with his parishioners; rumors circulated about dozens of others who he had slept with besides Elizabeth Tilton. Woodhull loathed that this beloved national figure secretly lived as a free lover while preaching against it from the pulpit. He was a hypocrite who was shielded from scorn by his position and family name. He was a coward who refused to change the social system so others could live freely the way he did. Woodhull wrote later that she "cast the thunderbolt into the very centre of the socio-religio-moralistic camp of the enemy and struck their chieftain, and the world trembled at the blow."[52] When newspapers failed to publish her revelation, Woodhull restarted the presses of *Woodhull and Claflin's Weekly* to print the whole story in an edition dated November 2, 1872. It was so popular that she printed 250,000 copies and issues sold for much more than their cover price of ten cents, possibly for as much as forty dollars each.[53]

Harriet Beecher Stowe defended her brother and attacked Woodhull but only privately; the Beechers decided not to dignify the accusations by taking public notice. Stowe maneuvered to censor Woodhull by preventing her from lecturing in Boston about the Beecher scandal. Stowe was friends with the wife of the governor of Massachusetts, and the pair persuaded the Boston Music Hall to cancel Woodhull's scheduled speech. Then Stowe boasted to her friend Annie Fields that Boston had "fought the good fight with those obscene birds so manfully" and that nothing had even appeared in the papers about the conflict.[54]

Woodhull expected personal retaliation from the Beechers and also arrest for libel charges. To ensure wide distribution, she sent copies of *Woodhull and Claflin's Weekly* with the Beecher story to subscribers before the issue was released to appear on newsstands, making printing and circulation of the story a deliberate act of civil disobedience.[55] Woodhull probably did not expect, however, that when she was arrested it would be for breaking a federal law prohibiting sending obscene material through the mails. Woodhull attracted another enemy who was much more determined to confront her directly and make an example of her: Anthony Comstock.

Comstock was at this time a self-appointed morality enforcer who was funded by the Young Men's Christian Association in New York. He brought police to shops that carried pornography and to saloons illegally open on Sundays. Comstock created a number of aliases he used to order items that were vaguely described in newspapers; many turned out to be pornographic or birth control material. He then worked with post office employees to identify the sender, who would be arrested. He was kept very busy since New York City in 1872 was awash in crudeness and exported it to the rest of the country; Woodhull and Claflin were in no way the worst offenders but after they printed the Beecher story, Comstock saw an opportunity to strike a blow against these celebrities. He failed to convince the New York district attorney to arrest Woodhull and Claflin for obscenity under state law. So after his agent sent copies of the newspaper in the mail, he turned to federal marshals who took the women to the federal prison on Ludlow Street for violating the 1872 postal code. When they were arrested early November of 1872, they were on their way to mail three thousand copies of their paper.[56] The federal marshals also raided the offices of *Woodhull and Claflin's Weekly*, seizing documents, breaking furniture, and scattering printing press type.[57] It is interesting to note that Harriet Beecher Stowe had more clearly broken the 1865 New York law against obscenity with her article about Lord Byron's incest and the distribution of it through the mail would have been illegal if it had been published after 1872.

Some recognized at the time that the sisters were being singled out for censorship. The court set their bail at ten thousand dollars, an incredibly high amount for the crime, and the women, who were nearly penniless, remained in jail for more than a month. Woodhull sat in prison the day of the presidential election. Publisher Frank Leslie, who over the previous three years probably sold millions of newspapers that featured the women, defended the right of journalists to free speech. Leslie argued that Beecher could sue for libel, but that journalists have a duty to expose corruption. He continued, "Woodhull & Co. have a right to public opinion, and public opinion depends on the press."[58] For his efforts, Leslie captured the attention and ire of Comstock, who had Leslie indicted for publishing advertisements in the *Days' Doings* for birth control items, which were considered obscene. Leslie agreed to cease running the advertisements and covering the activities of Woodhull and Claflin to avoid prosecution. He ironically ended up contributing to the censorship of the sisters with the editorial he hoped would help the cause of free speech.[59]

Comstock defeated Leslie, but Woodhull was not done fighting and she sensed that public opinion was turning her way. After her release in December, she revived *Woodhull and Claflin Weekly* and reprinted the Beecher story so all could judge for themselves whether it was obscene. Many other newspapers published the story with no consequences. Woodhull, however, found she was going to be arrested in New York City (again for obscenity) January 9, 1873, the day she was scheduled to give an evening lecture. She disguised herself, evaded the marshals, and dramatically revealed her identity on stage in the lecture hall. In her speech she held herself up as the sole defender of the written word and tried to shame others into joining her. She announced, "In my person, the freedom of the press is assailed, and stricken down, and such has been the adverse concurrence of circumstances that the press itself has tacitly consented, almost with unanimity, to this sacrilegious invasion of one of the most sacred civil rights." But she realized the importance of the arrest that the crowd would shortly witness and argued that Comstock and all the others involved in the campaign to silence her were actually her allies in bringing government harassment to light. Without their "recent active and well-calculated interference, no such vantage as the present revolution has attained could possibly have been granted."[60]

Woodhull returned to prison for a short period but won free speech battles and allies. She prevailed in a lawsuit against the Boston Music Hall for cancelling her lecture. She received more than two hundred dollars to cover the expenses she had incurred in preparation for the event. An editor in Boston called the action by the Music Hall bigotry and feared that it demonstrated that in the city "free speech has little or no chance of a hearing." "It is no crime to lecture," he argued, "and if she libels any one, let her be tried and punished if found guilty; but to punish her before trial is a mockery of justice." One minister of the city won over his reluctant congregation to Woodhull's right to free speech. Woodhull even spoke in the city four times during the February convention of the New England Labor Reform League.[61] Harriet Beecher Stowe must have been dismayed for the whole affair to progress that way.

Woodhull continued to reap the benefits of her free speech crusade. Comstock nudged a stronger anti-obscenity bill through Congress in March of 1873, which became known as the Comstock Law and had far reaching impact, but he failed to have Woodhull convicted or silenced. She was acquitted in the summer of 1873 because the judge ruled that the law under which she had been arrested did not apply to newspapers. Woodhull took her message on the road in the fall. She traveled through the Midwest, West, and South for the next three years, reaching possibly a half million people.[62] She attracted crowds because of her novel individual freedom topics but also because of her notoriety. People across the country recognized her name in 1873, but her lecture tours allowed Americans to become acquainted with her and her views. Woodhull delivered speeches that combined personal reflection and reform ideas. She also garnered sympathy with her explanation of the costs of her campaign for truth. Woodhull told a crowd in Chicago in 1873:

I am charged with seeking notoriety, but who among you would accept any notoriety and pay a tithe of its cost to me? Driven from my former beautiful home,
reduced from affluence to want, my business broken up and destroyed, dragged
from one jail to another, and in a short time am again to be arraigned before the
courts and stand trial for telling the truth. I have been smeared all over with the
most opprobrious epithets, and the vilest names, am stigmatized as a bawd and
a blackmailer. Now until you are ready to accept my notoriety, with its conditions—to suffer what I have suffered and am yet to suffer—*do not dare impugn my
motives;* as to your approval or dissent, your applause or your curses, they have
not a feather's weight with me, I am set apart for a high and sacred duty, and *I shall
perform it without fear or favor.*[63]

Some attempted to silence her during her tour, but they failed.
Many saw her as a victim and few could argue with her new argument
that the word obscene could be applied to the facts themselves but not
to the speaker who is trying to expose the behavior in order to eliminate it. The owner of the hall she rented in Bloomington, Indiana, cancelled her speech but she found another venue and sold out not just that
night but the next one as well. When authorities in Jackson, Michigan,
arrested her for corrupting audiences, people bought three hundred
copies of the speech she delivered. Woodhull earned between one hundred and three hundred dollars for each event, more than almost any of
the hundreds of other speakers on the over-crowded lecture circuit of
the early 1870s.[64]

Beecher and Tilton unwillingly helped increase her celebrity status also. Beecher finally broke the silence and denied the affair in 1873
but Tilton sued him the next year for alienating his wife's affections. The
trial, which lasted from January to June of 1875, was a national phenomenon. It ended in a hung jury (giving Tilton no money or satisfaction) but
after the trial was over, few believed that Beecher was innocent. Woodhull, as the little lady who had started this particular war, was popular
everywhere, even in the conservative South, because she had the courage to take on the elites. In 1876 she divorced her second husband and
closed down her newspaper. She and Claflin sailed for England, where
she was in demand as a speaker. She married a rich admirer and became
Victoria Woodhull Martin. She died in 1927.[65]

Harriet Beecher Stowe may have been the only person in the country convinced of her brother's innocence. She remained constant in
many other ways but she changed her mind about public speaking. Anna
Dickinson had in particular opened this avenue of reaching the public to
respectable women, but everybody seemed to be doing it in the 1870s.
Stowe decided to give it a try though she and her sister had strongly criticized women lecturers in the past. Stowe mostly read prepared remarks
and never captivated audiences like Dickinson, Woodhull, or others but

fans paid to just see the woman who had lead such an eventful literary life. Her celebrity came mostly from her articles and of course from her books, of which she wrote more than thirty. She died in 1896. It is interesting that the label of obscene faded for Stowe but remained a common one for Woodhull. It is all a matter of interpretation.

Select Bibliography

Carpenter, Cari M., ed. *Selected Writings of Victoria Woodhull: Suffrage, Free Love, and Eugenics.* Lincoln: University of Nebraska Press, 2010.

Fellion, Matthew. *Censored: A Literary History of Subversion and Control.* Montreal: McGill-Queen's University Press, 2017.

Frisken, Amanda. *Victoria Woodhull's Sexual Revolution: Political Theater and the Popular Press in Nineteenth Century America.* Philadelphia: University of Pennsylvania Press, 2004.

Gabriel, Mary. *Notorious Victoria: the Life of Victoria Woodhull, Uncensored.* Chapel Hill: Algonquin Books of Chapel Hill, 1998.

Hedrick, Joan. *Harriet Beecher Stowe: A Life.* New York: Oxford University Press, 1994.

Hirsch, Stephen A. "Uncle Tomitudes: The Popular Reaction to 'Uncle Tom's Cabin.'" *Studies in the American Renaissance* (1978): 303–330.

Horowitz, Helen Lefkowitz. "Victoria Woodhull, Anthony Comstock, and the Conflict over Sex in the United States in the 1870s." *Journal of American History* 87 (September 2000): 403–434.

Reynolds, David S. *Mightier Than the Sword: Uncle Tom's Cabin and the Battle for America.* New York: W.W. Norton, 2011.

Reynolds, Moira Davison. *Uncle Tom's Cabin and Mid-Nineteenth Century United States: Pen and Conscience.* Jefferson, NC: McFarland, 2012.

Werbel, Amy. *Lust on Trial: Censorship and the Rise of American Obscenity in the Age of Anthony Comstock.* New York: Columbia University Press, 2018.

SEVEN
◇◇◇◇◇◇◇◇◇◇◇◇

Sojourner Truth and
Sarah Winnemucca
Using Humor to Lighten the Mood

Sojourner Truth carried a scrapbook with her to document the activities of her celebrated self; she called it her Book of Life. She pasted in it laudatory newspaper clippings and letters from admirers. She asked famous people to sign their name within its pages; Harriet Beecher Stowe, Lydia Maria Child, and Anna Dickinson complied. By the time Truth was too ill to travel in the 1880s, she had filled at least three volumes. One can imagine a bedridden Truth, dealing with painful ulcers on her legs, paging through her books, needing to know from memory what each piece meant because she had never learned to read. Truth accomplished much in her life by fighting injustice wherever she encountered it because she was a woman or because she was black or because she was a black woman. Truth also, as the Book of Life demonstrates, sought to be a celebrity and to use that status in her causes. She deftly avoided being stereotyped as either a Jezebel or a Mammy; neither caricature so prevalent in her time would leave her any authority to do the work she desired. Born a slave but without an education, she would not be a classical poet like Phillis Wheatley. She acquired street smarts, but because she was a black woman, she could not use cons in the manner of Victoria Woodhull. She forged her own path with humor.

Truth never met Sarah Winnemucca, a Paiute Indian who became an entertainer of sorts on behalf of her people also. She must have known of her though; their lives and efforts were so similar. They certainly shared the same fans. Truth and Winnemucca, in the end, resembled Fanny Fern more than the other women we have considered because they caught the attention of America with caustic wit and fascinating stories. Whites respected the women's efforts for social justice but accepted them largely as entertainers. The women's otherness made them curiosities to white audiences and at times their celebrity over-shadowed and hindered their good works.

Truth was already in her forties before she became even the slight-est bit famous. She demonstrated early though a tremendous resolve to fight for justice. She lived enslaved, under the name Isabella, for nearly thirty years in New York and became free in 1827 when slavery largely ended in that state. Knowing the law and her rights, she went to court and won the release of her five-year-old son who had been illegally sold to people in Alabama. She also sued a couple in 1835 who falsely claimed she had tried to poison them. She embarked on an exploration of reli-gion and of the meaning of life during these years that resulted in her adopting the name Sojourner Truth in 1843. She proclaimed with this change that she would be a traveler who spoke out to reveal injustice and an itinerant preacher ordained not by any denomination but directly by God.[1]

Truth originally won acclaim as an abolitionist. She gave her first antislavery speech in 1844. By 1850 she also advocated women's rights, combining the two issues in ways that no other lecturer attempted. Truth toured New York and Ohio and spoke at reform organiza-tion meetings. She was prominent enough that both her allies and her opponents started to take notice. The *National Anti-Slavery Standard* reported that her speech at the 1845 annual meeting of the American Anti-Slavery Society was remarkable for its "strong feeling."[2] GWP felt that she had a "mind of rare power."[3] A correspondent for the *Southern Press* who wrote under the pen name A Southron, listed Truth, whom he labeled "a lady of color," among the "ruling spirits of this most detestable gathering of crazy fanatics" who had spoken at the 1850 Women's Rights Convention.[4]

Truth showed herself to be smart and passionate (which could be labeled crazy by those not reform minded), but she quickly realized that the way to spread her message most widely was to entertain. Fel-low black abolitionist Frederick Douglass noticed that she and oth-ers enjoyed her speeches most when she "put her ideas in the oddest forms."[5] Douglass spoke like white lecturers; Truth succeeded in being different. She reduced the complex issue of women's rights down to one of a matter of practicality and common sense. Truth delivered these ideas using blunt but also witty and quaint language. Newspa-pers started to label these Truth-isms and they began to take on a life of their own (not unlike the "Confucius say" quotes of the twentieth cen-tury). The *Oxford Democrat* out of Paris, Maine, for example, printed a string of them supposedly from the Woman's Rights Convention in Akron, Ohio, in 1851:

> "She had heard much of the equality of the sexes, but would not argue that question. All she could say was, if she had a pint of intellect, and man a quart, what reason was there why we should not have our pint *full*?"
>
> "She said she could not read, but she could hear. She had heard the Bible read, and was told that Eve caused the fall of man. Well, if woman upset the world, do give her a chance to set it right side up again."
>
> "She learned also from the new gospel that man had nothing to do with bringing Jesus into the world, for God was his father, but woman was his mother."[6]

Other sources quoted Truth as demanding, "Man, where is your part?" The *Anti-Slavery Bugle* listed additional Truth-isms from that same speech. "The men seem to be all in confusion," it quoted, "and dont know what to do. Why children, if you have woman's rights give it to her and you will feel better. You will have your own rights, and they [the women] wont be so much trouble." Many must have puzzled over just how to counter that logic.[7]

Truth used a similar tactic with her abolitionism. She spoke as if abolishing slavery was simple common sense but she also incorporated criticism of whites into her humor. Truth skillfully worked a white crowd at Farmington, Massachusetts, in 1854, until it was completely on her side. Her delivery included gestures, winks, and smiles that prompted the crowd to react the way she intended. She lectured following a white speaker, John Cluer, who had been jailed for protesting the capture of fugitive slaves in Boston. She said in relation to his incarceration that "it was good that white folks should sometimes feel the prick" and the crowd laughed and cheered! There is no record of how Cluer reacted to this comment. Truth went on to argue that God would punish whites for slavery but never lost the support of the crowd. She clearly had the ability to deliver a blunt message and make it memorable with the use of humor.[8]

Truth entertained even more effectively when she began to use her own story to create a personal connection with her audience. In 1850 she published her autobiography, which she dictated to Olive Gilbert. This first edition was titled *Narrative of Sojourner Truth, A Northern Slave, Emancipated from Bodily Servitude by the State of New York, in 1828*. She paid for the printing so could collect all of the proceeds from its sale, but chose to only charge twenty-five cents a copy when she sold it by mail or at her lectures. Truth regularly brought audiences to tears with her stories of three decades in slavery. She particularly emphasized how slavery affected the bond between a mother and child. She recounted for a crowd in New York in 1853 how her mother had tried to create a closeness and presence that would survive their inevitable separation. Truth's mother told her that when she looked up at the night sky to "remember that I shall see the same moon and stars that you look at." Truth was sold away from her family when she was nine years old.[9]

It is unclear at what age Truth decided to become a celebrity. She was always in need of money and as she aged she could no longer perform the domestic physical labor that provided the only employment for many black women in America. Surely, however, her fame did not just descend upon her as she claimed later in life. Truth told a crowd in Detroit in 1871 that her only aim was to simply tell the truth and to keep nothing to herself. To an interviewer in 1880 she similarly said that she intended to do her duty and "not to seek the applause of her fellow-beings." As an example, the interviewer recounted how she had resisted taking a visible place on stage at the Chicago Centennial of Freedom of 1876.[10]

Truth showed her ambition in many ways, however, especially by, in 1853, visiting the celebrity most visibly connected with abolitionism: Harriet Beecher Stowe. Truth traveled to Andover, Massachusetts, not long after the publication of *Uncle Tom's*

I SELL THE SHADOW TO SUPPORT THE SUBSTANCE.
SOJOURNER TRUTH.

Sojourner Truth (ca. 1797–1883). Truth posed for at least fourteen different photographs to use on cards such as this one printed in Detroit, Michigan. She had "I sell the shadow to support the substance" stamped on many of the cards. Truth used the money she earned from the sale of the cards and of her book for her causes, herself, and her family (Library of Congress, LC-USZ62-119343).

Cabin to ask Stowe to write an introduction for the next edition of her autobiography. Stowe hosted Truth and enjoyed her company. Stowe found her a natural entertainer, and invited family and friends to meet her. "An audience was what she wanted," she remembered later. "It mattered not whether high or low, learned or ignorant. She had things to say, and was ready to say them at all times, and to any one." Emphasizing Truth's apparent ease with being on display, Stowe wrote, "No princess could have received a drawing-room with more composed dignity than Sojourner her audience."[11] Stowe wrote the introduction, laying out three main reasons why people should read Truth's book. First, she argued that it was a story more interesting than other slave narratives that had been published. Second, she vouched for Truth and the narrative, saying that Truth was well-respected and had produced an accurate portrayal of her life. And third, Stowe pointed out that Truth was old and needed the money to buy a home for her elder years. This stamp of approval from the most famous author in America surely helped Truth sell more copies of her book.[12]

The real boost to Truth's celebrity from this visit, however, did not occur for another ten years. Truth continued to spread her message of social justice, and her Truth-isms independently traveled the country. She became a celebrity, however, when Stowe published an article in the *Atlantic Monthly* in 1863 about that earlier meeting. Truth was now much more closely connected with the famous Stowe than she had been before. Maria Driver, of Salem, Massachusetts, even inscribed her 1850 edition of Truth's narrative to connect it with Stowe and in a way reimagine her experience meeting Truth. She wrote in 1865: "Bought of 'Sojourner' herself in Grafton in the summer of 1852 when she was travelling thru Vermont to sell her books. She was a person of great interest both in appearance & manners. Fully all that Mrs. Stowe says of her in the 'Atlantic Monthly.'"[13] Driver may have always cherished the memory of that meeting but it seemed to hold much more importance to her now that Stowe had revealed that she had also met Truth. However Driver had felt about Truth, now it was Stowe's recollection of Truth's appearance and manners that were authentic.

Stowe portrayed Truth in some ways that Truth could not let stand. One of the most glaring was that Stowe quoted Truth as saying that she and her parents were born in Africa; hence the name of the article: "The Libyan Sibyl." Truth, who was living in Battle Creek, Michigan, corrected this mistake quickly in a letter to editor James Redpath, who published it in his Boston newspaper the *Commonwealth*. Truth clarified with "my grandmother and my husband's mother came from Africa, but I did not; she must have misunderstood me." And then, always the publicist, "You will find my book a correct history.... I have sold my books for twenty-five cents apiece. I will send you six copies today."[14]

Truth did not object in the letter to Stowe's general portrayal of her as, in Driver's words, "a person of great interest." Stowe character-ized Truth as strong and kind but most clearly as a simple woman with a child-like faith: one who spouted Truth-isms because her mind could not comprehend complexities instead of a smart lecturer who used sim-plicity as a sophisticated tactic. Stowe reinforced this image with one of the most enduring stories about Truth: the "Is God dead?" anecdote. Stowe wrote that the story originated from abolitionist Wendell Phillips. Frederick Douglass was speaking to a crowd in Boston, the tale went, describing all the ways that blacks were being abused. He became very excited and finally declared that the only way blacks would have justice is if they fought for it. "It must come to blood," Douglass proclaimed. After he sat down, the crowd was hushed as it contemplated his call to violence. Sojourner Truth broke this silence from her front row seat by asking loudly for all to hear, "Frederick, *is God dead?*" Immediately the feeling in the crowd changed. "Not another word she said or needed to say; it was enough."[15] Newspapers across the country reprinted it and theologians included it in their books as an example of "child-like sim-plicity of trust in the providence of God."[16] Truth was a woman of deep faith in God, but she also showed repeatedly that she was a woman of action.

Francis Dana Barker Gage objected to one of the Truth-isms Stowe used in her article. Gage felt that Stowe had downplayed Truth's com-mitment to women's rights by reporting that Truth had advised women at a suffrage convention to just take their rights and stop talking about it. Gage had presided over this meeting in Akron, Ohio, in 1851 and she now saw her opportunity to not only set the record straight but to increase the visibility of the women's rights movement with an arti-cle of her own on Truth. Like the "Is God dead?" anecdote, Gage's ver-sion of Truth's speech, written more than a decade after the convention, became intertwined with Sojourner Truth, the celebrity. Gage published her version of Truth in the New York *Independent* but it was widely reprinted as well. She not only proclaimed Truth a strong supporter of women's rights but set up her words as having saved the conven-tion from being overwhelmed by negative comments from anti-suffrage men in the audience. Gage recalled Truth slowly rising from her seat in the corner to be recognized to speak. Truth then dismissed one man's "women are the weaker sex" argument by exposing a muscular arm, say-ing she had performed labor equal of any man, and asking "and ar'n't I a woman?" Gage recounted Truth repeating this question three more times, coupling it with further evidence of her having earned the right to be treated equally. Gage concluded with "Amid roars of applause she turned to her corner, leaving more than one of us with streaming eyes and hearts beating with gratitude. She had taken us up in her great strong arms and carried us safely over the slough of difficulty, turning the whole tide in our favor."[17]

Stowe and Gage marked Truth with more than child-like faith and blunt practical arguments though; they put words into her mouth that further distinguished her from the readers of their articles. Stowe and Gage quoted Truth as speaking in a sort of southern dialect that she did not use. Truth complained in her letter to James Redpath in 1863 that she never addressed people as "honey"; Stowe recounted Truth calling her "honey" twice within the first thirty seconds of their meeting. Truth objected to that specific word, but Stowe did much more in the article to caricature Truth's speech patterns. Stowe said that when Truth sang, she mispronounced the words but seemed "to derive as much elevation and comfort from bad English as from good." She also described her singing voice as having the "strong barbaric accent of the native African, and with those indescribable upward turns and those deep gutturals which give such a wild, peculiar power to the negro singing." Gage mangled her words so completely it is hard to even read the quotes: "Bleeged to ye for hearin' on me, and now ole Sojourner ha'n't got nothin' more to say."[18]

Stowe had practiced a caricature of Truth's speech long before writing the article. While in Rome in 1857, she entertained her friends with stories about Truth and imitations of her voice, presumably in dialect. Phoebe Couzins incorporated her own impression of Truth into a speech she gave at a Woman's Rights Convention in Chicago in 1874. She told the well-known story of Truth pointing out that God and woman brought Jesus to the earth. Then she prompted prolonged laughter with her punchline: "man had nuffin to *do* with it."[19] Famous impersonator Helen Potter performed as Sojourner Truth and inspired Lizzie Champney to suggest that "any one with a genius for mimicry and extended opportunities for hearing the best speakers, might entertain a company in the same manner," by for instance, giving a "Lecture to Women; *a la* Sojourner Truth."[20]

White imitators assumed they could impersonate Truth but actually they probably did not even come close. Truth spoke Dutch as her first language and started learning English when she was nine; her accent would have been difficult to reproduce. Clearly she had a unique way of addressing a crowd, but she told reporters that she was proud that she had been able to learn fairly correct English. The *New York Tribune* reported in 1870 that Truth "wanted to be reported in a grammatical and smooth way, 'not as if I was saying tickety-ump-ump-nicky-nacky.'"[21] Lucy Larcom, one of the editors of *Our Young Folks*, knew in 1871 that Truth did not speak with a "dialect of the negroes of the Southern States"[22] but many writers and editors habitually portrayed her speech that way. Clearly one of the hazards for a black celebrity in the nineteenth century was an emphasis on stereotypical speech patterns, especially for one like Truth who sought to entertain.

While Truth's fame was tinged with racism, she was more famous than any other black woman of the time and her sayings penetrated society more effectively than the words of nearly anyone. Theodore Tilton offered to write her biography.[23] Sheep farmer A.F. Abernethy named one of his ewes Sojourner Truth.[24] Old Truth-isms continued to circulate. A Civil War soldier explained to a friend by letter his ideas about the importance of women in religion with "as old Sojourner Truth, the Lybian Sibyl, said, 'Was not Christ born of a woman?'"[25] Robert Taber began his paper for a meeting of gas engineers by saying that like Sojourner Truth had advised the women's rights reformers, they needed to "take their rights in this matter of increasing their gas supply."[26] New stories emerged from interviews, speeches, and new editions of her autobiography. One that was popular in 1864 explained how one day Truth was out raising funds for the Civil War soldiers in the 1st Michigan Colored Infantry. One man she encountered rudely refused to give her any money and in other ways revealed his bad character. As he was leaving, Truth asked who he was. He answered, "I am the only son of my mother." To that she responded, "Thank God there are no more."[27]

Truth-isms were able to start conversations just like the words of Fanny Fern. A good example is Truth's comments about the 1870 Woman's Rights Convention in Providence. She was amused by the fashion of many of the women speakers and said she wondered what kind of reformers they were, "with goose wings on your heads, as if you were going to fly." She felt that they could do little for their cause by wearing such ridiculous clothes. Many reprinted the comments, some adding their own opinion. *Good Health* magazine agreed with Truth and explained more fully the disconnect between the women's appearance and their cause. The woman's rights woman

> may be ever so eloquent, ever so logical; but what does it all amount to? There she is, a fashionable *fille de sol*; a thing of show, and not of sense; a *voluntary* slave pleading for emancipation; a self-degraded and self-disabled being, claiming to be entitled to self-government; an example of self-made inferiority.[28]

Truth was not Fern, however, and was always set apart because of race. White writers usually not only quoted her in dialect but also identified her as colored, as a negro/negress, as a former slave, or, after 1863, as the Libyan Sibyl, even though most readers already knew she was black. Some felt the need to distinguish her from other blacks, such as C.L.M. Sylvester who reported that Truth had convinced audiences in Wisconsin "that if the blacks as a race are inferior to the whites, she is an exception to the general rule."[29] The *New York Times* called her remarkable for showing "strong common sense, a simplicity of character, a sincerity of conviction, and a logical directness that have given her much influence as a public speaker."[30] When faced with racism, Truth won the battle as seen in the retelling of how she responded to a man who told her that blacks "were just fit for slaves, that God Almighty made them for slaves, and intended they should be slaves." She looked right at him and said, "Sir, you ain't acquainted with God Almighty! That's what's the matter with you."[31] Truth as a celebrity was able to not only avoid criticism but also being racially stereotyped as either a loose woman Jezebel or as a Mammy who was only useful to whites as a servant. In the white national press, there seemed to be an enormous amount of goodwill towards this old black woman celebrity that whites wanted to love.

Truth herself, however, always drew sharp racial distinctions in her public appearances before whites. She often asked her crowds how whites could hate blacks, the very people who loved them and had done so much for them. She sometimes argued that blacks were destined for heaven while whites needed to prove they were worthy of being saved. Truth alerted a white crowd in Syracuse, New York, to their peril by announcing that God would "do justice to ['the black race'], but whar will you all appear?"[32] In describing her religious journey, she often pointed out how before she became a Christian she hated whites. She told the same Syracuse crowd that sometimes her hate would diminish but then she would witness some act of brutality and she would get so mad at herself that she had not continued to hate whites. Truth often sang as well as spoke at her appearances and she sometimes expressed her anger and racial pride with music. One of the songs she wrote and sang implored whites to "sympathize with sighs and groans and scars, and note how base the tyranny beneath the stripes and stars."[33] She also composed and sang a song for black soldiers of the Civil War, among which was her own grandson. She demonstrated her pride with the lyrics, which included "We are the valiant soldiers who've 'listed for the war; We are fighting for the Union, we are fighting for the law; We can shoot a rebel farther than a white man ever saw; As we go marching on."[34]

Truth unsurprisingly expressed more strident race pride and anger when she spoke to black crowds. In the summer of 1874, a reporter for the *Wilmington Daily Commercial* attended a lecture for a white congregation and one for a black congregation and gives us a clue as to how the presentations differed. Truth spoke at the Bethel African Church in Wilmington, Delaware, then at the Unitarian Church. She spoke to the white Unitarians "in her own plain, practical manner" and "her address was divested of much of the acrimony" that had been present when she appeared at Bethel African Church.[35]

Josephine Franklin was a fan of Truth and shared her pride in being black. She addressed her as Dear Mother of Truth and wrote in 1864 that "our Colour was the first to inhabit the Earth and we are told that God made Adam after his own image, had not I ought to be proud." Franklin felt that blacks had also earned an exalted status and not simply been awarded it by God. She surpassed what Truth normally proclaimed by asserting that blacks had demonstrated a capability beyond what whites possessed. She wrote that the greatest men of all time were black and that "although crushed and enslaved, kept back and rejected their talents will shine and in some way show their superiority." She closed her letter in the typical fan style of concern for being a bother: "I must haste on least I weary your patience." Franklin sent her money and made it clear that she felt this was not just an act of kindness or gratitude to an individual but an important statement of support for a larger cause of racial justice. For her, and presumably many others, Truth was a symbol of the fight for racial equality.[36]

Other blacks, however, thought that Truth's expressions and manner of speaking made her an embarrassment. In 1874 Truth attended a concert at one of the black Sabbath schools in Washington, D.C. She was asked to perform for the crowd and of course she did. Truth sang two antislavery songs and made a short speech about her work for emancipated slaves. Truth was applauded but while she was speaking, "some young colored swells" laughed at her loud enough for others to hear. Truth ignored them until she was done with her remarks and songs. Then she addressed them directly and shamed them in front of the whole audience for not respecting her age and her sincerity to only accomplish something good. The crowd responded to her dressing down of the rude youngsters with thunderous applause.[37]

Truth risked alienating the people she was trying to help by her choice of presentation style. Sarah Winnemucca faced the same situation and had to deal with widely varying responses from other Native Americans. Many Paiutes felt that her alliances with whites had turned her against them. Being a celebrity and setting oneself apart from the group was not generally acceptable Paiute behavior in the nineteenth century. On the other hand, Winnemucca was a revered personality among Native Americans and sought after because of her fame. When she visited Carson City, Nevada, in 1884, for example, a crowd of Washoe Indian women followed her around town, not disturbing her but fawning over her every gesture. They waited outside her hotel on the night of her lecture to see her in her stage costume. Maybe not able to afford the twenty-five-cent entrance fee, this was their opportunity to see Winnemucca at her most glamorous. They showed their delight when she emerged from the hotel and were ecstatic when Winnemucca stopped to speak a few words to each of them, probably in their own language. Winnemucca, like Truth, knew how to properly respond to her varied public.[38]

Winnemucca became an entertainer when she was about twenty years old. She began interpreting her father's words for crowds and then, with her family, acted on stage in 1864. Her father was an important man among Paiutes, considered head chief by whites though this was not an actual office among her people. Winnemucca herself then became known as Princess Sarah. Winnemucca enjoyed a traditional childhood in the Great Basin desert of what became the state of Nevada but increasing conflicts with white miners and settlers forced her family and others to change their lifestyle. Winnemucca worked as a domestic servant in the home of a white family when she was a teenager, learning the customs of whites as well as how to speak, read, and write English. Northern Paiutes suffered desperate times after losing the Pyramid Lake War against whites in 1860. Their reservation at Pyramid Lake was not large enough for them to maintain a traditional hunting and gathering lifestyle, but most did not desire to acculturate into the white society emerging around them.[39]

Winnemucca and her family tried to obtain sympathy but more importantly cash to help their people. They traveled to Virginia City, Nevada, in September of 1864. Winnemucca translated her father's plea for help to a crowd in front of the Wells Fargo Express Company building. Sarah counted the money afterwards; they had collected twenty-five dollars. Winnemucca improved her performance the first time she and her father were on a stage to repeat the request for assistance. She appeared to have a severe case of stage fright, mangling her words and finally sitting down on the stage with her hands in front of her face. The audience probably knew what her father was going to say anyway; her shyness more effectively grabbed their attention and sympathy. They rewarded her with much applause and presumably generous donations. Winnemucca learned a lesson in acting that day whether or not she planned the outburst. As she became a seasoned lecturer she could not fake a bout of stage fright, but Winnemucca never hid her emotions when performing and many mentioned how often she cried for audiences.[40]

Winnemucca and her family soon developed a stage show that consisted of short skits, still scenes, and lectures on Paiute culture; this was decades before the enormously popular Buffalo Bill's Wild West. They appeared in Virginia City and then also for a week of October in San Francisco, California. The show presented what the family thought whites wanted to see. They performed in Plains Indian buckskin not more traditional Paiute attire made of rabbit fur; Winnemucca and her sister even wore Aztec-style headdresses made of feathers of a variety of colors. The family reenacted scenes of war councils, dances, and even the taking of a scalp—the victim was labeled a Confederate sympathizer, which made this act of violence against a white man not only acceptable but heartily applauded in the midst of the Civil War. They also incorporated scenes of Pocahontas saving John Smith from execution. Winnemucca probably played this other Native American princess but we do not definitely know this. We do know that Winnemucca continued to translate for her father or performed a speaking part since newspaper reports praised her voice.[41]

Winnemucca also skillfully provided publicity for the show. A reporter in San Francisco noticed her and her sister. When the family rode in open carriages down Montgomery Street in their stage costumes the day before their first performance, he noted that the daughters, besides the "chronic blush on their cheeks, comported themselves with a native dignity that bespoke them 'to the manner born.'" He also admired that their stage costumes were "calculated to display their native charms and graces to the best advantage."[42]

Winnemucca probably also realized that humor was an effective way to reach a crowd but, like Truth, found out that sometimes when you entertain the crowd laughs at you and not with you. Either Winnemucca or her sister provided a bit of humor during the show; whether it was intended or not is unknown. The sister who the reporter believed most resembled the scandalous actor Adah Isaacs Menken, pulled a bit too hard on the tail of the Coyote during one of the dances. She fell back onto the stage and the children, and probably many adults, laughed at the tumble. Others thought the whole show was nothing but a joke. The *San Francisco Golden Era* announced, with exaggerated pomp, that "Native Aristocracy" was in the city. It reported that the performance was to be a "*soiree*" at which the "Democracy" would be allowed to pay to "gaze upon their [the Paiutes'] war-worn liniments." The *Golden Hill Daily News* reprinted the piece and introduced it with a sarcastic prediction that soon P.T Barnum himself would send for the group to perform for him in New York City.[43]

Winnemucca and her family made only enough money to pay for their expenses and abandoned show business quickly. Winnemucca settled back into family life and stayed with her brother and his wife on the Pyramid Lake Reservation for a few years. She became an interpreter for the United States Army at Fort McDermitt late in 1869. She reemerged as a celebrity by writing a letter in 1870 about the conditions among Paiute peoples that made its way to the Commissioner of Indian Affairs in Washington, D.C. In the letter, she requested that her people be allowed to have permanent homes, access to education, and protection from whites. Newspapers around the country reprinted it, including the *New York Times* and the *Chicago Tribune*. *Harper's Weekly* published an article about the letter calling it "very sagacious" and pointing out many of its logical arguments. Closer to home, Winnemucca received less praise. The *Semi-Weekly News* out of Boise, Idaho, for example, questioned whether Winnemucca actually wrote the letter and provided a demeaning and racist description of her.[44]

Everyone was talking about Winnemucca now. Newspapers reported on her marriage to a white soldier; the couple had traveled to Salt Lake City, Utah, for the ceremony since Nevada had an anti-miscegenation law and local officials had refused to marry them. The press ran stories about a fight she had with a restaurant waiter and arguments she got into with other women that turned into a brawls; one headline read "Royalty on the Rampage" and another included "Fits! Faints!! Spasms!!!" Reporters tracked her movements and noted the "pale face admirers" and tourists who sought her out. They printed items about her falling ill, being thrown by her horse, having her house robbed, losing her horse and saddle to thieves, and being jailed for cutting a man's face with a knife when he tried to assault her.[45]

Often the coverage was mean-spirited (some mockingly elevated her title to "Queen") but occasionally journalists printed lengthy interviews that allowed Winnemucca to tell her story. A California reporter called Winnemucca a "well-informed, wide-awake woman" in 1870 and asked her serious questions about education and Pauite culture.[46] The *Nevada State Journal* praised Winnemucca's "excellent conversational powers" in 1873 and allowed her to tell her history but also express her opinions about the Indian reservation system. The reporter explained why she was and should be of interest to readers: "The high position you hold among the lodges of the Piutes, and the active interest you have taken in Indian affairs, have from time to time brought you into enviable notoriety, and a further knowledge would no doubt interest a great many."[47] When she travelled to the capital of Nevada in 1875 to try to interest state politicians in the conditions of Paiutes, the *Carson City Appeal* called for the state legislature to grant her a "full and respectful hearing."[48]

Winnemucca made a daring ride to help Paiute caught in the middle of the Bannock War of 1878 and became an even greater celebrity. She rode into the war camp to deliver instructions to her father from a general of the United States Army. Newspapers across the country reported on her heroism. The *Indian Journal* predicted that "her history will be a romantic episode of honor in savage warfare." A newspaper in Nebraska also called her action romantic and noted that "another Pocahontas may enroll her name on the pages of American history." The *Oswego Daily Times* hoped that, like Pocahontas, Winnemucca would find a "John Smith who can both appreciate and reward her heroism and self-sacrifice."[49] Winnemucca was probably more saddened by events than anything else because many Paiute had died in the war, but she came to embrace this romantic praise of her action. Years later she followed up a description of the Bannock War in her book with: "I, only an Indian woman, went and saved my father and his people" and a quote from a poem by the romantic poet Henry Wadsworth Longfellow.[50]

Winnemucca's critics became more vocal and harsh the more famous and outspoken she became. Some editors seemed angry at the recognition being given to Winnemucca.

Sarah Winnemucca (ca. 1844–1891). This photograph was taken when she was in Boston in the 1880s (PhotCL 275, The Huntington Library, San Marino, California).

The newspaper out of Austin, Nevada, called Winnemucca a "drunken strumpet" and accused her both of smuggling weapons to Bannock Indians as well as spying for the United States Army. It concluded that "there is about as much heroism in Sarah as there is in a coyote."[51] The *Idaho Avalanche* exploited Winnemucca's perilous racial position for crude laughs by printing that she "created considerable merriment among a number of her white admirers when she told them recently that she had to disguise herself *as a squaw* in order to gain admission to the camp of the hostiles." It seems unlikely she actually said this. It was well known that when she was among her people, she dressed in modest cotton dresses similar to the ones other women wore and she only wore her satin, wool, and velvet fashions when visiting the cities.[52]

Winnemucca had added reason to visit the cities because even though few Paiutes had helped or fought with Bannock Indians, after the war they were removed to the Yakama Reservation for punishment. Winnemucca traveled north on that horrible winter march, but found there was little she could do on the reservation. She returned to San Francisco to raise awareness about this latest injustice done to her people. She lectured for a month in late 1879. Belgian doctor J.J.F. Haine, who moved to California for the gold rush and never left, remembered that "everybody wanted to see and hear this young woman." She was by this time very bitter about the treatment of Paiutes. Winnemucca not only experienced exile but suffered personal loss: many of her family members, including her mother and baby brother, had been murdered by whites and her sister Mary had been raped. Like Sojourner Truth, Winnemucca refused to allow her audience to avoid blame for the brutality. She accused them of taking "all the natives of the earth to your bosom but the poor Indian, who is born of the soil of your land and who has lived for generations on the lands which the good God has given to them, you say he must be exterminated" and repeated the last phrase two more times. Winnemucca also strongly criticized the agents hired by the Indian Office in Washington, D.C., to run the reservations. She accused them of neglect and theft of the supplies that were intended for the people.[53]

Winnemucca used humor to get away with these very harsh words just like Truth had become accustomed to do. She used biting sarcasm as when she said that at first whites "lived with us peaceably, and we hoped more of our white brothers would come. We were less barbarous then than now." She lightened the dark mood by making a suggestion that would have been laughable for the time and that played with gender stereotypes; she proposed that Washington should send women to be reservation agents so that at least Indians would receive half of the goods sent for them. Winnemucca also made fun of a local celebrity, Joshua Abraham Norton, famously known in San Francisco as Emperor Norton, when he announced that he had declared Winnemucca Empress of all the North American Indians. She amused her crowds most, however with her physical comedy. As she skewered the reservation agents she pantomimed different money grubbing actions such as, with one arm appearing longer than the other, she pretended to pull cash from behind an Indian's back. One night she performed a ballet twirl as she was leaving the stage and proclaimed that if she were a ballerina instead of simply trying to help her people, everyone would come to see her.[54]

Winnemucca discovered a way to deliver a harsh message while entertaining a crowd. What she also found, however, is that once she became a celebrity, focus shifted to her and away from her message. The Commissioner of Indian Affairs invited Winnemucca and her father to visit Washington, D.C., and eastern periodicals focused on small details of Winnemucca's fashion choices. Newspapers always covered what she was wearing, but in 1880 the media reported the breaking news of her having hair bangs. She and the other Paiute visitors to Washington, D.C., all of them wearing mainstream style of clothing, sat for a portrait while they were in the city. Winnemucca stood beside her father with her arm on his shoulder and her hair is banged in front. This was an unusual hair style for 1880, and periodicals took note. While some simply included this detail in an overall longer description of Winnemucca, in Boston, for example, this was the story. Under "Table Gossip" the *Boston Daily Globe* printed the notice: "Sarah Winnemucca, the Piute princess, wears her hair banged."[55] The Washington, D.C., correspondent for the *Somerset Herald* liked her choice, writing that her hair is "piled up in the rear and banged in front in the most approved style."[56]

Winnemucca was probably not concerned with the scrutiny of her hairstyle choice, but reports of her bad behavior in Nevada that made their way to the eastern newspapers upset her considerably. The editor of the *Silver State* newspaper in Nevada printed a story that alleged that after one of her lectures, Winnemucca had become very drunk and that it was common for her to do so. Winnemucca sent him a telegram that he depicted as a challenge to a duel. She had reportedly written: "Your statement that I am a drunkard is an infernal lie, and you knew it was false when you wrote it. If you are anything of a man you will meet me and give me satisfaction. I will cram the lie down your throat at the point of a bowie knife. An early answer will oblige." He replied in his newspaper that "a drunken savage, who threatens to take the life's blood of a white person, should be given to understand that there is such a thing as a jail in the community."[57] Winnemucca was probably unaware, though, that one of the reservation agents she criticized had collected damaging statements and forwarded them to the Bureau of Indian Affairs. These enemies labeled her not only a drunk but a prostitute (who could be bought with a bottle of whiskey), liar, gambler, and "malicious schemer."[58] Being a celebrity certainly brought unwelcome attention.

Winnemucca wooed Washington, D.C., despite the scrutiny and libel. Reporters fawned over her and called her "Dashing Sarah." Many important people invited her to lecture but out of deference to the Commissioner of Indian Affairs, who had paid for her trip, she declined the requests. She believed she had won the right for Paiutes to leave the Yakama Reservation, but when she returned west, she found that she had been lied to. Even though Bannocks, who had been central to the war, had been allowed their freedom already, Paiutes would be prevented from returning to their homeland for years. Winnemucca regretted passing up the opportunity to speak to eastern audiences and she began planning a return trip.[59]

By the time Winnemucca first went east in 1880, Sojourner Truth's days of traveling were over. But before she had settled down in Battle Creek, Michigan, she had experienced a similar frustration with celebrity. She complained to newspapers in 1871 that she had "been hoping somebody would print a little of what I am doing, but the papers seem to be content simply in saying how old I am."[60] Traveling lecturers were so numerous in the 1870s (they included celebrities Victoria Woodhull, Harriet Beecher Stowe, and Anna Dickinson), it was difficult to capture the attention of the public. While she is most remembered as a lecturer, Truth fought injustice in a variety of ways and this is what she wanted reporters to write about. During the Civil War she traveled to Indiana, which had a law barring blacks from moving there, and was arrested after her speech caused a riot. Over the next ten days, she spent time in and out of jail until finally charges were dropped. She told one crowd there "it seems that it takes my black face to bring out your black hearts, so it's well I came."[61] Episodes like this were not widely shared because they could not be reduced to a Truth-ism or witty story.

Truth contributed to this trend and promoted herself as a celebrity because she relied on the money she earned from the sale of her book and eventually also her portrait. She sat for at least fourteen photos taken in seven different studio sessions between 1863 and 1875. She ordered fifty or one hundred prints at a time in two different sizes: the small ones were roughly two inches by three inches and the larger ones were about four inches by six inches. She charged about twice the production cost: thirty-three cents for the small and fifty cents for each large photo. Starting in 1864, she placed a copyright on the front to distinguish the photos she sold from counterfeits. As always, there was no shortage of people trying to make money from celebrities. Truth and her supporters always mentioned at her events that she had photos available for sale; as she put it "I sell the shadow to support the substance." She sold them at her appearances and sometimes people wrote on the back, just like Maria Driver had inscribed her copy of Truth's book. One fan wrote "bought of Sojourner Truth in a caboose car near Lansing Mar 5/78," another recorded "bought by Ann Heald at West Branch Iowa 1879 at the lecture by Sojourner Truth," and a third simply wrote, "I heard her." Fans also ordered copies through the mail. Josephine Franklin, who shared Truth's race pride, supported her by selling her photos among people she knew. Some fans collected the photos and included them in family photo albums.[62] In this way, Truth promoted the idea of creating celebrity but never intended for fascination with her to over shadow her causes; in fact her intention was that publicity for herself would bring support for her issues. As time passed, that became less likely.

Truth labored, during and after the Civil War, in Washington, D.C., where she faced both a flood of desperate black refugees and a racist institutional culture. She did what she could for former enslaved people, including preparing meals, finding clothes, and arranging transportation to cities where jobs were promised. She also battled every day to be treated as a citizen with rights. Truth particularly attacked the segregated transportation system in the city and faced problems when trying to use the horse drawn street cars. She often failed to convince the conductor to stop for her and was sometimes removed from the car. She sustained a shoulder injury in one instance and she sued the conductor. Truth reported that she had him and another conductor fired from their jobs. Her efforts were widely covered in the Washington, D.C., news and articles sometimes also appeared outside the city. The editors of those papers, however, put a comedic spin on the story by describing Truth stopping the cars by creating traffic jams or startling the horses. They also quoted Truth in dialect telling the story. "Dat driver paid no 'tention to me, an' was goin' right on when I gave such yelps!"[63] A fan, however, showed unconditional support for Truth by sending a letter to *Harper's Weekly*. The writer praised Truth's work among the refugees and concluded by arguing that "some horse-cars labeled 'Colored persons not admitted' collect fares from far less sensible ones than honest, earnest, and God-worshipping Sojourner Truth."[64]

In the early 1870s Truth traveled along the East Coast and all the way west to Kansas promoting a plan to have western lands set aside for newly freed people. She gathered signatures for a petition to Congress and some former abolitionists helped spread the word and arrange her lectures. Newspapers, however, reported her activities not as political news but nearly always humorously (describing how she bumped along in a wagon over rough Kansas roads for instance). She endorsed Ulysses S. Grant for president in the 1872 election and tried to both register and vote in Battle Creek, where she lived. Truth was described as both naïve for her allegiance and in assuming that a polling location had an actual pole that she wished pointed out for her. Americans still loved her, attended her lectures, and bought her merchandise, but they wanted to be entertained and seemed to have had enough talk about race by the end of the 1870s, just as Reconstruction was coming to an end. One consequence of celebrity is that it overshadowed the woman and the work she was still trying to do, especially if that work had lost the support of the mainstream.[65]

Americans enjoyed, however, endless speculation about how old Truth really was. For many the most entertaining thing about Truth was her age and how she seemed timeless. A.H. Hills wrote on the inside of the front cover of his copy of Truth's *Narrative* "Bought of Sojourner Truth Oct. 31, 1882. She was then 107 years old talked for 1½ hours, and Sang a Hymn of Seven or Eight verse that she learned of the first Minister that She ever heard Preach."[66] Truth was only in her mid-eighties when she died in 1883, but she had been declared a centenarian years earlier. Truth did not know exactly when she was born but she complicated the matter of her age when she began declaring that she had been a slave for about forty years. She became free in 1828 and everyone knew that; the date was even in the title of her *Narrative*. So, that meant she had been born in about 1788, which was ten years earlier than her probable birth year. By the end of the Civil War, people then assumed she was about eighty years old and incredibly spry and sharp minded for her age. The *Chicago Daily Tribune* reported that those who knew her declared she was actually growing younger: "Her face is full and smooth now, and her hair is growing black again. It was gray, and her face quite wrinkled some years ago."[67] Journalists always mentioned her age and people she met asked her about it. She told one pair who confronted her on the street that she was a hundred and fifty years old. For a time, she became very annoyed with the question, and the articles about it instead of her activities, and even began charging five dollars for an answer; she told this to the mayor of Washington, D.C., who apologized for his rudeness. One should never ask the age of a lady, he told her.[68]

Truth came to accept this element of celebrity just like she did all the others. In 1875 the *National Republican* reported that she had guessed her age to be ninety-eight but had been advised to set July 4,

1776, as her birthday so as to celebrate her centennial with the whole country.[69] She declined to add that many years, but on New Year's Day of 1881, she wrote a letter that was published in a Chicago newspaper declaring that many new ideas had come to her since she had reached a hundred years and that if her readers reached that age they might "have greater ideas than these."[70] By 1883 she was telling G.W. Amadon, who came to interview her, that she remembered seeing wounded Revolutionary War soldiers returning home and that she was a grown woman when George Washington died in 1799. Amadon was not completely convinced these things were true but did not fault Truth herself for any mistake. He wrote that Truth *"perhaps* is as old as this great American Nation" but that "whatever the facts are, we regard Sojourner Truth as an honest woman, scorning duplicity, and above misrepresentation."[71]

Many pulled out the Truth-isms and humorous stories for both premature reports and the actual event of her death in 1883. T. Thomas Fortune, however, lamented that her activities were not better known and remembered, especially among blacks. He wrote in the African American newspaper the *New York Globe* that even though "the name Sojourner Truth is familiar to many people," he believed that no more than one in ten black persons knew who she really was.[72]

Sarah Winnemucca faced a similar challenge as she also sought to keep the attention of the public and to keep them interested in helping Paiutes. She used many of the same techniques that Truth found useful. Winnemucca published an autobiography in 1883, sat for photographs, and gathered signatures for a petition to Congress—she even spoke before a committee of the United States House of Representatives. She also lectured nearly three hundred times in cities all along the East Coast in 1883 and 1884, from Vermont all the way south to Baltimore, where she appeared more than sixty times. She charged a fee of ten to twenty-five cents admission, and sold her book for a dollar or an autographed photo for fifty cents.[73]

By the 1880s, Easterners stereotyped Winnemucca in a way very different than how they had distinguished Truth. Winnemucca, as the *New York Times* put it "might have passed for a New-York ballet girl who had earned a sunburn by spending a Summer vacation in a row-boat" even though she often wore buckskin or some other Indian princess costume when she lectured. She blended in but possessed, the white media argued, personality traits common to her people. Truth was denigrated with offensive dialect; Winnemucca was confined within fanciful expectations. The *Boston Evening Transcript* supported her cause because she was of a "race of fine intellect, tender affections and noble integrity."

Another Boston newspaper declared she had "all the wild pathos of her people, with that subtle command of figurative language so peculiar to her race, coloring all she eloquently has to say." A newspaper from Providence, Rhode Island, reported that it was clear she had "native Indian eloquence." A writer for the *Philadelphia Inquirer* praised her "low, musical voice which is the almost universal excellence of the aboriginal woman."[74]

Winnemucca played on these stereotypes and used humor in the same sarcastic way as she had always. She concluded an article she published in the *Californian* with this bitterly pessimistic statement:

> I see very well that all my race will die out. In a few years there will be none left—no, not one Indian in the whole of America. I dare say the white man is better in some respects; but he is a bigger rascal, too. He steals and lies more than an Indian does. I hope some other race will come and drive him out, and kill him, like he has done to us. Then I will say the Great Spirit is just, and that it is all right.[75]

She also exploited for humor her white audience's racial prejudices when she told a crowd in Baltimore

> I want a right and a word in your courts such as the negro man has. [Great applause.] Why not give this to the Indian? Is he a brute? Has he not a mind? Is he not as good as a negro? Would he not know as well when a good man came along and said here is $2 or $2[.]50? Would he not know as well who to vote for?[76]

Sometimes she was self-deprecating with her humor as when she told a crowd in Philadelphia, "I think God made me as well as you, my white sisters, though He made you fair and beautiful, and thought it good that I should be brown and plain"; no one who described her called her plain.[77] She also joked about her weight, telling a reporter that her name meant "mirage," but then laughing and pointing out that she was "pretty substantial and the reverse of a mirage."[78]

She returned west in 1884 and now focused her sarcastic wit on easterners. Her trip had ended in disaster when her husband forged checks in the names of some of her supporters to cover his gambling debts. Winnemucca had no choice but to use her earnings to pay them back. Her enemies in the Indian Office added this damaging information to their old slanders of prostitution and drunkenness. Her celebrity status was unable to survive the truly bad publicity. The *Los Angeles Times* summed it up in familiar language when it printed that "this Piute princess is a humbug." Her appearance in Carson City, Nevada, in September drew a crowd of less than twenty people, but they were treated to a lively lecture. Winnemucca attacked her usual enemy, the greedy Indian agent. She also lampooned the fussy language of easterners as well as their lame attempts of assistance. "When I spoke in Boston my angel mother got up on the platform and began to talk and I had a hard time to choke that angel mother off."[79]

Clearly she was bitter that she had not accomplished more for her people. They remained in dire circumstances and her celebrity heft had not been enough to move the American people to action. She spoke in San Francisco in February of 1885 but this was probably her last public appearance in the West; little is known about a possible trip east later in the decade. She dedicated herself to creating and running a bilingual school for Paiute children. Winnemucca died in 1891 and her obituary was published widely in newspapers. Unlike Sojourner Truth, who remained an icon of social justice, especially after being rediscovered by feminists of the 1970s, Winnemucca has largely faded from public memory.[80]

Select Bibliography

Carpenter, Cari. "Choking off that Angel Mother: Sarah Winnemucca Hopkins's Strategic Humor." *Studies in American Indian Literatures* (Fall 2014): 1–24, 101.

Carpenter, Cari M., and Carolyn Sorisio, eds. *The Newspaper Warrior: Sarah Winnemucca Hopkin's Campaign for American Indian Rights, 1864–1891.* Lincoln: University of Nebraska Press, 2015.

Fitch, Suzanne Pullon, and Roseann M. Mandziuk. *Sojourner Truth As Orator: Wit, Story, and Song.* Westport, CT: Greenwood Press, 1997.

Grigsby, Darcy Grimaldo. *Enduring Truths: Sojourner's Shadows and Substance.* Chicago: University of Chicago Press, 2015.

Hopkins, Sarah Winnemucca. *Life Among the Piutes: Their Wrongs and Claims.* Boston: Cupples, Upham and Co., 1883.

Mabee, Carleton. *Sojourner Truth: Slave, Prophet, Legend.* New York: New York University Press, 1993.

Painter, Nell Irvin. *Sojourner Truth: A Life, A Symbol.* New York: W.W. Norton, 1996.

Painter, Nell Irvin, ed. *Narrative of Sojourner Truth.* New York: Penguin Books, 1998.

Scherer, Joanna Cohan. "The Public Faces of Sarah Winnemucca." *Cultural Anthropology* 3 (May 1988): 178–204.

Sorisio, Carolyn. "Playing the Indian Princess?: Sarah Winnemucca's Newspaper Career and Performance of American Indian Identities." *Studies in American Indian Literature* 23 (Spring 2011): 1–37.

Zanjani, Sally. *Sarah Winnemucca.* Lincoln: University of Nebraska Press, 2001.

EIGHT

◇◇◇◇◇◇◇◇◇◇◇◇◇

Annie Oakley and
Women of Action

Sojourner Truth and Sarah Winnemucca competed for attention with many lecturers but none as successful as Anna Dickinson. She mesmerized audiences at her first public lecture in 1860; at the time she was only seventeen years old. Dickinson matured in the spotlight and quickly became the most famous lecturer in America. By the 1870s, however, even she was finding it difficult to maintain public interest in her speeches about women's suffrage, black equality, and workers' rights as she competed with the likes of Harriet Beecher Stowe and Victoria Woodhull, as well as Truth and Winnemucca. Dickinson met Sojourner Truth in 1869, and was clearly willing to share the public stage with her, writing in her Book of Life what she labeled an Arabic blessing: "May you live to be a thousand years old, and may your shadow never grow less."[1]

While Truth and Winnemucca turned to personal stories and humor to garner publicity, Dickinson burnished her celebrity status by becoming an actor, even playing male roles such as Hamlet, and by becoming a woman of action. In 1873 she ascended Longs Peak in Colorado. While she was not the first woman to reach the top, she was the most famous and her mountain climbing exploits made great news. She sensibly wore pants and the newspapers gleefully reported how she ripped them sliding down a hill in the snow. Before leaving Colorado she ascended five other of the tallest Rocky Mountain peaks (all higher than fourteen thousand feet) and one nearly twelve thousand-footer was later named in her honor.[2]

Women in America longed for activity in the last decades of the nineteenth century. They attended college, joined clubs, played sports, and marched for the vote. Authors disagreed on whether these activities were helpful or harmful for women, but enough of them recommended physical fitness to be noticeable. Women's education advocate Catharine Beecher published a fitness manual in the 1850s; in it she argued that women in particular neglected their health. She reported that the fitness level of women was so dire that doctors believed that before long there would be "no healthy women in the country." She proposed in her manual an exercise routine that could prevent this catastrophe. Beecher continued to fear for women's health into the 1870s and gathered statistics from the women she met as she traveled. She compiled information about the health of women in two hundred communities throughout the North and argued that very few women were not sickly in some way. She also used the statistics of her acquaintances to prove her point. She concluded that among her extended family and friends she could only name ten married women who were "perfectly sound, healthy, and vigorous."[3]

Homeopathy doctor Dio Lewis agreed that women should improve their health and also advocated physical activity in his lectures and books of the 1870s. He argued that "exercise is the great law of development" and when girls did not have enough activity, they suffered for the rest of their lives. He was frustrated by the misplaced priorities of parents: "elegance, education, rank, aspiration, prayer—these will not produce a strong, full, muscular body. They are not the appointed means. *Exercise, exercise! work, work!*—this produces strong muscles, full chests, and physical beauty." Women took up a variety of activities such as calisthenics at school but also croquet, tennis, and archery.[4]

Anna Dickinson (1842–1932). This photograph was taken at Brady's National Portrait Gallery probably in the 1860s (Library of Congress, LC-DIG-ppmsca-53271).

Women and men wanted their celebrities to be even more active than they were. Lecturers and writers continued to attract attention, but Americans admired more those who performed feats of courage or skill like they read about in the extremely popular dime novels. Calamity Jane became one of the most famous daring women in America but she probably led a much less outrageous (though maybe equally dangerous) life than the one attributed to her in books and articles.[5] Besides, there was no shortage of women, like Dickinson, who sought fame this way by methods more easily documented, such as in front of live audiences. Daredevil women adopted all of the emerging sports and activity fads to become famous. They could grab the spotlight for a time but it was Annie Oakley, skilled in both shooting and in cultivating her celebrity, that became the superstar. Fans of these extraordinary women of the last decades of the century often felt inspired to emulate the activities. Oakley and others became advocates for their sports at the same time that they bolstered their own celebrity.

Maria Spelterini risked her life above the rapids of Niagara Falls to become a celebrity. She started performing in her family's circus acts in Italy when she was three years old and quickly showed great skill as a tightrope walker. She established a reputation as the world's best funambulist by performing in the great cities of Europe. Spelterini arrived in the United States in 1876, looking for a feat that would increase her fame even further. She desired to tightrope between towers of the Brooklyn Bridge, which was still under construction, but failed to receive permission to do so. She performed during the early summer of 1876 at the Jones Wood Coliseum, which had been completed a few years earlier and was located between Sixty-Eighth and Sixty-Ninth Streets along the East River in Manhattan. It held fourteen thousand spectators. Spelterini did not simply walk across the tightrope but, as a program printed in the *New York Herald* shows, she marched, carried and used a chair, ran backwards, read poetry aloud, and cycled all while one hundred feet above the crowd. Each spectator paid twenty-five cents to be amazed by her courage and skill.[6]

Spelterini continued to search, however, for a newsworthy feat that would earn her copious amounts of publicity. She visited Niagara Falls in June of 1876 and decided that was the location she had been searching for. No woman had ever walked a tightrope across the falls and she hoped to outdo the first man to have done it, Charles Blondin of France. Newspapers across the country reported that she was going to make the attempt. She completed the crossing on July 8, 1876, using a rope just over two inches in diameter but so heavy that it could not be made completely tight, forcing her to start and end the one-thousand-foot-long journey with a steep decline and incline. Spelterini crossed the gorge in a drizzling rain, which made the rope slick and diminished the spectators, who paid twenty-five cents each. She told her manager that she did not mind that she had not earned much money since she felt she had accomplished what she wanted to do: "out Blondin-Blondin."[7]

The Female Blondin certainly attracted publicity with her crossing that rainy day, dressed in a flamboyant costume of green boots, flesh-colored tights, and scarlet tunic, but she was not done. She performed additional feats that July. Spelterini crossed the gorge backwards, blindfolded, wearing wicker baskets on her feet, with her wrists and ankles in chains, and carrying a stove that she used to cook an omelet halfway across. She copied some of these, including the last, from Blondin and so encouraged the newspapers to connect her with him, and they did with relish. The *New North-West* out of Montana joked that "if she and Blonden [sic] would marry they could keep house and raise a family on a clothes line." Papers printed other amusing quips about her, including the *National Republican* with its terrible pun about

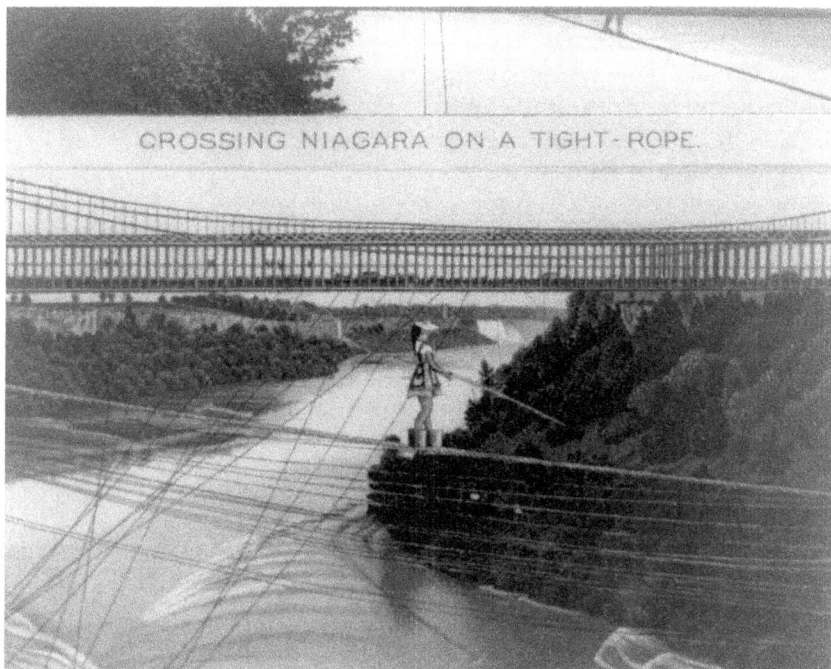

CROSSING NIAGARA ON A TIGHT-ROPE

Maria Spelterini (1853–1912). In this photograph Spelterini is crossing Niagara Falls while wearing baskets on her feet (Library of Congress, LC-USZ62-82800).

the rain during her first crossing: "The rope acted badly, but it failed to Spelterini water." Other newspapers put her in the category of humbug by reporting that she was not really Italian but was actually called Sarah McGinnis. Even risking one's life could not keep the skepticism at bay.[8]

Audiences increased as the summer progressed, however, and women in particular were enthralled with Spelterini. Five thousand spectators witnessed her July 12 crossing, so many in fact that they knocked down the fencing that was designed to prevent those who had not paid from seeing the event.[9] The *New York Herald* reported that ten thousand arrived to see her last performance two weeks later.[10] Newspapers noted how women sometimes had to look away "in painful suspense" during some of Spelterini's maneuvers.[11] A writer from Niagara Falls, New York, reported that Spelterini was "much petted by the ladies, as they thoroughly appreciate the magnitude of the performance." Before she left Niagara Falls, female fans held a gathering for her at the International Hotel and gave her a present, which was reported as both a gold medal and as a gold locket.[12]

Spelterini fell quickly out of the national spotlight when she was no longer performing in New York, but was not completely forgotten. She may have performed in Philadelphia but just where she appeared and when she returned to Europe is a mystery. She posed for photos while on the tightrope and copies of those, especially of her with baskets on her feet, continued to be printed in books such as the 1883 *30 Views of Niagara Falls*. British politician W.S. Caine found that people were still talking about her when he visited Niagara Falls in 1887. Spelterini remains the only woman to cross the gorge on tightrope so authors of articles and books about daring feats mention her, such as Orrin Dunlap who published pieces early in the twentieth century in *Cosmopolitan* and *The Scrap Book* about stunts at Niagara Falls. As we have seen, celebrity usually needs to be fostered and Spelterini seems to have lacked interest in maintaining fame in the United States. She last made widespread news in America in 1886 by participating in a stunt in Brussels. She ascended in a balloon while trapeze artist Leona Dare held on by her teeth.[13] By that time Americans had a new daredevil celebrity: Carlotta the Lady Aeronaut, who was herself a balloon specialist.

Fifteen thousand spectators came out on another rainy day, this one in early July of 1880, to see Mary "Carlotta" Myers make her first ascent into the sky, which was the first solo flight by any woman. As she rose, Myers first noticed the crowd and thought "what a sea of faces!" but fame was not her main concern. Her husband was engaged in experimentation with balloons, and Myers knew that, while other aeronauts were "addicted to exaggeration," she could provide the scientific evidence that would help his research. She carried a barometer and other instruments and knew how to read and interpret them.[14] She confessed she had so little experience in self-promotion that when landing her second flight, she chose a spot distant from the crowds instead of thrilling them by coming down among them. Myers figured out how to please the crowds by the fall of 1880, however, and even resorted to trickery to give them a thrill. At one fair, she dressed up as an elderly woman and demanded to go up in the balloon so she could "sweep the cobwebs down from the skies." She jumped into the basket as the balloon was rising and pretended to consider leaping out of it when she dropped her broom, prompting shouts of alarm. Then she threw off her disguise revealing her identity and continued her flight. "With a realizing sense that they also had been 'taken in' by the fascinating aeronaut, such a shout and babel arose as was probably never before heard at any balloon ascension."[15]

Myers performed for eleven years, becoming increasingly a show woman. She began wearing costumes with gold braid and a sailor cap. She liked to announce to the crowd where she would descend and was often correct even though predicting and riding air currents was far from a science. In the summer of 1882, Myers gave the spectators in Watertown, New York, a thrill when she maneuvered the balloon back to pass over them before flying off to her destination. She developed the habit of waving a white handkerchief as she floated up and away. Myers provided captive ascensions that allowed her passengers to experience the thrill of flying but, since the balloon was tethered, not the danger of drifting away or landing poorly. She raced other balloonists and also did trapeze tricks on a horizontal bar while aloft. Myers most often performed at rural fair grounds, in states as far west as Minnesota, as far south as Virginia, and north into Canada, but in the late 1880s she also entertained city crowds. In 1888, she ascended from Coney Island and Washington Park in Brooklyn. In 1886 she performed her most daring feat; she floated up four miles above the earth, setting a new altitude record.[16]

Myers completed more than three hundred lower altitude flights and all without a major accident. Aeronauts of the 1880s often died although a Saratoga, New York, newspaper concluded that ballooning was a "dangerless amusement."[17] Myers had a very close call in 1883 when her balloon split into pieces two miles above the ground but she was able to land safely by using the scraps that remained.[18] She nearly landed in a lake once when she was carrying her eleven-year-old daughter Aerial.[19] Myers and her balloon sometimes needed to be rescued when she was not able to find a clear landing zone and ended up entangled in a tree. She occasionally endangered those whom she asked for help in bringing her in for a landing. One woman in Connecticut nearly fainted at the prospect of being lifted in the air if she helped anchor Myers's balloon. In 1884 Myers persuaded two of the three boys she encountered outside of Saratoga, New York, to grab hold of her basket when she landed. The boys, no doubt wishing they had refused like their friend had, were carried aloft when a gust blew the balloon up and along for another mile. Myers landed them all safely, but must have been terrified for the boys hanging over the edge of her basket.[20]

Of all her fans, she seemed to enjoy the children the most. Newspapers reported crowds of up to thirty thousand spectators clamoring to see Princess Carlotta.[21] Children followed her about the fair grounds and even cried when they watched her ascend in her balloon. "I am told," she wrote in her memoir, "that many [adults] were present, but I confess that I failed to observe them particularly till later."[22] She did begin to notice when crowds grew troublesome or demanding. A fan in Massachusetts accidentally pulled the gas release cord before she could ascend, making it impossible for her to get enough lift. At an event in Canada the crush was so extreme she had to ascend to prevent a trampling. When she landed in Brooklyn for one of her flights of 1888, she needed help to prevent the crowd from cutting up her balloon for souvenirs.[23]

Myers and her husband tired of travelling the fair circuit in 1889. They bought a mansion near Frankfort, New York, for their research and experiments and invited the public to visit them. Carlotta retired from professional aeronautics in 1891 but continued to take guests aloft at their home, which became known as Balloon Farm since it sprouted deflated balloons each spring. Tourists soon arrived and the farm became a well-known destination. Like Spelterini, Mary Myers will always appear in books about daring women since she also has a first to her name. She was the first woman to fly solo. But, when she was not actively risking her life, her fame quickly faded.[24]

Few were inspired to walk tight ropes or take to the air, but many emulated celebrities made famous by less dangerous feats. During the 1870s and 1880s, the most popular spectator sport was pedestrianism. Competitive walking was an old sport, but bringing it inside, holding multi-day events, and charging for admission turned it into a phenomenon. Athletes competed against each other to see how far they could walk in a designated period; six-day races were common. Well-known professionals also held exhibitions in which they attempted to walk a very long distance in very short, frequent stages; a quarter mile every fifteen minutes was part of a typical performance. For the best pedestrians, speed was important but endurance and the ability to deal with sleep deprivation were also key.[25]

Ada Anderson was one of the early stars of the sport who used her appearances to encourage women to walk for health reasons. Her example also inspired many women to compete in the sport. Anderson was born in London and began competitive walking in 1877 when she was in her mid-thirties. She quickly became the top woman pedestrian in Great Britain, having completed at least nine strenuous performances.[26] She decided to travel to the United States, like Speltarini and many others we have examined in this book. Madame Anderson, as she began to call herself, proposed to walk a quarter of a mile every fifteen minutes for twenty-eight days (officially 2,700 quarter miles in 2,700 consecutive quarter hours), a more strenuous feat than she had yet attempted and something that had never been done in the United States by a woman or a man. She started at eight pm on December 16, 1878, in Brooklyn's Mozart Garden, as hundreds of spectators cheered and a band played from the stage. Anderson made seven laps around her three-foot-wide mulch track every fifteen minutes for nearly the next month.[27] Every day and night she walked: Christmas, New Year's, every week day, every weekend.

When Anderson was not on the track she was usually in her dressing tent. Newspaper reporters found her there wrapped in a robe, lounging on a couch. She ate often and well, consuming oysters, lobster, mutton, potatoes, bread, and peanuts as well as drinking beef broth and port.[28] She slept when she could and told a reporter for the *New York Herald* that her only obstacle was blisters. She said "she never experienced any very great difficulty in waking up, and if her feet lasted out she would not have the slightest difficulty in performing the feat that she had commenced."[29] Dealing with the sleep deprivation was not as easy as she claimed though. The *Herald* reported that she sometimes needed help getting out of her tent and appeared to be asleep while walking "judging from the way she rolled about the track."[30]

Anderson did not just walk, though; she also entertained. She dressed in brightly colored flamboyant costumes, which she changed often. She wore multi-colored tunics over silver or pink tights. Her hair was braided down her back and partly covered with a cap that matched her outfit. She sometimes played the piano and sang for the audience, gave speeches, or answered questions from the crowd. Anderson also played pranks on members of the audience who had fallen asleep; she would paint their faces or blow a horn in their ears. Other celebrities sometimes visited Mozart Garden to walk with her. Boxer John Dwyer, for instance, joined her for many laps over a four-hour period late in December.[31]

Even though she was an entertainer, it seems hard to believe that people would show up to see a woman walk, much less pay to watch her, but thousands did. To increase attendance, organizers offered one hundred dollars to any spectator who caught Anderson cheating. Many also placed bets on whether she would finish or not. By the end of the month as many as four thousand people daily paid the twenty-five cent admission to Mozart Garden. Demand was so great that the price was eventually increased to fifty cents and then to one dollar, with also the option of paying two dollars for a reserved seat.[32] Inside, spectators sat on chairs within or outside the track, up in the balcony, which was reserved for ladies, or in grandstands that had been added to increase seating above the original capacity of eight hundred. The crowd chatted and amused itself while Anderson was in her tent, but when she emerged all eyes fixed on her. The *Brooklyn Daily Eagle* gave an account of the crowd's attentions one night. It remarked how many women were in the crowd that filled the interior of the track. "When the brave Englishwoman stepped upon the tanbark, their demeanor changed. Every voice was hushed. Smiles of encouragement illuminated their faces, their eyes sparkled with enthusiasm and their jeweled fingers waved delicate lace handkerchiefs approvingly."[33] Millions of others around the country followed her progress in their local newspaper, where her daily accomplishment was reported in box scores.[34]

Anderson specifically wanted to connect with women and to encourage them to walk for exercise. She was not alone. Fitness advocate Dio Lewis argued that "if you carry yourself erect and swing your arms freely, [walking] is, on the whole, the best, the most healthful exercise in the world" for women.[35] On the first night before Anderson began her performance, she gave a short speech to the crowd, which according to the *Brooklyn Daily Eagle* included an expression of "hope that more of her lady friends would attend to encourage her in her arduous feat." It continued that she said "it was always pleasant to her to see a large representation of her own sex at her exhibition, and it would greatly encourage her on her long journey."[36] The *New York Times* added that women responded to her request in droves. It reported that the "crowds are largely composed of women, and of these no small portion are ladies. For it is now quite the correct thing in Brooklyn to drop into Mozart Hall and watch Anderson for an hour or so." The paper continued that the women so admired Anderson they had come to regard her "as one of the most wonderful of their sex."[37] Some women even joined Anderson on the track to chat with her as she walked, which was allowed by the rules. Anderson reportedly seemed "to enjoy communion with her sex, and she graciously adapts her step to that of the unskilled ladies."[38] In fact, her whole performance was advertised as an encouragement to women to become more healthy. When she completed her final quarter mile in front of a cheering sellout crowd on January 13, 1879, an exhausted Anderson "advised ladies to walk more and use horse cars less."[39]

Some newspapers reported that walking had actually increased but it is impossible to determine whether women of Brooklyn took Anderson's advice. It is clear, however, that competitive walking for women became very popular. Women across the country (specifically in Boston, Chicago, Cincinnati, New York, San Francisco, Washington, and Wheeling) tried to match or even exceed Anderson's feat. Exilda La Chapelle is the only one to succeed. She amazingly walked three thousand quarter miles in three thousand consecutive quarter hours in Chicago—performing for three more days than had Anderson.[40] Women also headlined competitions, such as the women's six-day race at Gilmore's Garden (later known as Madison Square Garden) in March 1879. Bertha von Berg won the one-thousand-dollar prize and championship belt by walking 372 miles. Only four other of the eighteen contestants finished the grueling race. There was another at the same venue in December of 1879.[41]

Ada Anderson did not rest long after her feat in Brooklyn. She spent much of the remainder of January walking a quarter mile every fifteen minutes for crowds in Pittsburgh. During 1879 in total she spent 116 days walking around a track, performing also in Chicago, Cincinnati, Detroit, and Buffalo.[42] In December she entered the six-day race in New York's Gilmore's Garden but she was an endurance athlete not a speed walker. She could not keep up with the younger competition and came in sixth out of seventeen racers, 40 miles behind new champion Amy Howard who completed 393 miles.[43] Anderson considered then decided against trying to take the belt from Howard at the next six-day race.[44] She may have taken the first few months of 1880 off but was back on a track in Baltimore in May for an exhibition. There she sped up her pace, walking quarter miles every twelve minutes for thirteen straight days. After that it seems she retired and pedestrianism also declined not long after. It was racked by bribery scandals but ultimately superseded by the excitement of bicycle racing as well as live action theater such as the Wild West, with stars like Annie Oakley.[45]

Annie Oakley (Phoebe Ann Moses) taught herself to shoot to earn money for her poor Ohio farm family. Her widowed mother struggled so much to feed her family that she sent Oakley away to the county poor farm. Oakley took a domestic servant position with a farm family but she experienced harsh conditions and abuse from her employer. Oakley ran away from that family at the age of about eleven and started making money by selling game. By 1880, when Ada Anderson retired from pedestrianism, Oakley was making a name for herself as the best shot in the county. Oakley beat touring professional rifleman Frank Butler in a shooting match in 1881 and married him in 1882. She remained in his shadow as he toured with a shooting partner, but once she appeared on stage, she quickly attracted attention and became the headliner.[46]

Oakley convinced Buffalo Bill to give her a tryout for his Wild West in 1885. Buffalo Bill questioned her stamina; he could not imagine that the five foot, one hundred ten-pound Oakley could entertain twice a day, every day. So Oakley practiced to prove to herself she was up to the job. She hit nearly 5,000 thrown glass balls in a nine-hour session. Then on the same day, Oakley attempted to shoot an additional 1,000 balls and broke 984 of them, which was a record in target shooting for the time.[47] Buffalo Bill's business partner witnessed the endurance session and offered her a job in the show on the spot. Oakley performed with the Wild West for seventeen years and joined the group just as its popularity exploded. The show found a home for the summer of 1886 in an open-air amphitheater on Staten Island, attracting on average fourteen thousand visitors a day. Then for the winter they adapted an indoor version of the show for Madison Square Garden witnessed by six thousand spectators on the first day. Oakley also toured Europe with the Wild West, becoming the symbol of a woman of the American West for an international audience as well.[48]

Oakley did not start out as the star of the show. She quickly gained prominence because of her skill but also because of her acting. She lived up to her nickname of Little Sure Shot by performing amazing tricks such as shooting an apple off the head of a dog, the ash off a cigarette held in her husband's teeth and a dime from between his fingers, a target behind her using a mirror, and glass balls not when she was standing still but after jumping over a table and picking up her gun while the balls were already in the air. Oakley rode very well and performed shooting tricks while lying on her back on a galloping horse. She also knew how to connect with the massive crowds by doing more than just hitting her targets. Oakley sometimes missed, maybe on purpose. When this happened, she pouted and stamped her foot. She mostly, however, exuded a feminine charm that was appealing to both the men and the women of the audience. She told a reporter in 1888 that what she strived for was "to be considered a lady." She wore practical but not masculine costumes and blew kisses to the crowd. Oakley always rode side saddle and signaled the end of her act with a cute leg kick that propelled her into a run out of the arena.[49] She received even rave reviews for her style of running and a number of newspapers printed an article that argued "she is one of the most graceful and strong runners among women. It is a perfect picture to watch her, and if more women could run like Annie Oakley there wouldn't be half so much use for doctors in this world."[50] She was as nonthreatening as a woman could be who could kill you with a gun from a great distance.

Oakley quickly became a celebrity, with all of the hassles and benefits evident to that status by the 1880s. She experienced others trying to make money off of her name by marketing themselves as Little Sure Shot or their foot powder as her exclusive choice.[51] Men proposed marriage—when a Frenchman calling himself a count delivered a photograph of himself with his proposal, she shot a hole through the head and sent it back with the answer "respectfully declined."[52] She often received medals from gun or horse clubs and personal gifts of jewelry, dresses, china and serving pieces, clocks, dogs, and horses. Oakley most appreciated, however, the press reports of her activities. She started a scrapbook of the clippings in 1887 and continued it for the next forty years. She said, "I guess the press has made me famous" and she realized how much a celebrity relied on publicity to be able to continue to make a living.[53] While she always maintained that being famous was important because it allowed her to earn money, she

Annie Oakley (1860–1926). Richard K. Fox photographed Oakley in 1899 for this souvenir card (Library of Congress, LC-DIG-ppmsca-24362).

continued to periodically tend her celebrity status even after she was
wealthy enough to ensure she would never again experience the poverty
of her youth.

Oakley's real passion though was hunting and she relished the ability to both serve as a role model and to overtly encourage women to
learn how to shoot. Women were looking for athletic pursuits but many
wanted to maintain their femininity while exercising; Oakley demonstrated of course but eventually also argued how her sport could be pursued this way. She wrote in 1894 that women should not

> sacrifice home and family duties merely for outside pleasure, but that, feeling how
> true it is that health goes a great way toward making home life happy, no oppor-
> tunity should be lost by my sex of indulging in outdoor sports, pastimes and rec-
> reations, which are at once healthy in their tone and results and womanly in their
> character. Under this category the use of firearms must come, for does not this
> practice, as a rule, bring one out into the open, where not only the fresh air may be
> breathed, but oftentimes the beauties of nature be also enjoyed?

Oakley considered shooting good for physical health but believed that it
brought other worthy benefits as well. She argued that targeting engaged
the "mind in exercising judgment when aiming and firing at an object.
When learning the use of firearms, a woman learns at the same time
confidence and self possession." Oakley also felt it was important for
women to be able to protect themselves.[54]

Fans were convinced and showed her how influential she was. A
woman from Florida sent Oakley a note explaining how much she
enjoyed watching her perform. She was an "indifferent but enthusiastic" shooter herself and was amazed by Oakley's proficiency with a
gun.[55] One man wrote her that his wife became interested in hunting
and shooting after seeing Oakley perform in the Wild West. He had
attempted to get her to try it for years. Another husband thanked Oakley
for also getting his wife interested. She became "head over heels" about
it after seeing Oakley shoot and even challenged him to a competition.[56]
A father informed her that his daughter admired her and enjoyed shooting. Even while with the Wild West, Oakley gave private exhibitions and
entered shooting matches. Women made up a large part of her audience at some of these events. The *Boston Daily Globe* reported that half
of the crowd for a performance at the Boston Gun Club in 1888 were
women. The Club had sent out invitations to members that said that
women were "specially invited to participate," possibly because Oakley had requested it. Others commented that the number of women at
shooting grounds had increased because of Annie Oakley's influence.[57]

Women even started gun clubs named after her. Oakley attended
the inaugural ball of the Annie Oakley Rifle Club of Newark, New Jersey,

in 1889. She socialized with members and gave a speech, but apparently did not shoot. While this club included both women and men, female hunters of Butte, Montana, formed a woman-only Annie Oakley Rifle Club. Emma Schatzlein served as the secretary in 1892. Schatzlein was a hunter and wife of western artist Charles Schatzlein.[58] With this honor, the women of Butte demonstrated that they accepted Oakley as an exemplary symbol of the West though she had been born in Ohio and rarely even visited the region.

Oakley tried to make it easier for women to officially join her on the shooting match circuit and it seemed to work. An article on women athletes from 1893 profiled a number of prominent markswomen besides Oakley, including Winnifred Leale and Mrs. Frank Class. It also complimented the twenty women of the Miller Rifle Club of Hoboken, New Jersey, who "make very creditable scores. They have several times beaten the men's third class."[59] Another writer proposed in 1898 that there were seven outstanding American shooters who could claim the title of "champion woman shot." Oakley was deemed on par with, for example, Emma Rock, who had won a hundred contest medals and Tillie Hunt, who had challenged not only any woman but any man in the world to a shooting match.[60] Oakley included in her scrapbook an article about having competed against Wanda Lindsley in a match in 1899.[61]

Oakley left the Wild West to enhance and then to save her celebrity status at the turn of the twentieth century. She was very successful on stage in the winter of 1902 and spring of 1903 as the star of *The Western Girl*, a play which one newspaper characterized as a "dashing, sparkling, not to say sensational, melodrama" that was also "clean and wholesome throughout."[62] People across the country must have been shocked to read later that summer a widely published newspaper article that claimed that Annie Oakley had been arrested in Chicago for stealing to get money to buy cocaine. Oakley immediately informed the newspapers of the error. The woman in jail was an impostor who the police assumed was the real Annie Oakley. Newspapers of the time were not above printing lies but in this case it seems to have been simply an error, though a very sloppy one. Any investigation would have proved the story false. Newspapers printed retractions, but as Oakley had written to the *Philadelphia Press*, "someone will pay for this dreadful mistake."[63] She relied on the newspapers to maintain her good name but she was going to have to make special effort to reclaim it now that they had trashed it.

Oakley spent the next six years in what must have been the most bizarre period of celebrity of her life. She personally sued for libel fifty-five newspapers and received monetary settlements from fifty-four of them. Oakley testified in each case that went to trial, traveling at her own expense. Spectators jammed the courtrooms to hear and see up close a woman they had admired from afar for years. Newspapers often reported her testimony and how dignified she appeared under the sometimes hostile cross-examinations. One lawyer argued, for instance, that she was simply seeking publicity with her lawsuits and that it was wrong of her to attack the newspapers since they had been "the means of her greatness."[64] Oakley knew she owed much to the newspapers but she worked her whole life to be an unquestioned moral woman; she just wanted that confirmed. William Randolph Hearst owned many newspapers, including the Chicago one that first published the story. He hired a private detective to find something damaging to use against Oakley but the man found nothing. Hearst ended up paying her the largest amount of all of the owners, more than $27,000. Oakley received possibly a quarter of a million dollars from the lawsuits. Considering her travel costs, lawyer fees, and loss of income for six years, she successfully defended her name but probably did not profit from the ordeal.[65]

Oakley returned to familiar pursuits after this weird episode in her life. She traveled widely with Vernon Seaver's Young Buffalo Show from 1911 through 1913. She performed her old tricks and added new ones, such as twirling a lariat with her left hand as she hit targets with a gun in her right hand. As always, she was the hit of the show and not at all slowed down by having passed her fiftieth birthday. Oakley and her husband began spending their winters in Pinehurst, South Carolina, in 1915, to hunt and spend time with other shooting enthusiasts. Oakley found here an opportunity to devote time to another passion of hers: teaching women to shoot. She had given shooting demonstrations, taken on some students, and written articles and pamphlets with shooting advice for women, but at Pinehurst Oakley found large numbers of the eager students she longed to reach. Oakley charged no fee and apparently began instruction after simply overhearing a woman lament, "I wish I were a man so that I could shoot." Oakley introduced herself and invited the woman to the range for a lesson. At the end of the day, the woman carried home a target card with a clean shot through the bull's eye, proof of the fact that she did not have to be a man to have good aim.[66]

Oakley was soon spending two hours each morning with students. She taught not only target shooting but gun safety as well. Oakley warned never to point a gun at a person unless you meant to kill them. She had written years earlier that she would indeed "forever shun" any person who turned a firearm in her direction or otherwise carelessly handled guns.[67] Oakley instructed more than seven hundred women by the end of that first season. She returned to Pinehurst each winter into the early 1920s. Some argued she taught thousands of women to shoot during her time at Pinehurst. She was most proud of one Boston woman who became comfortable with a gun after having originally been "as frightened at the sight of a rifle as a rabbit is of a ferret." But she seemed most happy taking women hunting and wrote about one enjoyable trip with three of her students. They failed to bag much prey, but thoroughly enjoyed cooking and eating out in the field those birds they killed.[68]

Annie Oakley believed hunting a perfect exercise of body and mind for women, but she also enthusiastically advocated cycling once manufacturers developed the modern styled safety bicycle to replace the cumbersome and difficult to ride high-wheeled vehicles. Oakley bought her first in 1892 when she was in London touring with the Wild West. She rode through the streets of the city, claiming she was the first woman to do so. She loved that bicycle so much that she brought it back with her to the United States and even incorporated it into her act. Oakley designed her own cycling costume that kept her skirt free of the spokes as well as always appropriately covering her legs. She was the proper lady but other cyclists were less interested in decorum and more interested in riding fast, defying the apparent intentions of naming the new vehicles safety bicycles. By 1895, four million American women were cyclists. Many relished the exercise and freedom the vehicles brought, but others sought the thrill of speed and the cash they could win by being the best.[69]

These racers risked their lives for fame even more clearly than did Marie Spelterini. The tightrope walker controlled many of the variables; the cyclists controlled none. They competed in almost unbelievably dangerous competitions and Americans, who knew nothing close to these spectacles, loved them. Women rode in straight course distance races, but the phenomena of 1896 to 1902 was banked oval track competitions. Men competed in six-day around the clock events, which could degrade into sleep deprivation farces, but women, deemed not physically fit enough for that style of competition (despite the success of Ada Anderson and other pedestrians) raced in heats over the same six-day period. They rode for no more than two hours at a time or a total of three hours a day, thus maintaining incredible speeds while jostling five or six other women on tiny wooden tracks of only 125 feet long. The racers averaged about twenty miles an hour, sprinting to take a lead, and circled the track in less than nine seconds. They seemed to defy gravity as they leaned into each curve, banked at about a forty-five-degree angle.[70] The women nearly always jumped right back on their bikes after a crash, which occurred usually at least once during a heat, though they were often bruised and bloody; they wore no safety equipment or pads.

A rider occasionally rose high on the wall and even went over the top. Spectators at the events numbered in the thousands and included large numbers of women. Fans sat in grandstands but could also cross above the track on a bridge and descend steps to sit inside the oval, or pit, where they could be among the referees and trainers, but also the riders before and after heats. Admission was usually twenty-five cents and clearly worth it. A *Chicago Daily Tribune* reporter captured the crowd at the climax of a race in 1896 this way:

> People in tight places quit mopping perspiration to yell. Everybody, both in the pit and without, surged a bit closer to the track. Women, numbers of them with children and even babies, spoke of discomfort, but the men and boys had lost all faculties but sight and voice.[71]

Tillie Anderson, who won that race in Chicago, bought the least expensive bicycle she could find in 1894, using precious money earned from hard labor in a commercial laundry and at a sewing machine. She later recalled that she started riding not for health reasons but for the speed. Anderson loved biking more than most, becoming a scorcher on the streets of Chicago for hours in the morning and again in the late afternoon, logging forty to eighty miles a day. She was in training. Anderson wanted to ride faster than anyone, inspired by 1893 national bicycle champion John Johnson, who was from her home country of Sweden. Johnson covered a mile in less than two minutes, the first person to ride that fast. Anderson quickly began setting records of her own. In the summer of 1895, she finished the Elgin-Aurora Century Course in Chicago faster than any previous woman. Anderson had found her calling. She acquired a sponsor, manufacturer of the Thistle bicycle, and rode a sleek racer in her next competition.[72]

Anderson dominated women's bicycling from her first race until the sport ceased in 1902. She fell five times the first day she practiced on a banked oval but soon improved; during her career she entered 130 races and lost only 7. She set speed records in both sprints and endurance races and was well known, especially throughout the Midwest where most of the competitions took place. Anderson did little to cultivate celebrity though; she mostly left that to lesser racers. She was interested in winning. She did give interviews and pose on her bike for publicity photographs in her racing costume of snug woolen sweater, tights, and shorts. Anderson even allowed the circulation of glamor shots showing how she could look feminine in a fashionable hat and fur cape. But newspapers dubbed her Tillie the Terrible Swede, coined the term bicycle face to describe her look of concentration while racing, and used her as an example of the unattractive masculinizing effects athletic training had on women. Spectators cheered her on with shouts of "Good boy, Tillie!" An admiring poet praised her stamina and cool nerves as well as appreciated the thrill of watching her race: "The goal in sight— How wild her flights, And how our senses reel, To see the rush, And hear the hush, When Tillie rides her wheel!" The poet also, like many others, however, noted her "firm-set face." She had fans but she was never the darling of the press or of audiences.[73] They both seemed to want celebrities who were athletic but who did not appear to be so, like the Gibson Girl image that was so popular in the 1890s. Annie Oakley walked this fine line perfectly. Women racers had a more difficult time with it, but some succeeded.

Dottie Farnsworth could not beat Anderson on the track but overshadowed her often with publicity. Farnsworth bought her first bicycle in 1895 and decided to delay a career on the stage when she found success on the track. She held the record for the most miles covered by a woman in eighteen hours when she first competed against Anderson. After that first meeting, however, Farnsworth was never again considered the better racer. She was named the victor in one controversial race against Anderson and lost to her twenty times. Farnsworth knew how to act and to attract attention. She, more than Anderson, became the focus of fan and reporter adoration.[74]

Farnsworth worked the crowd the first time she competed against Anderson. She appeared on the track for the initial heat in a long white robe but when she was introduced, she revealed she was wearing a red satin racing suit tied at her waist with a white belt. The other women must have looked rather frumpy in their dull colored woolen outfits. The Chicago crowd loved the suit and reporters gave Farnsworth the nickname Red Bird because of it. She tried to further curb Anderson's popularity in her own hometown by racing another heat in a suit showing the colors and symbol of one of the local male cycling clubs, members of which had shown up in large numbers to spectate and probably support Anderson. Farnsworth, heavily cheered on, won some heats during the competition but Anderson beat Farnsworth in the last night head-to-head as all other riders had dropped out, unable to catch them. A newspaper reported how Farnsworth collapsed "woman-like" into the arms of her trainer at the end of the race.[75]

Farnsworth continued to foster this image of femininity, which was easy to do in contrast to the athletic Anderson. In addition to her satin suit, she impractically wore jewelry, including rings on her hands, while racing, sometimes resulting in injuries. She was the only one to actually use on the track the gold and pearl jeweled handlebar given to the women during the 1897 season. Reporters in many cities deemed her the most beautiful of the racers, with a pretty face and dark curly hair. The *Cleveland World* gushed that her "black eyes and midnight hair are quite as much an attraction as her powers of pedaling."[76] Dottie Farnsworth's looks alone often were enough to also make her a favorite of the crowd. Fans taunted supporters of other racers at a competition in Columbus, Ohio, in 1897: "Why, you're not so warm. Why's hot? Who's hot? Dot, Dot, Dot, Dot." In her hometown of Minneapolis, fans were positively smitten and rioted in 1896 when they found she was not going to be racing only after they had paid admission to the final night of a competition.[77]

Farnsworth's celebrity loomed particularly large at a six-day competition in Cleveland in early 1897. On display were her femininity, crowd support, and newspaper partisanship. Pearl Keyes was just seventeen and new to the circuit; she seemed determined to displace Farnsworth for second place and repeatedly over the week worked on her own and with others to block Farnsworth's advances. On Friday night Keyes fended off a Farnsworth pass by forcing her high for several laps, the two circling higher and higher to the horror of the crowd. Finally, Keyes grew tired and Farnsworth got by to tuck in behind Anderson, who as usual was in the lead. Keyes kept it up the final night of competition and faced both the ire of the crowd and of the *Cleveland Plain Dealer* the next day. It wrote:

> The evening was a sensational one in many ways, and when the schemes to defeat Farnsworth developed one after another, the plucky little girl found it too much for her, and breaking down completely, she burst into tears, but still kept riding. Then there was a scene that has seldom been equaled on a race track. The audience cheered Farnsworth, hissed Keyes and cool headed people had all they could do to keep the more excitable ones from breaking on to the track and causing a small riot. Some threatened to throw chairs and some made incipient attempts to do it, but the race was too great a one, even as it stood, to be interrupted, and thousands of people watched it in wild excitement.[78]

Other newspapers reported that Keyes illegally pocketed Farnsworth and the referees agreed. They ruled that Farnsworth should receive some of the first-place earnings even though she again trailed Anderson at the end. Anderson replied that she would not give up the money but that Farnsworth could earn the prize with a head-to-head competition. Farnsworth accepted the challenge but lost the race. When Anderson invited her to take a victory lap anyway, Farnsworth shyly responded that nobody wanted to see the loser. Of course her fans screamed for her to ride and she was able to enjoy their adulation, secure again as fan favorite even though a perennial second best.[79]

Farnsworth did not always exhibit grace and sparred with Anderson in front of reporters as well as with letters to the editor. This drama, which was possibly staged, increased crowd interest in the races but hurt Farnsworth's celebrity status. Critics emerged who complained that she was a poor loser. Due to this and to her aggressive on track behavior that contradicted her image as the more feminine racer, over time she lost a bit of her glow. Other racers garnered their own attention, especially Helen Baldwin. She was known as the Queen of the Wheel and often scandalously ripped off torn tights though the other women managed to always keep their legs covered.[80] But when Lisette came from France to challenge the American racers, crowds truly fell in love.

Newspapers first reported in 1897 the rumor that Lisette (Amelie Le Gall) would compete in the United States. Seemingly bored with the American women after only a few seasons of racing, they puffed Lisette as thoroughly as any previous visiting celebrity from Europe. They printed highly speculative and widely varying biographies and descriptions, reporting on her incomparable beauty. They also marveled at her accomplishments: she challenged and sometimes beat men, she held multiple world championships, and she could cover twenty-seven and even twenty-nine miles in an hour, which was much faster than even Tillie Anderson.[81] The frenzy was on.

Lisette arrived in New York in August of 1898, and, while not quite as beautiful as many had claimed, with her petite features and frame she seemed to embody femininity in a way the American racers could not. She charmed reporters and fans with her stories about her little eccentricities, telling a confused reporter for the *Minneapolis Times* that she had forgotten that "everybody does not know the habits and fancies of Lisette."[82] She competed in what was billed as a world championship in Minneapolis in September of 1898. All the top Americans were there. Lisette mostly raced on flat courses and was not accustomed to the banked tracks. She also rode a bicycle not as well suited to those conditions, but the press and the fans, nudged by Lisette herself, saw every set back as an evil plot of the Americans to deny her victory. When Dottie Farnsworth fell and Lisette crashed after running right over her, both were badly injured. Dottie could not be removed from the track for half an hour and it turned out she had a cracked rib. Lisette remained unconscious for minutes but when she was revived seemed in better shape. Reporters ignored Farnsworth and followed Lisette back to her hotel to be able to gather whatever they could. She told them that no matter how badly she was injured, she would ride the next day. She would "not have them trick me."[83] Dottie Farnsworth previously benefited from chivalry, now it was Lisette's turn. The reporters turned on the women they had been covering for years by accusing them of foul play.

Lisette further enhanced her celebrity the next night by riding hard and, on the occasions when she made it to the front, the crowd went wild. She always acknowledged the applause and even responded with sprints when the spectators called for them. She contrasted with the Americans, even drama student Farnsworth, who remained largely professional and serious while riding. Fans loved it. Lisette moreover was not accustomed to the jostling of the close quarters of banked track racing and her small size made it seem that the Americans were intimidating and blocking her; maybe at times they were. Spectators definitely believed it and started to hiss riders who appeared to be harassing Lisette; the *Tribune* explained the partisanship by saying that it was easy to sympathize with the "oppressed and downtrodden."[84] Racers tried to defend themselves in the newspapers. Ida Peterson claimed that Lisette was actually the dirty player because she swung her elbows out but Peterson also showed her frustration when she said that "American people like to worship foreigners."[85]

On the fourth night of racing, Dottie Farnsworth fended off a Lisette pass and the referees disagreed on which one of them had violated rules by swinging an elbow. The crowd and the *Times*, however, sided with Lisette over their own, homegrown star. The newspaper accused Farnsworth of "un–American tactics." Tillie Anderson won all six heats and, though the crowd chanted Lisette's name on the last night, Anderson took home the championship medal and four hundred dollars.[86]

Lisette joined the circuit, rarely winning even heats, but remaining the top celebrity. She continued to be touted as a feminine woman among the burly athletes who resorted to cheating to beat her. A spread in the *New York Journal* in November of 1898, printed photos of her in many different alluring poses. Author Roger Gilles joked that "everything she did—even crashing—was ladylike and endearing." Newspapers reported that after a fall, she checked the state of her hat and hair. Lisette even admitted to cheating to keep a rival from being able to attempt a challenge on Tillie Anderson at a crucial time in the final heat.[87] Nothing could affect her popularity. Except the decline of racing itself.

By the turn of the twentieth century, fans were lured to automobiles and away from what now seemed the slow pace of bicycle racing. Attendance was not the only problem though. Critics increased their claims that such intense athletic training made women masculine and could not be good for them. A lady riding her bicycle through the park was proper, but female competitive racing was an abomination. A common damning analogy was a competition that was held on a dirt track; Martha Frazer of St. Louis proclaimed that "God intended women to be better than horses."[88] The death of Dottie Farnsworth in 1902, however, proved to be the final straw. Farnsworth married and largely retired from racing in 1901, but finally made it on the stage. Not as an actor but performing on a cycle whirl, a track banked so steeply that it was small enough to fit on an indoor stage. It is unknown whether she was riding by herself or against others, but in late May of 1902, she flew up and over the edge. She had been performing on the track for less than a month. She suffered internal injuries and died June 6.[89] Tillie Anderson and the others all retired that year and the early era of women's racing was over.

Select Bibliography

Algeo, Matthew. *Pedestrianism: When Watching People Walk was America's Favorite Spectator Sport.* Chicago: Chicago Review Press, 2014.

Carlotta, Lady Aeronaut. *Aerial Adventures of Carlotta, or Sky-Larking in Cloudland, Being Hap-Hazard Accounts of the Perils and Pleasures of Aerial Navigation.* Mohawk, NY: C.E. Myers, 1883.

Cherches, Peter. *Star Course: Nineteenth-Century Lecture Tours and the Consolidation of Modern Celebrity.* Rotterdam: Sense Publishers, 2017.

Gallman, Matthew. *America's Joan of Arc: The Life of Anna Elizabeth Dickinson.* Oxford: Oxford University Press, 2006.

Gilles, Roger. *Women on the Move: The Forgotten Era of Women's Bicycle Racing.* Lincoln: University of Nebraska Press, 2018.

Kasper, Shirl. *Annie Oakley.* Norman: University of Oklahoma Press, 1992.

Riley, Glenda. *The Life and Legacy of Annie Oakley.* Norman: University of Oklahoma Press, 1994.

Stanley, Gregory Kent. *The Rise and Fall of the Sportswoman: Women's Health, Fitness, and Athletics, 1860–1940.* New York: Peter Lang Publishing, 1996.

NINE

◇◇◇◇◇◇◇◇◇◇◇◇

Jane Addams
and Mary Fuller
and the Power of Film

In the summer of 1922, Annie Oakley, now sixty-one years old, came out of retirement to perform in a charity event in New York. As always, the newspapers widely reported her actions, including printing photos of her providing shooting instruction to the daughters of others involved with the show. Predictably, she was the hit of the event; the *New York Tribune* reported that she "cavorted around the ring, skipping and blowing kisses with the coyness she learned forty years ago" even though she now had white hair and wore glasses. The newspapers also reported that she was about to appear in movies. She may have used the charity event as a sort of screen test and a film exists of not only her performance but of her acting for the camera, making faces and walking around. Sadly, Oakley was badly injured in a car accident later that year. She recovered enough to resume shooting but would never again cavort while doing it. If she had hopes of becoming a movie star, they were dashed. After her brief recovery, her health declined until she died in 1926.[1]

In 1909, Jane Addams, the most famous social worker in America, also took note of the importance of movies and argued that films turned children into criminals. Girls stole for movie ticket money and boys hatched plots of murder in imitation of movies they had seen. The woman who became a celebrity by being useful urged Americans to quench outside of the fantasy world of theaters their children's thirst for adventure. What Addams failed to understand was that Americans could both become obsessed with a movie character and still embrace her philosophy of making a difference. She and the actor Mary Fuller were opposites in many respects but for a brief time were the most beloved women in an America beginning to discover the power of film.

Jane Addams was born into wealth but she would never have been happy with a life of leisure. Even volunteer work would never have satisfied her need to be useful. Addams was born in Cedarville, Illinois, in 1863. After earning a bachelor's degree from Rockford Female Seminary in 1882 and traveling extensively in Europe, she faced a world in which an educated woman had few professional options. After surviving a nervous breakdown, she made a career for herself and used work to maintain her mental health. By founding Hull House in Chicago, she was able to not only help people of the immigrant neighborhood but to provide meaningful employment for herself and others like her. It was a bonus that she found that she was very good at the work.[2]

Jane Addams also discovered that she was an excellent writer and it was through her essays and books that she became a celebrity, though a carefully crafted one. Certainly Addams spoke eloquently to crowds but she often found herself too busy in the Hull House neighborhood to accept all of the speaking engagements offered. Her written words could much more efficiently accomplish what she lacked the time to do in person. She emerged at a time when Americans avidly read not only pulpy fiction but also large quantities of nonfiction in an effort to better understand the world around them and the rapid changes occurring. Through her publications, Addams endeavored to not only publicize her ideas and work but to shape public opinion on the proper role of the individual in society. In other words, to use her experiences to convince people that it was their duty to work for social justice for all people. Audiences loved *Democracy and Social Ethics* and *The Spirit of Youth and the City Streets,* but *Twenty Years at Hull-House* was the book that made Addams a star and is still her best-known work. She reached even more readers by allowing excerpts to be printed in the *Ladies Home Journal,* the most popular magazine in America at the time. Addams used the book specifically to reinforce her own public image as a hero and "lady bountiful bent on aiding the lowly."[3] The book has never gone out of print since its publication in 1910.

But what did it mean to be a star social worker in early twentieth century America? Certainly it meant winning accolades. Club women of her adopted home named her "the best woman in Chicago" in 1906. The *Ladies Home Journal* acknowledged her widened importance two years later with the title "America's foremost living woman." By 1913 her fame had transcended gender as the Twilight Club of New York, using the results of a survey of three thousand "representative Americans," declared Addams the country's "most socially useful American," man or woman. A Rockford, Illinois, florist even named his new bright rose pink chrysanthemum variety after her and exhibited it at the National Flower Show in Chicago. Prestigious colleges bestowed on her honorary degrees. The author of *Child's Book of American Biography* included her among the persons profiled.[4]

Being a celebrity also meant, however, inspiring millions of individuals. Whether they were young or old, involved in social work or not, Americans placed her photo on their mantel pieces and composed verses of admiration, such as this one that appeared in *Pearson's Magazine*:

> MOTHER of races fusing into one,
> And keeping open house with presence sweet
> In that loud city where the nations meet
> Around thy ample hearth when day is done,
> When I behold the wild tribes thou hast won
> And see thee wooing from the witching street
> By thy own saintly face the erring feet,
> I know Love still has power beneath the sun.[5]

Some of these fans wrote directly to Addams though they did not personally know her. A few asked for money or other favors often requested of celebrities, but most wrote to express their gratitude and explain how she had moved them. Canadian Rose Cullen, a fellow social worker, wrote to Addams in December of 1911:

> I have just finished reading "Twenty Years at Hull-House" and feel as if I had received a great gift for which I must say "thank you." Miss Addams, I wish you could know how your self-sacrifice and devotion and striving after righteousness have strengthened others who are endeavoring to live their lives in a "neighborly way." I do hope that although the care of thousands are passed on to you, there may be in your life a deep joy which nothing can ever take away.

After explaining some of her own work, she concluded with "Please forgive me for daring to write to you, but there are some people in this world whom we consider as friends because they draw out the best that is in us, and you know, one must write to her friend sometime."[6]

Grace Hebard wrote that she had used *Twenty Years at Hull-House* "to such splendid advantage" in her sociology class that she had to "send just a word of greeting to a very busy and useful woman." Hebard, a professor at the University of Wyoming, thanked Addams for writing the book but also for the work that she had accomplished.[7] Hannah Lislerude, an immigrant from Norway, specifically appreciated Addams writing in *McClure's Magazine* about the plight of domestic servants and how they sometimes resorted to prostitution to survive. She herself had faced similar hardships: "I have tramped the streets, bewildered and weary, looking for work. Have been cheated by employment offices, insulted by mistresses and I have known the bitter, bitter loneliness of the hired girl."[8]

In these articles in *McClure's Magazine,* which became her fifth book, *A New Conscience and an Ancient Evil,* Jane Addams implicated movie theaters in the problem of forced prostitution. Movie star hopefuls could be trapped by their vanity as they were convinced to follow flattering young men who claimed they could introduce them to the right people. A poor young girl, "to whom life has offered few pleasures," she argued, could be "induced unthinkingly to barter her chastity for an entrance fee."[9] In *Twenty Years at Hull-House,* Addams despaired that on her very first visit to Halstead Street, where she hoped to set-

tle, she saw large lines at the movie theater and noted that the children talked of nothing else but the latest films. She also told the story of two girls who schemed to steal gold crowns from a dentist in order to be able to buy movie tickets; one of the girls actually had a healthy tooth pulled to carry out the plot. They were caught trying to pawn the gold.[10]

Jane Addams more fully explained the myriad dangers of motion pictures in another of her books. She explained that the darkened theater was "filled with the glamour of love making" and the accompanying songs were vulgar and celebrated immoral behavior such as flirting. Children not only stole money to afford to buy tickets, but were induced to break

Jane Addams (1860–1935). This photograph of Addams at her writing desk was taken in 1912 when her celebrity status was at its highest point (Library of Congress, LC-USZ61-144).

the law in much more serious ways. She recounted this incredible story: "Three boys, aged nine, eleven and thirteen years, who had recently seen depicted the adventures of frontier life including the holding up of a stage coach and the lassoing of the driver, spent weeks planning to lasso, murder, and rob a neighborhood milkman." The boys bought a gun and one morning put their plan into motion. "Fortunately for him, as the lariat was thrown the horse shied, and, although the shot was appropriately fired, the milkman's life was saved."[11]

Addams, who titled the chapter "The House of Dreams," believed the problem was larger than simply a few cases of juvenile delinquency. She reported that doctors in Chicago had begun to blame the vividness of movies for eye problems, hallucinations, and even mental illness. She also argued that the general idea of movies as an escape from reality held its own dangers. It was natural she argued for children to need a "transition between the romantic conceptions which they vainly struggle to keep intact and life's cruelties and trivialities which they refuse to admit." Movies, however, served this purpose poorly in comparison to literature or self-expression. She argued that the reliance on revenge plots and on rewarding characters for doing evil warped children's sense of reality. "Is it not astounding" she wrote, "that a city allows thousands of its youth to fill their impressionable minds with these absurdities which certainly will become the foundation for their working moral codes and the data from which they will judge the proprieties of life?"[12] Children who watched movies became adults who had suspect moral codes.

Even Jane Addams with her belief in the spellbinding effects of movies could not have predicted how obsessed Americans would become with *What Happened to Mary*. It started late in July of 1912 when thousands of subscribers received their copy of the *Ladies' World*. They were delighted that the cover portrait of Mary had been created by none other than Charles Dana Gibson and intrigued by the announcement of a one-hundred-dollar prize for the person who could write the most interesting short account of what happened to Mary next. Once inside they were snared by the first of twelve monthly installments of Mary's story and made aware that within the week the beginning of her adventure would appear on screen at their local movie theater and run monthly for the next year. While poet and early movie critic Vachel Lindsay of Springfield, Illinois, considered the serial "flip" and saw through the ploy to keep fans "jollied along," millions of Americans became hooked. Nearly a million people subscribed to the *Ladies' World* and the twenty thousand Edison Company movie theaters screened movies for twenty million people.[13]

Lucy Proctor Armstrong of Palo Alto, California, was one of the millions. This mother of four small children wrote the winning three-hundred-word entry for the contest and, according to her local newspaper, carried "Mary into further adventure, stimulating the imagination as to what the outcome is going to be." Armstrong's story appeared in the October edition of the *Ladies' World* and is an early example of fan participation in the creation of the popular culture they loved.[14] Armstrong's story was in addition to and not a replacement of the professionally written regular monthly installment. T.C. Strickland of New York wrote a story similar to Armstrong's but in rhymed verse; it too was published in the magazine. Also appearing in October was a story by Charles Connolly (Ph.D. from Pennsylvania) that jumped right to the end, having Mary already wed within minutes of where the story had left off. Clearly he did not understand the concept of a serial story that is revealed slowly! The editor explained that it was difficult to choose the winner and which of the additional entries to publish. He easily eliminated some stories though because they were "in the spirit of burlesque." Many contestants clearly had fun and had let their imagination go wild. "We mean our Mary to be taken seriously," the editor argued, "and we want only legitimate and fairly logical things to happen to her."[15] It seems many were taking the whole thing much less seriously.

The publicity stunt was so popular, two thousand readers entered, that the *Ladies' World* held additional plot contests, which eventually drew ten thousand responses each. The magazine printed two or three entries in each issue. In November, Ruth Scott of Massachusetts won the prize and Sara DuBois of Pennsylvania also had her story printed. In January of 1913, Irma Edwards of New Orleans won the prize. Helen Lathrop Swayer of Honesdale, Pennsylvania, and Eve DeVore of Toledo, Ohio, submitted stories also published that month; these clearly contributed plot points used in the February installment. In that month's edition, stories by Ruth Roberts of Georgia, who had won the prize, and by Grace Stephens Capers of New York appeared. When the series concluded, the magazine held a contest for the best answers to how readers would spend a million dollars, which is what Mary ended up inheriting.[16]

Entering the writing contests and reading the *Ladies' World* were not the only ways that Mary's friends could show their obsession with the movie. Even before the serial had concluded, fans could attend a stage version of the story in cities across the country. In addition, the *Ladies' World* and the Edison Company made available some of the first movie fan merchandise, expecting it to be popular especially among female fans. Many theaters gave away picture postcards of Mary, sometimes only to the women attending. Women could be like Mary by buying a replica of her rose adorned wide-brimmed hat, designed by C.M. Phipps. Fans could amuse themselves between serial releases by playing the *What Happened to Mary* game or watch an illustration of Mary disappear when they spun the puzzle created by Sam Loyd. They could also perfect a rendition of the Mary song: "Mary had a dainty little fad of making boys feel very kindly t'ward her. Ruby lips, that Cupid created, baby eyes, but so educated. Mary was a very wary fairy, so nothing ever happened to her!"[17]

The song was not very closely connected to the serial plot points; plenty of things happened to Mary in each twenty-minute episode but she was smart and strong enough to triumph in the end.[18] The serial is about an orphaned heiress who was kidnapped as a baby. Mary grows up not knowing of her true birth situation but she has a vague feeling that she does not belong in the life of poverty she is living. She escapes from the island where she is being held and has many adventures in New York and Europe. She becomes a chorus line star, exposes not one but two separate robbery/embezzlement schemes, and does a bit of spying for the United States. Mary also discovers the truth about her status and is able to remain a step ahead of her captors. She proves her identity on her twenty-first birthday, the deadline for her to claim her inheritance.[19]

Theater owners across the country thrilled in the success of *What Happened to Mary*. In Albert Lea, Minnesota, one reported that interest in the "fortunes of this young lady is at the boiling point all the time." The Rex Theatre of Coeur d'Alene, Idaho, broke attendance records when it showed the fourth and fifth installments together. Managers of the Princess Theatre in Cape Girardeau,

Mary Fuller (1888–1973) *What Happened to Mary* publicity card. Edison Studios distributed souvenir cards like this one at movie theaters (author's collection).

Missouri, had to add seats to meet the demand. In Hattiesburg, Mississippi, movie goers felt they were among millions of others following Mary's story. The Kozy Theater in Chickasha, Indian Territory, declared the movie "one of the best drawing cards" that had ever been to town. Mary's friends filled the Empire Theater in Bridgeport, Connecticut, for the tenth episode even though the circus was in town. Mr. Lavender, manager of a theater in Laurens, South Carolina, assured movie goers that they would have ample time after prayer meeting to attend the showing of episode two. Those theaters that initially passed on *What Happened to Mary*, such as the Lyric in Annapolis, Maryland, raced to catch up and show the serial "that all asked for."[20]

The craze did not subside but theater owners took pains to make sure Americans stayed interested and continued to attend showings. The Kozy in Chickasha, Indian Territory, offered five dollars in gold to the person who could guess the ending of the serial. One common ploy used by theaters was to designate a weekly Mary Day and play nothing except one or more episodes of the serial repeatedly through the afternoon and evening. Theaters usually showed a varied program of films to entice viewers, but managers found they could ensure a steady stream of five-cent ticket sales with just *What Happened to Mary* fans. Other theaters maintained a program format but added special features, such as performances of that flirtatious Mary song (which Jane Addams undoubtedly would have hated if she had heard it). When communities faced hardship, theaters used the movies to raise relief funds for, as an example, flood victims in Oregon in 1913. Even the lack of electricity could not deny movie fans of Dundee, Michigan, the enjoyment of watching Mary. When the electric plant broke down, the manager used a car engine to run the projector and sent a photo of the rigged-up power source to the Edison Company with the caption "We would not have gone to so much trouble for anyone but Mary."[21]

And go to trouble fans did. Clara Beffrey of Denver, Colorado, wrote to the *Motion Picture Story Magazine* specifically to say how much she enjoyed the serial; it is "just as interesting as can be, and every character so true to life." A dozen friends of a shoe factory worker in East Belfast, Maine, held a What Happened to Nina? surprise party for her. They ate ice cream and cake as well as played games. Her friends actually prevented Nina from attending that night's showing of *What Happened to Mary* but it seems she forgave them.[22]

With millions like Nina watching and re-watching Mary's adventures, the serial reached a level of cultural saturation rare for popular culture in early twentieth century America. When newspapers reported the tragic story coming out of Los Angeles of Bertha Walters the headline was "What Happened to Mary, Beaten: Girl Who Seems to have more Trouble than a Bumble Bee on Fly Paper."[23] Even the world of politics had taken note of the plucky girl overcoming setbacks in her search for her identity. Perhaps forecasting defeat for Woodrow Wilson in the upcoming 1912 presidential election, the newspaper from Roundup, Montana, ran a notice about three previous Democratic Party presidential nominees who had all been defeated: Horace Greeley, Alton Parker, and William Jennings Bryan. It concluded with "What happened to Mary wasn't a circumstance to what happened to them in November."[24]

Behind the fictional Mary was of course a real Mary. Initially movies lacked credits but by 1911 fans had successfully convinced the studios to provide at least the names of the players.[25] It did not take long for favorites to emerge. Mary Fuller was one of the recognizable stars in 1912 but playing the title role in *What Happened to Mary* made her a dear friend to millions of Americans. Born in Washington, D.C., in 1888 Fuller was performing on stage by the age of seventeen; as did Addams, she lost her father early but her life choices were more limited. Also like Addams who believed in surrounding everyone with beauty, Fuller saw art as a necessity of life. Fuller quickly grew tired of the travel and inconsistency of a career in theatrical productions so in December of 1907, out of work and without money to visit her family for Christmas, she decided to try to break into movies. One Friday she stopped in at the Vitagraph Studio in Brooklyn. Because she had a relaxed and natural manner on camera, she was hired for a part that would shoot when the weekend was over. After making more than a dozen one-reel shorts for Vitagraph, Fuller signed with Edison Studios, located in new facilities in the Bronx. She quickly became the studio's leading lady, appearing in more than 150 and possibly up to 500 one reelers during her four years there.[26]

Fuller maintained a grueling schedule of shooting, making costumes, writing scene scenarios, and appearing in public in part to keep loneliness and possibly clinical depression at bay. Edison shorts were sometimes filmed in twenty-four-hour continuous sessions; an actor could even be starring in multiple movies at once. Adding to the excitement, Fuller did her own stunts, including using knotted sheets to climb out of a seventh-floor window in *What Happened to Mary* that left her hands callused and torn. She experienced some truly close calls, such as when the crew used a bit too much dynamite for a scene in one of her later shorts for Edison. Fuller wrote in her diary, excerpts of which were reprinted in *Motion Picture Story Magazine*, "They blew me up with a Black Hand bomb today.... The shack was wrecked, my clothes were torn and blackened, and blood ran from a scalp wound. It was exciting. I hope my 'fans' will like it."[27]

Her fans didn't simply like her and her movies, they loved them and her popularity only grew. In 1912 and 1913 fans ranked Fuller behind about a dozen other actors in the *Motion Picture Story Magazine* popular player contests. By 1914 when *What Happened to Mary* had concluded and been replaced with the sequel *Who Will Marry Mary?*, readers were flooding the magazine with votes for Fuller, moving her consistently into the top five most popular actors. She outright won popularity contests at theaters in Dallas, Texas, and Buffalo, New York. Fans bought Mary Fuller Perfume and other products simply because she endorsed them. While she could still sometimes attend the classical music concerts that she loved (another thing she had in common with Jane Addams) without being recognized, by 1914 trying to film movies on location was nearly impossible; crowds developed instantly and she marveled "how they do eat me up!" Fuller was so famous that a letter from Australia addressed simply "Mary Fuller, United States" actually found its way to her in 1914.[28]

This was just one letter though of a daily torrent. While friends thanked and praised Jane Addams, fans adored and gushed over Mary Fuller. Some, like George Matthews of Hartford, Connecticut, sketched admiring pictures of her. A ten-year-old simply called her a "big sugar lump." Emilia Caprini, of Pittsburgh, Pennsylvania, wrote that she would have to be ill or "bound by bonds which she couldn't break" to miss a Mary Fuller movie. Others wrote poems such as this one:

Mary Fuller (1888–1973). Edison Studios hired Floyd Photography in New York to take glamor shots of Mary Fuller and other stars (author's collection).

How I adore her, no one knows; I see her oft in the picture shows. When I see her play upon the screen, I sit as if in a lovely dream. She's the girl that has such a winsome way; She's always sweet and always gay. She wears such becoming hats and frocks, they're almost as sweet as her pretty, dark locks. She has large eyes and a cute little nose; She's really a doll, from her head to her toes. I'll give you a hint, if you cannot guess—It's the loved Mary Fuller, I confess.[29]

In addition to admiring letters, fans sent her gifts as well. These could be practical items like hat pins, pin trays, handkerchiefs, or calendars. Some fans tried to distinguish themselves from the hordes by sending Fuller more unusual items such as ornaments from South Africa, ostrich plumes, and a bouquet of violets from Mississippi. Others sent typical romantic gifts like candy or a volume of poems by John Keats. Once fans knew she loved animals they burdened her with pets, both typical and not. One summer on location in Pennsylvania fans gave her a bulldog puppy, but also a butterfly, a pigeon, a grass snake, a pig, an angora goat, and a flock of ducks.[30]

While people admired Jane Addams for her usefulness, fans loved Mary Fuller for seeming like a real person on screen and off. Dorothy Kelley of Piedmont, California, wrote that she loved her because she was so talented as an actor that she was able to play many different parts well. She could be a strong-willed queen, a young girl "brimful of romance and mischief," or an "inexpressibly tender" woman. M. Iventge however felt that one could take real inspiration from Fuller and her performances because watching her on screen convinced one "that all the world was not to be distrusted yet; in short, to be uplifted and gain faith in ideals." Others seemed to think they actually knew what Fuller was like as a person though clearly they had never met her. Margaret Dittmann wrote that Fuller was unaffected. An anonymous admirer felt Fuller was modest and that there was not "anything put on about her."[31]

Like Addams, Fuller tried to craft her own image but she was less successful than America's social worker. Fuller wrote diary excerpts and articles for publication in fan magazines as well as gave interviews but allowed for two conflicting personalities to emerge from them. It seems that Fuller wanted fans to see her as similar to many of her characters on the screen: courageous, independent, and strong. She reinforced this image with stories about how hard she worked and what obstacles she overcame to be successful. Some fans seemed convinced. M. Iventge felt sure that Fuller "could and would do the same things in real life that she did in the silent drama." Fuller also, however, appeared to be fragile. Interviewers commented on how she seemed melancholy or sat with her feet tucked under her like a child. Fuller may not have realized that telling stories about loneliness, attending concerts alone, her family being so far away, or her love for her pet pig Wilfred created an image of vulnerability. This is the Mary Fuller that fans believed was real. Heroines who could do it all on their own belonged up on the screen for most Americans in 1913. Real women needed to be protected.[32]

The closeness that fans felt to not just Fuller's characters but to the real her became a bit excessive by 1914. One admirer who was a frequent letter writer to fan magazines became so angry that Fuller would not give him her autograph that he apparently tore up all her photographs. Fuller received so many requests for locks of her hair that she asked a fan magazine to explain that she simply could not send away all her curls.[33] The most personal intrusions that crossed the line though were the marriage proposals. Fuller requested interviewers to include in their stories that she was not thinking about marriage, hoping that the flood of proposals would stop. Fan magazine writers made fun of the love struck who sought their advice. To Maurice one wrote, "So you boldly state that you are in love with Mary Fuller. Can't do anything for you. *E. pluribus unum.* Hopeless." And to Three Love-Sick Guys one chided that Fuller "was single, but there is not hope for you."[34] J. Webb Gaynor of Grand Rapids, Michigan, wrote a toast to Fuller that started innocently: "Saw your picture on the screen, sweetest girl I've ever seen, in our hearts you reign as queen; Mary, here's to you! Just can't help but like your style, made me cry and made me smile, showed me life is worth the while; Mary, here's to you!" But he ended with phrases a bit too personal: "Should you wish to try your fate, and go looking for a mate, put me in as candidate; Mary, here's to you! Simple guise or more complex, dimple eyes and elfish grace, slender form and fair of face, gentle acme of your sex; merry Mary, here's to you!"[35]

Jane Addams actually had her own episode with an obsessed fan in 1913 that explains much about her public image. Always believing in the power of the written word, she answered a letter from troubled Henry Leunker in 1911. For the next two years she was the recipient of increasingly personal and apparently offensive notes from him. Convinced he suffered from mental illness, she attempted to find help for him by contacting a social worker in New Orleans, where Leunker lived. When she felt he had threatened to kill himself, Addams urged authorities to take him into custody. He had written "you know that the very moment that you give me up I shall be lost and dead." Even though Leunker was apparently armed, newspapers across the country ran the story with an amused and light tone; he was arrested, they reported, for "annoying Miss Jane Addams by persistently writing love letters to her."[36]

Addams had maintained her image as the "lady bountiful," which helped explain to the public her continued single status; when would this woman have found time for a husband and children when she was already taking care of so many and their needs? Americans could easily see Addams also as prudish and offended by overtures of love, such as it was assumed were coming from Leunker, since she did not seem to have romantic relationships with men. Because of prevalent gender ideas of the time, most would not have been able to imagine Addams having deep love relationships with female partners. Those so-called Boston marriages, which may or may not have been sexual, had been common before the turn of the century but the country had become more insistent on heterosexual relationships in the teens.[37]

Obsessive fans and oppressive fame may have been the only similarities between the lives of Fuller and Addams in 1912 to 1913. Jane Addams did break into show business in 1912 by giving an entertaining speech at the Majestic Theater and by playing herself in the movie *Votes for Women,* which was incorporated into a newsreel. (The *New York Tribune* declared that with the movie, suffragists were now so visible that "pretty soon they'll be breaking into baseball against the Giants and we won't be able to get away from 'em anywhere.")[38] Addams, like Fuller, was at the pinnacle of her power, but for Addams it was in the world of politics not film. Theodore Roosevelt asked her to second his nomination for president at the Progressive Party convention. She was the first woman ever to present a major candidate for the highest office in the land. In addition to writing her nomination speech, as a member of the platform committee she helped write planks supporting many actions such as granting women the vote and abolishing child labor. Addams campaigned for Roosevelt across the country that fall, traveling by train and giving speeches every day. She was often greeted by choruses of women wearing red handkerchiefs and singing new songs set to old tunes from the *Jane Addams Songbook* in support of Roosevelt.[39] Progressives applauded her contribution to the convention, campaign, and political discourse though Roosevelt lost in the election that fall. (Though Mary Fuller said in 1912 she would like to vote for Roosevelt, she felt she had not studied the woman suffrage issue enough to have a strong opinion. She said politics did not interest her because politicians were not artistic, "except the lies they tell."[40])

In 1914 Addams changed her focus and lost the support of her public. She turned her efforts to the peace movement. Long dedicated to pacifism, one of her first books had dealt with the subject, she felt a renewed sense of urgency as war raged in Europe. She made repeated trips to witness the impact firsthand and felt compelled to make Americans aware of the dangers of joining the fight. On her anti-war stance she was unable to bring her fan base with her, especially once the United

States entered World War I. Her outspoken opposition to the war turned her from beloved to pariah. She was widely criticized for one particular speech in which she tried to explain the understandable reluctance of men to fight and the use of alcohol to induce them out of the trenches for charges. She argued that it was not that they lacked courage; they would rather kill themselves than kill another human being. Americans, whether or not they had husbands or sons among those who would be in those trenches, did not see her point and felt she was insulting the heroic soldiers.[41] After the United States joined the war, she turned her attention to food distribution but that work could not restore her reputation.

General criticism came in many forms. One man wrote, "My dear Miss Addams, believe me, you are an awful ass, truly awful." He continued,

> You take yourself and your opinions with such solemn seriousness that only the ass is your equal. Continue to bray my dear woman. Each time you open your mouth nowadays and each time you write one of your unpatriotic and pro–German speeches you proclaim yourself an ass.[42]

Among her papers is an anonymous limerick accusing Addams of creating even more annoyance with her constant complaining about the war than any German could do. It ends with "Eternal ennui you have inspired, No Hun from Hun-land e'er made us so tired." Organizations cancelled her speeches and when she did face crowds she experienced being booed for the first time in her life.[43]

Criticism of her in newspapers was often gendered. Writers argued not only that her views on the war were wrong but that as a woman she was unable to even hold opinions on this matter. Or conversely, if she insisted on involving herself with war matters, maybe she was not a woman at all. One critic called her a "silly, vain, impertinent old maid" and another argued that she needed "a strong, forceful husband who would lift the burden of fate from her shoulders and get her intensely interested in fancy work and other things dear to the heart of women who have homes and plenty of time on their hands."[44]

After the war criticism became even more acute as Addams pushed for humanitarian aid for Germany and criticized harassment of political protesters. She faced public wrath as an atmosphere of suppression of dissent grew. Critics now saw her not only as wrong but as a traitor; one newspaper labeled her the "most dangerous woman in America." Some linked Addams and many of her organizations to communism.[45] The Daughters of the American Revolution revoked her honorary membership. Someone sent her a news clipping about the social worker Charlotte Anita Whitney who courts convicted for being a member of the

California Communist Labor Party. The anonymous sender underlined the words "social and charity worker" in the article and wrote on the newspaper, "It is sometimes well to read 'the handwriting on the wall.'"[46] She received many critical letters but her attempted public appearances must have been the most difficult for her. Before Addams could speak in Detroit in 1919, for instance, she endured forty-five minutes of heckling.[47]

While Addams chose to take stances that she knew were likely to diminish her influence, Fuller decided to retire from public life altogether. She moved to California in 1914, leaving Edison Studios for Universal Pictures, but stayed only a few years. One of her last movies was *The Public Be Damned*, a condemnation of food trusts that included an introduction by Herbert Hoover, United States Food Administrator. (Addams continued to work for food distribution in 1917 but no connection between the two women is apparent.) Fuller moved back to Washington, D.C., to live with her mother because she needed a rest and possessed enough money to live comfortably. Critics and fans knew Fuller was experiencing health problems leading to weight loss. They gossiped, however, that she retired due to a nervous breakdown brought on by a failed affair with a married opera singer. Though a Pittsburgh Suburbian had concluded a poem about her with "from photo fame she'll never fade," fade she certainly did.[48]

Fuller tried to conceal her new location, but a *Photoplay Magazine* reporter tracked down Fuller's mother in 1924 by using the city directory. Fuller told the reporter that she never intended to retire permanently and was now ready to resume her career. Fuller, however, never made another movie. She admitted she was rather old fashioned and averse to publicity compared to the actors of the 1920s.[49] Since she retired before sound pictures were made, the public never heard her voice, which had a slight southern accent from her upbringing in Washington, D.C.[50] Fuller endured extreme fan attention but it seemed very mild in comparison to what future stars experienced. Honeymooners Mary Pickford and Douglas Fairbanks were mobbed in 1920, for example. Pickford was nearly pulled from a moving car by fans and both lost buttons, handkerchiefs, and other items to souvenir hunters when they moved through crowds. Pickford also survived a kidnapping attempt in 1925.[51]

Addams weathered the criticism and eventually regained her good name by the 1930s. Americans again wrote poems in her honor and included her in children's books, such as *When I Was a Girl*. Colleges such as Mt. Holyoke awarded her honorary degrees. Supporters pushed for her consideration for the Nobel Peace Prize during the 1920s and they were successful in 1931. Jane Addams was the first woman to be awarded this exclusive honor; however, she shared the prize with a co-recipient who was a supporter of United States entry into World War I. In 1933 she was named one of the twelve greatest women leaders of the last one hundred years in a poll conducted by the National Council of Women, *Ladies' Home Journal*, and the *Christian Science Monitor*. Nearly 100,000 women voted for her and only Mary Baker Eddy, founder of the Christian Science Church, received more votes.[52] Jane Addams was back on top in the eyes of the world and stayed there through her death in 1935.

Mary Fuller never reacquired fame in her lifetime but has since reclaimed her status as one of the great queens of the silent films. She apparently suffered a nervous breakdown when her mother died in 1940. Fuller's sister took care of her as long as she could but felt the need to institutionalize her. Fuller died in 1973 at St. Elizabeth's Hospital in D.C., her home for the final twenty years of her life. Finding no family members, the hospital buried her in an unmarked grave. Persistent researcher Bill Capello rediscovered her and writer Billy Doyle used his Lost Players column of *Classic Images* to try to erase Hollywood amnesia of the star who for a whole year kept audiences enthralled with the first movie serial.[53] Recently, fans installed a bench at her grave with a Hollywood Walk of Fame–like star. It includes her own quote characterizing her strength: "A personality of eloquent silence."[54] In this as in so many other ways, Fuller was an opposite of Jane Addams, but for a brief time, no two women in America were more beloved.

Jane Addams (1860–1935) later in life. This photograph of the famous social worker is undated but was probably taken in the 1920s (Library of Congress, LC-DIG-hec-21664).

Select Bibliography

Addams, Jane. *The Spirit of Youth and the City Streets.* 1909. Reprint, New York: The MacMillan Company, 1930.

Addams, Jane. *Twenty Years at Hull-House with Autobiographical Notes.* New York: The Macmillan Company, 1912.

Booth, Paul, ed. *A Companion to Media Fandom and Fan Studies.* New York: John Wiley and Sons, 2018.

Davis, Allen F. *American Heroine: The Life and Legend of Jane Addams.* New York: Oxford University Press, 1973.

Diliberto, Gioia. *A Useful Woman: The Early Life of Jane Addams.* New York: Scribner's, 1999.

Enstad, Nan. *Ladies of Labor, Girls of Adventure.* New York: Columbia University Press, 1999.

"Extracts from the Diary of Mary Fuller." *Motion Picture Story Magazine* 7 (July 1914): 80–84.

"Extracts from the Diary of Mary Fuller." *Motion Picture Story Magazine* 8 (August 1914): 97–99.

Firkus, Angela. "What Happened to Mary." In *Reforming America: A Thematic Encyclopedia and Document Collection of the Progressive Era,* edited by Jeffrey Johnson, 742–744. Santa Barbara: ABC-CLIO, 2017.

Fuller, Mary, and Bailey Millard. "My Adventures as a Motion-Picture Heroine." *Collier's* 48 (December 30, 1911): 16–17.

Conclusion

Celebrity women constantly command our attention. Cleopatra, Pocahontas, and Queen Victoria are historical icons discovered anew by each generation. Beyoncé, Taylor Swift, and Hillary Clinton could not escape their fame if they tried. The current social media sensation will have long ago ceased to be a celebrity by the time these words are published. Loved or hated, celebrated or scorned, these women are not ignored. Without a doubt, celebrity is a phenomenon that cannot be avoided in the twenty-first century but it had its origins long ago.

Phillis Wheatley and Martha Washington were among the first women of the Americas to command attention. Slave poet Wheatley earned a reputation with her genius and Lady Washington personified a dutiful wife at the end of the eighteenth century. They became symbols that filled a need for Americans looking for reassurance as they threw off British rule. While the details of the women's lives could not have been more different, they both understood well how celebrity worked. Wheatley and Washington each created a public persona that overshadowed her actual personality and thus became a symbol: one of genius and the other of amiability. Americans of the time were happy to accept the women as representations of these types rather than as complex women with a variety of impulses, roles, and desires. They honored the women with gifts and treasured meeting them whether or not they received poems or mementos in return. Still, Americans would not have dreamed of intruding on the women's privacy or of demanding more information than the women willingly provided. As a result, Wheatley and Washington easily crafted their own image for their contemporaries and have made it difficult for historians to add much to that portrayal. Americans would become much more curious and demand more from future celebrities.

Susanna Rowson and Elizabeth Patterson Bonaparte instinctively knew that to maintain celebrity took work and a willingness to lay bare the self. They also deftly skirted the line between respectability and disgrace; Americans largely accepted and forgave their transgressions. Author Rowson ingeniously used personal revelations to try to keep her fans intrigued. She worked biographical details into her novels and connected with readers through confessional prefaces and epilogues. Ultimately though, Rowson was unable to generate lasting interest in her story though she had unwittingly created the perfect self-perpetuating fictional celebrity in the character of Charlotte Temple. Bonaparte internalized disappointments but exposed her physical body to generate the publicity she needed for her quest for celebrity. As Napoleon's sister-in-law and mother of his nephew, she entered society seemingly located in the eye of a hurricane, with rumor, innuendo, and chaos swirling around her. When she acquired the aristocratic connection she sought, she turned her back on celebrity but it would not leave. She did little to foster her fame for most of her life but rather than be resented, she was celebrated by many for her ability to dismiss so easily the benefits of public reputation.

Lecturer Fanny Wright and author Lydia Maria Child captured American attention through their ideas and words but with very different styles. They joined a chorus of voices of the 1820s and 1830s advocating justice and equality but as women they needed to break through what Frances Trollope called a "shield of habitual insignificance" in order to become influential. Scotland-born Wright made the United States her home and mesmerized audiences with her speaking abilities. Few respectable women of the age dared to appear on stage before a mixed-sex crowd, called promiscuous by contemporaries. Wright attracted attention with her antislavery lectures and activities, but others were also making a plea for abolitionism. When Wright attacked organized religion and clergy as part of her individual rights message, she crossed a line deemed improper for all but especially for women. Lydia Maria Child came to feel indifferent about fame but also used her celebrity status to advocate for the worst off in American society. She damaged her widespread respectable reputation with a blunt antislavery book though a careful reading of her literature would have given her fans clear evidence of her racial equality leanings. Like Wright, Child faced complicated gender norms: a woman could attack racial discrimination with fictional stories without repercussions but could face condemnation if she addressed the same issue in the logical prose at the time reserved for men. Child loathed having drawn attention to herself, and for the rest of her life tried to overcome that decision to be so direct and to rebuild her ability to persuade with a more subtle style. Wright and Child faced gender-based limits on their public activities but ironically these limits also brought more attention to their message. They broke through the shields of insignificance on purpose and by accident; they paved the way for other women to follow.

Women used some degree of hype to enhance their fame but dancer Fanny Elssler and singer Jenny Lind benefited from full-blown humbug to become superstars and subsequently rich in mid–nineteenth century America. The women we have considered certainly also understood this requirement of celebrity. Martha Washington allowed her husband's secretary to solidify her amiable reputation with well-placed letters. Phillis Wheatley enjoyed the public praise of Wheatley family members as well as of their connected friends. Susannah Rowson used her personal story to intrigue her fans. Elizabeth Patterson Bonaparte used style to tap into an inexplicable American fascination with royalty that went against its founding republican ideals. Fanny Wright provoked ire for publicity. Lydia Maria Child orchestrated a female public show of support to save the life of accused murderer Amelia Norman. Austrian Fanny Elssler, however, made these efforts appear small. She promoted her dance performances in the 1840s with a campaign designed to create a craze and it worked beyond imagining. Many Americans caught Elsslermania and gladly lost themselves and much cash in a frivolous but satisfying bit of humbug that others were disgusted with. By the time that Jenny Lind arrived from Sweden, the public was more jaded about cultural celebrity but overall not less eager to participate in the phenomenon. Americans largely did not share a national identity at mid-century but outsiders like Elssler and Lind created an opportunity for a common experience that clearly many in the United States longed for but many others decried.

In many ways though, the 1850s must have been ripe for female celebrity worship because the number of prominent women is astounding. The early 1850s was a golden age for women wanting fame and fortune though the publicity campaigns of previous celebrities had created excessive expectations of fan familiarity. Women who wanted to keep a private life found it impossible to maintain a secret identity. Fans demanded to know not only their idol's work and public persona, but to feel the privilege of a personal connection to a celebrity's authentic self. Author Fanny Fern generated veritable hysteria when she tried to conceal her identity. Dancer Lola Montez desperately obfuscated through books, trial testimony, letters to the editor, and plays she represented as autobiographical. Montez embraced the scrutiny and abuse directed at her by an adoring and vilifying public; she used it all as celebrity-generating publicity. Fern shied away from celebration and scorned the spotlight, ever philosophical about the price of fame and its differing burdens for men and women. She enjoyed her newspaper column persona and rather than reveal her authentic self, she became Fanny Fern: dispenser of wit and advice. Adah Menken learned from both women and perfected a method of completely shedding one identity for the next, not simply for the public but also on a personal level. Eventually she created a private self and revealed it in poetry in such a skillful manner that after her early death many respectable women deeply regretted the disdain they had previously felt toward her. Celebrity had reduced women to symbols, emphasized transgressive elements of their lives, moved women to hype their stories, and finally convinced women even their own identity did not belong to them.

Women willing to put up with these intrusions experienced power and influence during the latter half of the nineteenth century but continued to navigate a confusing landscape of rules about celebrity. World famous author Harriet Beecher Stowe arguably single handedly turned the North against slavery with her novel *Uncle Tom's Cabin*. Politician Victoria Woodhull was the first woman to run for president of the United States and disseminated the ideas of the woman suffrage movement more effectively than most women involved in the cause. These two women, who were among the best known and celebrated Americans of the period, faced censure for obscenity when they simply told the truth about despicable male behavior. Stowe exposed the scandalous life of poet Lord Byron and Woodhull revealed an affair of preacher Henry Ward Beecher. While the men maintained their reputations, Stowe faced ridicule and Woodhull suffered imprisonment. Their stories were linked and reveal even more clearly how confusing were the standards since Stowe herself labeled Woodhull obscene.

Two extraordinary women of color forged their own paths of celebrity during the latter half of the nineteenth century. Black activist Sojourner Truth fought injustice all of her life. She demanded an end to slavery, equal access to public transportation, and the vote. Truth found that she could deliver a blunt message to white crowds more effectively if she used witty and quaint language. She attracted publicity with her Truth-isms, which could not easily be dismissed and were amusing enough to warrant steady repetition. Truth also used her own story of slavery and religious conviction to reach audiences. While Truth succeeded in publicizing her issues, she played into the racism of the time and was dismissed by some as simply an entertainer. Paiute Indian Sarah Winnemucca faced a similar challenge to grab and hold the attention of white America. She devoted her life to requesting assistance for Native American tribes of the West facing dire circumstances. She too turned to humor and used racist attitudes to her advantage. In her case, she appeared to white audiences as an Indian princess who delivered biting criticism of American treatment of her people but with sarcasm and a smile. Winnemucca though, like Truth, could not escape racial stereotypes that marred her publicity.

In the latter part of the nineteenth century Americans still adored celebrity authors and lecturers, but a new standard emerged. Fans wanted women of action to obsess over. Daredevil women completed all manner of activities to attract attention. Italian Maria Spelterini tight roped into the hearts of Americans. Aeronaut Carlotta Myers thrilled spectators with her antics and balloon ascensions. Pedestrian Ada Anderson inspired women to walk for their health. Racers Tillie Anderson, Dottie Farnsworth, and Lisette risked their lives for the thrill of speed and cash prizes, though they could face gender stereotyping and criticisms. Sharpshooter Annie Oakley eclipsed them all in both skill and celebrity manipulation. She became a superstar because she was able to walk the thin line of being a woman of action who always maintained her femininity.

Women celebrities of the beginning of the twentieth century faced new challenges that made them reevaluate whether fame was worth the price. Social worker Jane Addams devoted her life to helping people but found herself buffeted by the winds of fame. When faced with the decision in 1918 of whether to follow American attitudes toward favoring participation in the war in Europe or to strike out alone in support of pacifism she did not hesitate. What good was fame if it could not be used to garner support for a cause you held dear? She took an extremely unpopular stance and faced cruel criticism. Addams willingly gave up her celebrity status on principle. Actress Mary Fuller arrived at the same estimation of the excessive price of fame. She walked away from her acting career when she was among the most famous and popular women in film.

Fans allowed these celebrities to earn money and a sense of security in precarious economic times for women. Fans emerge also from this story as increasingly unforgiving. They held these women to impossible standards and forced them to navigate confusing rules that they constantly changed. Anti-fans expected these celebrities to respect the same gender norms they themselves ignored; women who acted in public could be treated as if they were not women at all. Fans demanded of their objects of adoration a level of exposure they themselves would probably never have tolerated. They doled out celebration and scorn easily and for sometimes mystifying reasons.

Besides these hypocrisies however, fans in early American history demonstrated a charming optimism in the power of personal relationships. If one simply told Elizabeth Patterson Bonaparte or Mary Fuller how much one loved her, she might realize how perfect a husband one would make. If one could personally experience the genius of Phillis Wheatley, the beauty of Lola Montez, the grace of Fanny Elssler, or the goodness of Jenny Lind one could be transformed. If one could only present a treasured item to Martha Washington or Lydia Maria Child she would understand just how much she was admired. If one could get advice from Fanny Fern, buy a photograph from Sojourner Truth, take shooting lessons from Annie Oakley, or share tales from the life of a social worker with Jane Addams one could know that one's life held deep meaning. Fans realized celebrities made their lives worth living and they imagined they could enrich the lives of those they adored, if only they could get the chance.

Ironically it was just this assumption of closeness that lead celebrities to create (and sometimes re-create) public personae to distance themselves from fans. This identity might be a one-dimensional, symbolic representation of genius or amiability. It might be a full-blown fictional biography or personality. It might be a veneer of humor or bravado. Fans may or may not see or think they see through this creation. While this dialogue between fans and celebrities is still evolving, it clearly was already in existence in early America, before the age of Hollywood. Lacking anything else to base their decision on, fans celebrated or scorned famous women based on the personae they portrayed.

Chapter Notes

Preface

1. Cora Sutton Castle, "A Statistical Study of Eminent Women" (PhD diss., Columbia University, 1913).

2. Frances Trollope, *Domestic Manners of the Americans* (1832; repr., New York: Dodd, Mead and Company, 1901), 1: 97.

3. See Sharon Marcus, *The Drama of Celebrity* (Princeton: Princeton University Press, 2019) and Greg Jenner, *Dead Famous* (London: Orion, 2020).

4. Antoine Lilti, *The Invention of Celebrity: 1750–1850* (Cambridge: Polity Press, 2017) is a wonderful overview and Julia Fawcett, *Spectacular Disappearances: Celebrity and Privacy, 1696–1801* (Ann Arbor: University of Michigan Press, 2016) nicely compares male and female celebrities in London.

Chapter One

1. Vincent Carretta, *Biography of a Genius in Bondage* (Athens: University of Georgia Press, 2011), 11–22.

2. Carretta, *Biography*, 26, 35, 39–40; Henry Louis Gates, *The Trials of Phillis Wheatley: America's First Black Poet and Her Encounters with the Founding Fathers* (New York: Basic Books, 2003), 18–20; G.J. Barker-Benfield, *Phillis Wheatley Chooses Freedom* (New York: New York University Press, 2018), 65–66; John C. Shields, ed., *The Collected Works of Phillis Wheatley* (New York: Oxford University Press, 1988), 282.

3. Carretta, *Biography*, 94.

4. Leo Braudy, *The Frenzy of Renown:*

Fame and Its History (New York: Vintage Books, 1986); Antoine Lilti, *The Invention of Celebrity: 1750–1850* (Cambridge: Polity Press, 2017), 3–10, 102–104, 276; Julia Fawcett, *Spectacular Disappearances: Celebrity and Privacy, 1696–1801* (Ann Arbor: University of Michigan Press, 2016), 1–2; Heather McPherson, *Art & Celebrity in the Age of Reynolds and Siddons* (University Park: Pennsylvania State University Press, 2017), 7–15.

5. Jennifer Rene Young, "Marketing a Sable Muse: Phillis Wheatley and the Antebellum Press," in *New Essays on Phillis Wheatley*, eds. John C. Shields and Eric D. Lamore (Knoxville: University of Tennessee Press, 2011), 217; Carretta, *Biography*, 102.

6. Shields, *Collected Works*, 212–213.

7. Carretta, *Biography*, 83–85; William H. Robinson, *Phillis Wheatley: A Bio-bibliography* (Boston: G.K. Hall, 1981), 11. She corrected the pronouns when publishing the poem in her book.

8. "Deborah Cushing to Thomas Cushing, September 19–21, 1774," Massachusetts Historical Society Online, accessed March 17, 2020, http://www.masshist.org/database/viewer.php?item_id=792&mode=large&img_step=1#page1.

9. Robinson, *Phillis Wheatley*, 13.

10. Phillis Wheatley, *Poems on Various Subjects, Religious and Moral* (London: A Bell, 1773), 7; Joann Brooks, "Our Phillis, Ourselves," *American Literature* 82 (June 2010): 7–10.

11. Carretta, *Biography*, 133–134.

12. Barker-Benfield, *Phillis Wheatley*

Chooses Freedom, 78; Carretta, *Biography*, 105.

13. Samuel Johnson wrote in *Rambler* (October 15, 1751), "I did not find myself yet enriched in proportion to my celebrity" and this is considered by the Oxford English Dictionary to be the first modern use of the word in print. McPherson, *Art & Celebrity*, 9.

14. Gates, *Trials of Phillis Wheatley*, 22, 31; Carretta, *Biography*, 95–99.

15. Carretta, *Biography*, 105.

16. Makhtar Ali Isani, "The Contemporaneous Reception of Phillis Wheatley: Newspaper and Magazine Notices during the Years of Fame, 1765–1774," *Journal of Negro History* 85 (Fall 2000): 268; *New Hampshire Gazette*, June 18, 1773, printed the poem by request.

17. Carretta, *Biography*, 120–123.

18. Robinson, *Phillis Wheatley*, 14; Carretta, *Biography*, 123.

19. Isani, "Contemporaneous Reception," 262, 269–270.

20. *London Magazine, or Gentleman's Monthly Intelligencer* 42 (September 1773): 456; *Scots Magazine* 35 (September 1773): 484; *Critical Review: Annals of Literature by a Society of Gentlemen* 36 (July-December 1773): 232–233.

21. Zach Petrea, "An Untangled Web: Mapping Phillis Wheatley's Network of Support in America and Great Britain," in *New Essays on Phillis Wheatley*, 296; *Monthly Review* 51 (July-December 1774): 387–390.

22. Isani, "Contemporaneous Reception," 271.

23. Carretta, *Biography*, 94.

24. Shields, *Collected Works*, 143; researchers speculate that Wheatley may have written this poem. See Barker-Benfield, *Phillis Wheatley Chooses Freedom*, 143–153.

25. Daniel Ennis, "Poetry and American Revolutionary Identity: The Case of Phillis Wheatley and John Paul Jones," *Studies in Eighteenth-Century Culture* 31 (2002): 85–98.

26. Wheatley, *Poems on Various Subjects*, 4.

27. Barker-Benfield, *Phillis Wheatley Chooses Freedom*, 127.

28. Carretta, *Biography*, 137–138.

29. "Poetical Essays," *Pennsylvania Magazine, or American Monthly Museum*

(April 1776), 193; Shields, *Collected Works*, 145–146.

30. Helen Bryan, *Martha Washington: First Lady of Liberty* (New York: John Wiley and Sons, 2002), 49.

31. Alice Curtis Desmond, *Martha Washington: Our First Lady* (New York: Dodd, Mead and Company, 1966), 142.

32. Elswyth Thane, *Washington's Lady* (New York: Meredith Press, 1954), 101; Martha Washington to Elizabeth Ramsay, December 30, 1775, in *"Worthy Partner": The Papers of Martha Washington*, comp. Joseph Fields (Westport, CT: Greenwood Press, 1994), 164.

33. Patricia Brady, *Martha Washington: An American Life* (New York: Penguin, 2005), 201; "The Valuable and Extraordinary Collection of Books From the Library of Genl. Geo. Washington and other things To be sold Wed. and Thurs. Feb. 11 and 12, 1891 by Birch's Sons, Philadelphia" lists among the books to be sold a copy of *Charlotte Temple* and a volume of *The Jilts; or, Female Fortune Hunters*. The later has Martha Washington's name in it and the auctioneers reported they were "pained to say this Volume is very indecorous."

34. Shields, *Collected Works*, 304–306.

35. Benson Lossing, *Mary and Martha: The Mother and the Wife of George Washington* (New York: Harper and Brothers, 1886), 151–152; Anne Hollingsworth Wharton, *Martha Washington* (New York: Charles Scribner's Sons, 1897),102; Benson Lossing, *The Pictorial Field-book of the Revolution Volume I* (New York: Harper & Brothers, 1860), 555–556.

36. Gates, *Trials of Phillis Wheatley*, 68.

37. Barker-Benfield, *Phillis Wheatley Chooses Freedom*, 132–143.

38. "Elegy on the Death of a Late Celebrated Poetess," *Boston Magazine* (December 1784): 619–620.

39. Desmond, *Martha Washington*, 251.

40. "Martha Washington and the American Revolution," Mount Vernon Website, accessed March 17, 2020, https://www.mountvernon.org/library/digitalhistory/digital-encyclopedia/article/martha-washington-and-the-american-revolution/; Lossing, *Pictorial*

Field-book of the Revolution Volume II, 106; Barker-Benfield, *Phillis Wheatley Chooses Freedom*, 164.

41. Cokie Roberts, *Founding Mothers: The Women Who Raised Our Nation* (New York: William Morrow, 2004), 116–118.

42. Fields, *Worthy Partner*, xxiii.

43. "Martha Washington," Mount Vernon Website, accessed March 17, 2020, https://www.mountvernon.org/library/digitalhistory/digital-encyclopedia/article/martha-washington/; Allison Lange, "Picturing Tradition: Images of Martha Washington in Antebellum Politics," *Imprint* 37 (Autumn 2012): 26.

44. "Martha Washington and the American Revolution"; for the lyrics see American Antiquarian Society Digital Assets Archive, accessed March 17, 2020, https://gigi.mwa.org/netpub/server.np?quickfind=285719&site=public&catalog=catalog&sorton=filename&template=detail.np&offset=0&TabletNPResults=/netpub/server.np%3Fquickfind%3D203762%26site%3Dpublic%26catalog%3Dcatalog%26sorton%3Dfilename%26template%3Dresults.np&TabletNPResultsCount=1&playMode=stop.

45. Richard Frothingham, *History of the Siege of Boston, and the Battles of Lexington, Concord, and Bunker Hill* (Boston: Charles C. Little and James Brown, 1851), 313; Roberts, *Founding Mothers*, 116; *Pennsylvania Evening Post*, July 10, 1777.

46. Martha Washington to Arthur Lee, September 15, 1780, Fields, *Worthy Partner*, 184; Desmond, *Martha Washington*, 192.

47. Martha Mortier to Martha Washington, June 15, 1781 and George Washington's reply, Fields, *Worthy Partner*, 186–187.

48. Desmond, *Martha Washington*, 206, 210.

49. "For Sale, The Lady Washington," Charleston (SC) *Morning Post and Daily Advertiser*, November 7, 1786; "To be Let, that licensed tavern known by the sign of Lady Washington," *Pennsylvania Mercury and Universal Advertiser*, October 6, 1786.

50. *Gazette of the United States* (New York), May 30, 1789.

51. Desmond, *Martha Washington*,

217; *New York Daily Gazette*, May 27, 1789.

52. *New York Daily Gazette*, May 27, 1789; *Pennsylvania Mercury and Universal Advertiser*, May 28, 1789; *Gazette of the United States* (New York), May 30, 1789.

53. Bryan, *Martha Washington*, 295–296.

54. Enos Hitchcock, *Memoirs of the Bloomsgrove Family. In a Series of Letters to a respectable Citizen of Philadelphia. Containing Sentiments on a Mode of Domestic Education, Suited to the present State of Society, Government, and Manners, in the United States of America: And On the Dignity and Importance of the Female Character. Interspersed With a Variety of interesting Anecdotes* (Boston: Thomas and Andrews, 1790), iii–v.

55. "General Washington's Birth Day," *Bartgis's Maryland Gazette*, May 22, 1792.

56. Fields, *Worthy Partner*, 235, 236, 242, 283.

57. Roberts, *Founding Mothers*, 264.

58. "Covered Cup," Mount Vernon Website, accessed March 17, 2020, https://www.mountvernon.org/preservation/collections-holdings/browse-the-museum-collections/object/w-1497ac/.

59. John Lamb to Martha Washington, December 10, 1790, Fields, *Worthy Partner*, 227.

60. Martha Washington to Mary Ann Aitken, February 24, 1794, Fields, *Worthy Partner*, 259. A draft of this note is in the handwriting of Tobias Lear.

61. John Trumbull to Martha Washington, October 7, 1796, Fields, *Worthy Partner*, 292.

62. Countess of Buchan to Martha Washington, January 8, 1794, in Fields, *Worthy Partner*, 254.

63. "Account of an Elegant Fancy Piece," *Columbian Centinel* (Boston), March 14, 1795.

64. Wharton, *Martha Washington*, 197; "To the Printers of the *Albany Register*," *Daily Advertiser* (New York), June 15, 1789; Bryan, *Martha Washington*, 295–296, 299.

65. Henry Lee to Martha Washington, April 10, 1800, Fields, *Worthy Partner*, 374.

66. David Humphreys to Martha Washington, July 5, 1800, Fields, *Worthy Partner,* 388–390.

67. Fields, *Worthy Partner,* 352, 363, 369.

68. A. Gray to Martha Washington, April 28, 1800, Fields, *Worthy Partner,* 379–380.

69. John Adams to Martha Washington, December 27, 1799; Martha Washington to John Adams, December 31, 1799, Fields, *Worthy Partner,* 327–328, 332–333. Copies of this letter are in the handwriting of Tobias Lear.

70. *Washington Federalist* (Georgetown, D.C.), May 24, 1802.

71. *Philadelphia Repository and Weekly Register,* May 29, 1802.

72. *Spectator* (New York), May 29, 1802.

73. Bryan, *Martha Washington,* ix.

74. Martha Washington to Fanny Bassett Washington, October 23, 1789, Fields, *Worthy Partner,* 219–220.

75. Martha Washington to Janet Livingston Montgomery, January 29, 1791, Fields, *Worthy Partner,* 229–230.

Chapter Two

1. Cathy Davidson, ed., *Charlotte Temple* (New York: Oxford University Press, 1986), xx–xxii.

2. Davidson, *Charlotte Temple,* xx–xxii.

3. Marion Rust, ed., *Charlotte Temple: A Norton Critical Edition* (New York: W.W. Norton, 2011), xxii.

4. R.W.G. Vail, *Susanna Haswell Rowson, the Author of Charlotte Temple, a Bibliographic Study* (Worcester: American Antiquarian Society, 1933), 56–58.

5. Davidson, *Charlotte Temple,* xxiv.

6. Melissa Homestead and Camryn Hansen, "Susanna Rowson's Transatlantic Career," *Early American Literature* 45 (2010): 630.

7. Davidson, *Charlotte Temple,* xxix

8. Marion Rust, *Prodigal Daughters: Susanna Rowson's Early American Women* (Chapel Hill: University of North Carolina Press, 2008), 117–118, 144–158.

9. Susanna Rowson, *Slaves in Algiers; or, A Struggle for Freedom: a Play, Interspersed with Songs, in Three Acts* (Philadelphia: Wrigley and Berriman, 1794), epilogue.

10. Susanna Rowson, *Mentoria; or, the Young Lady's Friend* (Philadelphia: Samuel Harrison Smith, 1794), preface.

11. Rowson, *Slaves in Algiers,* epilogue.

12. Camryn Hansen, "A Changing Tale of Truth," in *Charlotte Temple: A Norton Critical Edition,* ed. Marion Rust (New York: W.W. Norton, 2011), 184.

13. Thomas Clark Pollock, *The Philadelphia Theatre in the Eighteenth Century* (1933; repr., New York: Greenwood Press, 1968), 279.

14. Rust, *Prodigal Daughters,* 121–123; William Cobbett, *Porcupine's Works; Containing Various Writings and Selections Exhibiting a Faithful Picture of the United States of America* (London: Cobbett and Morgan, 1801), 82–89.

15. *A Rub from Snub; or a Cursory Analytical Epistle: Addressed to Peter Porcupine* (Philadelphia, 1795), 78–79.

16. Dorothy Weil, *In Defense of Women: Susanna Rowson* (University Park: Pennsylvania State University Press, 1976), 5.

17. Homestead and Hansen, "Susanna Rowson's Transatlantic Career," 637.

18. Susanna Rowson, *The Inquisitor, or, Invisible Rambler: In Three Volumes* (Philadelphia: Mathew Carey, 1794), 3:189.

19. "America, commerce & freedom. Together with the Soldier and his fair maid," *Isaiah Thomas Broadside Ballads Project,* accessed March 17, 2020, http://www.americanantiquarian.org/thomasballads/items/show/213.

20. Elias Nason, *A Memoir of Mrs. Susanna Rowson, with Elegant and Illustrative Extracts from Her Writings in Prose and Poetry* (Albany: Joel Munsell, 1870), 90.

21. *American Watchman and Delaware Advertiser* (Wilmington), March 26, 1824.

22. Nason, *Memoir of Mrs. Susanna Rowson,* 194.

23. Nason, *Memoir of Mrs. Susanna Rowson,* 193; Francis Halsey, ed., *Charlotte Temple* (New York: Funk and Wagnalls Company, 1905), xxvii–xxviii.

24. Vail, *Susanna Haswell Rowson,* 77–78; Rust, *Charlotte Temple,* 424.

25. Cathy Davidson, "The Life and

Times of Charlotte Temple," in *Charlotte Temple: A Norton Critical Edition*, ed. Marion Rust (New York: W.W. Norton, 2011), 243.

26. *American Watchman and Delaware Advertiser* (Wilmington), April 18, 1823 has reprint of *Columbian Centinel* piece.

27. Davidson, "The Life and Times of Charlotte Temple," 250.

28. Davidson, *Charlotte Temple*, xii–xiii; Cathy Davidson, *Revolution and the Word* (New York: Oxford University Press, 2004), 145, 147.

29. Rust, *Charlotte Temple*, 413.

30. Nason, *Memoir of Mrs. Susanna Rowson*; Francis Halsey, *Charlotte Temple*; Caroline Dall, *The Romance of the Associations; or, One Last Glimpse of Charlotte Temple and Eliza Wharton* (Cambridge: Press of John Wilson and Son, 1875); Ellen Brandt, *Susanna Haswell Rowson: America's First Best-selling Novelist* (Chicago: Serbra Press, 1975).

31. Brandt, *Susanna Haswell Rowson*, 75.

32. Linda Kerber, "Women's Reading," in *Charlotte Temple: A Norton Critical Edition*, ed. Marion Rust (New York: W.W. Norton, 2011), 214.

33. "Race News," *Richmond* (VA) *Enquirer*, September 29, 1835; Davidson "The Life and Times of Charlotte Temple," 255.

34. "To Correspondents," *Wilmingtonian* (DE), April 1, 1824.

35. Davidson, *Revolution and the Word*, 145.

36. Davidson, *Revolution and the Word*, 145.

37. Rust, *Prodigal Daughters*, 48–49.

38. Davidson, *Revolution and the Word*, 144–145.

39. *Liberty* (MS) *Advocate*, July 25, 1839.

40. Lydia Maria Child, *The Mother's Book* (Boston: Carter, Hendee and Babcock, 1831), 90–91.

41. Halsey, *Charlotte Temple*, xlix–lxii. An excavation in 2008 found no burial chamber under the slab. C.J. Hughes, "Buried in the Churchyard: A Good Story, at Least," *New York Times*, Dec. 12, 2008, https://www.nytimes.com/2008/12/13/nyregion/13trinity.html.

42. Halsey, *Charlotte Temple*, l-lii.

43. P.D. Manvill, *Lucinda; or the Mountain Mourner* (1807; repr., Erie, PA: Rufus Clough, 1831), 76.

44. Thomas Man, *Picture of a Factory Village* (Providence: n.p., 1833), 86, 87.

45. P.T. Barnum, *Struggles and Triumphs: Forty Years' Recollections* (Hartford: J.B. Burr and Company, 1869), 153–155.

46. "Charlotte Temple: Trinity Church Cemetery," History Underfoot, January 22, 2016, http://historyunderfoot.blogspot.com/2016/01/charlotte-temple-trinity-church-cemetery.html.

47. William Charvat, *The Profession of Authorship in America, 1800–1870* (1968; repr., New York: Columbia University, 1992), 20; James Hadden, *A History of Uniontown* (Uniontown, PA: New Werner Company, 1913), 38; Scott Martin, *Killing Time: Leisure and Culture in Southwestern Pennsylvania, 1800–1850* (Pittsburgh: University of Pittsburgh Press, 1995), 164–165; J. Thomas Scharf, *History of Saint Louis City and County, Vol. 1* (Philadelphia: Louis H. Everts and Company, 1883), 961; Ulana Lydia Baluk, "Proprietary Museums in Antebellum Cincinnati," (EdD Thesis, University of Toronto, 2000), 109, 129, 130; Samuel Hadley, "Boyhood Reminiscences of Middlesex Village," *Contributions of the Lowell Historical Society, Vol. 1* (Lowell: Butterfield Printing Company, 1913), 240.

48. *National Intelligencer and Washington* (D.C.) *Advertiser*, March 4, 1805.

49. Charlene M. Boyer Lewis, *Elizabeth Patterson Bonaparte: An American Aristocrat in the Early Republic* (Philadelphia: University of Pennsylvania Press, 2012), 117–118, 189; Carol Berkin, *Wondrous Beauty: the Life and Adventures of Elizabeth Patterson Bonaparte* (New York: Alfred A. Knopf, 2014), 26.

50. Berkin, *Wondrous Beauty*, 31.

51. [Thomas] Law to Elizabeth Patterson Bonaparte, 1804, *Elizabeth Patterson Bonaparte Papers, 1785–1879*, MS 142, Maryland Historical Society, Baltimore, MD.

52. Berkin, *Wondrous Beauty*, 26–27; "Elizabeth Patterson Bonaparte: Nineteenth-Century Fabulous," The Penn Press Log, July 14, 2012, https://pennpress.typepad.com/pennpresslog/2012/07/elizabeth-

paterson-bonaparte-nineteenth-century-fabulous.html.

53. Sarah Seaton diary excerpt January 2, 1813, in *William Winston Seaton of the National Intelligencer*, ed. Josephine Seaton (Boston: James R. Osgood and Company, 1871), 90; Berkin, *Wondrous Beauty*, 28–31.

54. Lewis, *Elizabeth Patterson Bonaparte*, 82.

55. Aaron Burr to Theodosia Burr Alston, January 17, 1804, in *Memoirs of Aaron Burr* (New York: Harper and Brothers, 1837), 2: 269.

56. Lewis, *Elizabeth Patterson Bonaparte*, 49.

57. Mrs. Smith to Mrs. Kirkpatrick, January 23, 1804, in Gaillard Hunt, ed. *The First Forty Years of Washington Society, Portrayed by the Family Letters of [Margaret Bayard Smith]* (New York: Charles Scribner's Sons, 1906), 46–47.

58. Lewis, *Elizabeth Patterson Bonaparte*, 82.

59. Lewis, *Elizabeth Patterson Bonaparte*, 18.

60. Berkin, *Wondrous Beauty*, 73.

61. Helen Jean Burn, *Betsy Bonaparte* (Baltimore: Maryland Historical Society, 2010), 211.

62. Berkin, *Wondrous Beauty*, 32.

63. Lewis, *Elizabeth Patterson Bonaparte*, 82.

64. Lewis, *Elizabeth Patterson Bonaparte*, 90–91.

65. Lewis, *Elizabeth Patterson Bonaparte*, 86–94.

66. R. Gilmore to Elizabeth Patterson Bonaparte, Feb. 5, 1802, *Elizabeth Patterson Bonaparte Papers*.

67. Sir George Dallas to Elizabeth Patterson Bonaparte, 1827, *Elizabeth Patterson Bonaparte Papers*.

68. ECH to Elizabeth Patterson Bonaparte, Nov. 1842, *Elizabeth Patterson Bonaparte Papers*.

69. Nicholas Nemo to Elizabeth Patterson Bonaparte, Oct. 25, 1812, *Elizabeth Patterson Bonaparte Papers*.

70. ECH to Elizabeth Patterson Bonaparte, April 1802, *Elizabeth Patterson Bonaparte Papers*.

71. Lewis, *Elizabeth Patterson Bonaparte*, 80, 166.

72. Lewis, *Elizabeth Patterson Bonaparte*, 218–220.

73. "The Late Jerome Bonaparte. 'Miss Patterson's' Husband," *Harper's Weekly*, July 28, 1860, 465–466.

74. Lewis, *Elizabeth Patterson Bonaparte*, 121.

75. Lewis, *Elizabeth Patterson Bonaparte*, 225.

76. Burn, *Betsy Bonaparte*, 245.

77. *New North-west* (Deer Lodge, MT), May 12, 1876.

78. *Gold Hill Daily News* (Nevada Terr.), July 6, 1878.

79. Lewis, *Elizabeth Patterson Bonaparte*, 228.

Chapter Three

1. Frances Trollope, *Domestic Manners of the Americans* (1832; repr., New York: Dodd, Mead and Company, 1901), 1:97.

2. Carolyn Karcher, ed., *A Lydia Maria Child Reader* (Durham: Duke University Press, 1997), 97.

3. The friend was Lois Curtis, a relative of Ticknor. Lydia Maria Child to George Ticknor, March 29, 1825, in *Lydia Maria Child Selected Letters, 1817–1880*, eds. Milton Meltzer and Patricia Holland (Amherst: University of Massachusetts Press, 1982), 3–4; Carolyn Karcher, *The First Woman in the Republic: A Cultural Biography of Lydia Maria Child* (Durham: Duke University Press, 1994), 39.

4. Lydia Maria Child to Mary Preston, Jan. 6, 1827, Meltzer and Holland, *Selected Letters*, 8.

5. Lydia Maria Child, "The First and Last Book," in *The Coronal* (Boston: Carter and Hendee, 1832), 283.

6. Child, "The First and Last Book," 284; William Osborne, *Lydia Maria Child* (Boston: Twayne Publishers, 1980), 21.

7. Karcher, *First Woman in the Republic*, 66.

8. "Works of Mrs. Child," *North American Review* 37 (July 1833): 139, 142.

9. Lydia Maria Child, *The Frugal Housewife* (1829; repr., Mineola, New York: Dover, 1999), introduction to the Dover edition; Deborah Clifford, *Crusader for Freedom: A Life of Lydia Maria Child* (Boston: Beacon Press, 1992), 78.

10. Karcher, *First Woman in the Republic*, 78.

11. Osborne, *Lydia Maria Child*, 24; Lori Kenschaft, *Lydia Maria Child: The Quest for Racial Justice* (New York: Oxford University Press, 2002), 23.

12. Anna Hallowell, "Lydia Maria Child," *Medford Historical Register* 3 (July 1900) 101.

13. Child, "The First and Last Book," 283.

14. Lydia Maria Child, *An Appeal in Favor of that Class of Americans Called Africans* (Boston: Allen and Ticknor, 1833), preface.

15. Kenschaft, *Lydia Maria Child*, 23; Lydia Maria Child to Mary Preston, June 11, 1826, Meltzer and Holland, *Selected Letters*, 7; Lydia Maria Child, *The Rebels: Or Boston Before the Revolution* (Boston: Cummings, Hilliard, and Company, 1825), 246.

16. Hallowell, "Lydia Maria Child," 101.

17. Clifford, *Crusader for Freedom*, 54.

18. Karcher, *First Woman in the Republic*, 58.

19. Child, *An Appeal*, preface, 232.

20. Karcher, *First Woman in the Republic*, 173.

21. Clifford, *Crusader for Freedom*, 102–104, 106; Kenschaft, *Lydia Maria Child*, 37.

22. [Leonard Bacon], "Mrs. Child's Appeal in Favor of the Africans," *Quarterly Christian Spectator* ser. 3 v. 6 (Sept. 1834): 446, 448, 450, 455–456; Kenschaft, *Lydia Maria Child*, 43.

23. Clifford, *Crusader for Freedom*, 103.

24. Rev. of *An Appeal, North American Review* 41 (July 1835), 170, 193.

25. Clifford, *Crusader for Freedom*, 102.

26. Karcher, *First Woman in the Republic*, 193, 194.

27. Charles Wilkes to James Fenimore Cooper, Sept. 30, 1828, in *Correspondence of James Fenimore Cooper* (New Haven: Yale University Press, 1922), 1:151; Celia Morris Eckhardt, *Fanny Wright: Rebel in America* (Cambridge: Harvard University Press, 1984), 41, 46.

28. Eckhardt, *Fanny Wright*, 76–79.

29. A.J.G. Perkins, *Frances Wright, Free Enquirer: The Study of a Temperament.* (1939; repr., Philadelphia: Porcupine Press, 1972), 111.

30. Eckhardt, *Fanny Wright*, 81.

31. Perkins, *Frances Wright, Free Enquirer*, 112.

32. Bernhard, Duke of Saxe-Weimar Eisenach, *Travels through North America, During the Years 1825 and 1826* (Philadelphia: Carey, Lea and Carey, 1828), 1:41–42; Eckhardt, *Fanny Wright*, 82.

33. Eckhardt, *Fanny Wright*, 66, 85–98.

34. Eckhardt, *Fanny Wright*, 143, 168, 172.

35. Karlyn Kohrs Campbell, ed., *Women Public Speakers in the United States, 1800–1925* (Westport, CT: Greenwood Press, 1993), xi.

36. Jane Elmes Cranhall, "Deborah Sampson Gannett (1760–1827), Revolutionary War Veteran and Early Lecturer," in Campbell, *Women Public* Speakers, 381–385.

37. Trollope, *Domestic Manners of the Americans*, 1:97–98, 100.

38. Horace Traubel, *With Walt Whitman in Camden* (New York: Mitchell Kennerley, 1915), 2:205, 445; F.O. Matthiessen, *American Renaissance: Art and Expression in the Age of Emerson and Whitman* (New York: Oxford University Press, 1941), 541, 550.

39. Eckhardt, *Fanny Wright*, 141.

40. Eckhardt, *Fanny Wright*, 176.

41. Emma Rogers, ed., *Life and Letters of William Barton Rogers* (Boston: Houghton, Mifflin and Company, 1896), 1: 69–70.

42. Robert Connors, "Frances Wright: First Female Civic Rhetor in America," *Journal of College English* 62 (Sep 1999): 36–39; Perkins, *Frances Wright, Free Enquirer*, 249.

43. Trollope, *Domestic Manners of the Americans*, 2:77–78.

44. William Randall Waterman, *Frances Wright* (New York: Columbia University Press, 1924), 172–173.

45. Eckhardt, *Fanny Wright*, 163, 176–187, 199.

46. Waterman, *Frances Wright*, 162.

47. Perkins, *Frances Wright, Free Enquirer*, 215.

48. Eckhardt, *Fanny Wright*, 222.

49. Waterman, *Frances Wright*, 169.

50. Eckhardt, *Fanny Wright*, 185–186.

51. Eckhardt, *Fanny Wright*, 220–222.

52. Eckhardt, *Fanny Wright*, 187.

53. Waterman, *Frances Wright*, 219–220.

54. Eckhardt, *Fanny Wright*, 204, 217, 222.

55. Karcher, *First Woman in the Republic*, 76, 118–119; Clifford, *Crusader for Freedom*, 89.

56. Eckhardt, *Fanny Wright*, 232–233.

57. Eckhardt, *Fanny Wright*, 235.

58. Eckhardt, *Fanny Wright*, 224.

59. Eckhardt, *Fanny Wright*, 244.

60. Eckhardt, *Fanny Wright*, 258, 265.

61. Catharine Beecher, *Letters on the Difficulties of Religion* (Hartford: Belknap and Hamersley, 1836), 22–23; Eckhardt, *Fanny Wright*, 249.

62. Eckhardt, *Fanny Wright*, 247–248, 258, 266–268; Perkins, *Frances Wright, Free Enquirer*, 355.

63. Eckhardt, *Fanny Wright*, 273.

64. Kenschaft, *Lydia Maria Child*, 50.

65. Kenschaft, *Lydia Maria Child*, 50, 57; Karcher, *First Woman in the Republic*, 208, 271.

66. Andrea Hibbard, "Law, Seduction, and the Sentimental Heroine: The Case of Amelia Norman," *American Literature* 78 (2006): 337- 338, 341–342.

67. Osborne, *Lydia Maria Child*, 12.

68. Clifford, *Crusader for Freedom*, 181, 209.

69. Karcher, *First Woman in the Republic*, 148.

70. Karcher, *First Woman in the Republic*, 311.

71. Karcher, *Lydia Maria Child Reader*, 17.

72. Karcher, *First Woman in the Republic*, 423.

73. Karcher, *First Woman in the Republic*, 605–607.

Chapter Four

1. Ivor Guest, *Fanny Elssler* (Middletown, CT: Wesleyan Press, 1970), 133.

2. Mary Grace Swift, *Belles and Beaux on Their Toes: Dancing Stars in Young America* (Washington, D.C.: University Press of America, 1980), 224.

3. Meredith McGill, *American Literature and the Culture of Reprinting, 1834–1853* (Philadelphia: University of Pennsylvania Press, 2003), 1–3, 132.

4. *New York Herald*, May 4, 1840.

5. *New York Herald*, April 30, 1844. For the publicity campaign see Michael Lueger, "Henry Wikoff and the Development of Theatrical Publicity in America" (MA thesis, Tufts University, 2011). Bennett printed Wikoff's letters in his paper in 1844.

6. *New York Mirror, A Weekly Journal of Literature and the Fine Arts,* May 16, 1840, 375; Guest, *Fanny Elssler*, 132.

7. Guest, *Fanny Elssler*, 130, 134; *New York Morning Herald*, May 7, 1840.

8. *New York Morning Herald*, May 7, 1840; *New York Morning Herald*, August 15, 1840; Guest, *Fanny Elssler*, 134.

9. Swift, *Belles and Beaux on Their Toes*, 43–44; "Correspondence from Washington, DC," *New York Morning Herald*, May 23, 1840.

10. "From the *New Orleans Picayune,*" *New York Mirror, A Weekly Journal of Literature and the Fine Arts*, July 25, 1840, 38.

11. *Spirit of the Times*, June 13, 1840, 180.

12. "Fanny Elssler: Extract of a Letter from New York," *Alexandria* (VA) *Gazette*, May 22, 1840.

13. *New York Mirror, A Weekly Journal of Literature and the Fine Arts*, May 23, 1840, 382.

14. Swift, *Belles and Beaux on Their Toes*, 199; Guest, *Fanny Elssler*, 12–13. Video reconstructions can be easily found on the internet.

15. *Alexandria* (VA) *Gazette*, May 22, 1840.

16. *Ladies' Companion* (New York), 13 (July 1840): 157.

17. *New York Mirror, A Weekly Journal of Literature and the Fine Arts*, May 23, 1840, 383.

18. Lois Banner, *American Beauty* (New York: Knopf, 1983), 63–64; Swift, *Belles and Beaux on Their Toes*, 209; *Baton-Rouge Gazette*, June 20, 1840; Guest, *Fanny Elssler*, 133.

19. Swift, *Belles and Beaux on Their Toes*, 214; *Baton-Rouge Gazette*, June 20, 1840; Guest, *Fanny Elssler*, 178.

20. *Pilot and Transcript* (Baltimore, MD), May 22, 1840.

21. *New York Morning Herald*, May 25, 1840; *New York Morning Herald*, May 30, 1840; Tom Picton, *Fun and Fancy in Old New York* (San Bernardino: Borgo Press, 2007), 43–44.

22. Maureen Needham Costonis, "The Personification of Desire: Fanny Elssler and American Audiences," *Dance Chronicle* 13 (1990) 47–67.

23. *New York Morning Herald*, May 7, 1840.

24. *New York Mirror, A Weekly Journal of Literature and the Fine Arts,* June 13, 1840, 407.

25. *Spirit of the Times,* May 30, 1840, 156.

26. *Alexandria* (VA) *Gazette*, May 22, 1840.

27. Maud Howe Elliott, *Uncle Sam Ward and His Circle* (New York: MacMillan Company, 1938), 263.

28. Guest, *Fanny Elssler*, 185; *New York Morning Herald*, May 15, 1840.

29. *Ladies' Companion* (New York), 13 (July 1840): 157.

30. Guest, *Fanny Elssler*, 133–134; "Advertisement Olympic Theatre," *New York Morning Herald,* May 30, 1840; Abram C. Dayton, *Last Days of Knickerbocker Life in New York* (New York: George W. Harlan, Publisher, 1882), 223–224.

31. Robert C. Allen, *Horrible Prettiness: Burlesque and American Culture* (University of North Carolina Press, 1991), 102; Later in the decade minstrel acts also parodied Elssler. See William John Mahar, *Behind the Burnt Cork Mask* (Urbana: University of Illinois Press, 1999), 370.

32. *Macon* (MS) *Herald*, August 28, 1841.

33. *New York Mirror, A Weekly Journal of Literature and the Fine Arts,* July 25, 1840, 35.

34. Neil Harris, *Humbug: The Art of P.T. Barnum* (Boston: Little, Brown and Company, 1973) 113; Daniel Cavicchi, "Loving Music: Listeners, Entertainers, and the Origins of Music Fandom in Nineteenth Century America," in *Fandom: Identities and Communities in a Mediated World* eds. Jonathan Gray, Cornel Sandvoss, and C. Lee Harrington (New York: New York University Press, 2007), 244.

35. Swift, *Belles and Beaux on Their Toes*, 218–220.

36. "The Elssler Serenade and the Elssler Jackasses," *Native American* (Washington, D.C.), Sept. 19, 1840. This was reprinted from the *New York Sunday Morning News*.

37. H.N. Moore, "The Heart Overtasked," *Philadelphia Visitor and Parlour Companion* 6 (Dec. 1840): 266.

38. *The Pilot and Transcript* (Baltimore), October 22, 1840.

39. Margaret Armstrong, *Fanny Kemble: A Passionate Victorian* (New York: The MacMillan Company, 1938), 255.

40. Guest, *Fanny Elssler,* 136; *New York Morning Herald,* July 17, 1840.

41. *Madisonian* (Washington, D.C.), June 11, 1840.

42. *New York Morning Herald*, July 21, 1840.

43. *New York Morning Herald,* August 1, 1840; Guest, *Fanny Elssler,* 139; *Native American* (Washington, D.C.), August 8, 1840.

44. George Washington Warren, *The History of the Bunker Hill Monument Association* (Boston: James R. Osgood and Company, 1877), 311. Rumors of her shoes being buried with the cornerstone persist but it had been installed years earlier.

45. Edward M. Cifelli, *Longfellow in Love: Passion and Tragedy in the Life of the Poet* (Jefferson, NC: McFarland, 2018), 155–156; Guest, *Fanny Elssler,* 146.

46. "Municipal Court, Boston," *Alexandria* (VA) *Gazette*, June 22, 1841.

47. A.H. Saxon, *P.T. Barnum: The Legend and the Man* (New York: Columbia University Press, 1989), 81–82.

48. Guest, *Fanny Elssler,* 165–166; *Richmond* (VA) *Palladium*, March 27, 1841.

49. *Bloomington* (IA) *Herald,* May 7, 1841.

50. N.M. Ludlow, *Dramatic Life as I Found It* (St. Louis: G.I. Jones and Company, 1880), 537.

51. *Madisonian* (Washington, D.C.), April 6, 1841.

52. Author of "Straws" [Joseph Field], "La Deesse, an Elssler-atic Romance," reprinted in *Fanny Elssler in America: Comprising Seven Facsimilies of Rare Americana*, ed. Allison Delarue (New York: Dance Horizons, 1976), 71–114.

53. *The Yazoo* (MS) *Whig and Political Register*, March 26, 1841.

54. "The Memphis Enquirer is out

upon 'the divine Fanny' like a tornado," *Conservative, and Holly Springs* (MS) *Banner*, April 2, 1841.

55. "Memoir of Fanny Elssler," Delarue, *Fanny Elssler in America,* 13–36; Guest, *Fanny Elssler,* 25, 52–53; *Mississippi Creole* (Canton), July 24, 1841.

56. In 1845 Wikoff published *The Letters and Journal of Fanny Ellsler* but these were in his words not hers. In his memoir of 1880 he wrote that Elssler told him she did not care about making money but only wanted Americans to applaud her. It is doubtful that she said this. "The Letters and Journal of Fanny Ellsler, Written Before and After Her Operatic Campaign in the United States," in Delarue, *Fanny Elssler in America;* Henry Wikoff, *The Reminiscences of an Idler* (New York: Fords, Howard and Hulbert, 1880), 578.

57. [Peter Pindar], "A Short and Correct Sketch of the Life of Mad'lle Fanny Elssler," Delarue, *Fanny Elssler in America,* 121–128.

58. *New York Tribune,* June 9, 1841.

59. *Mississippi Creole* (Canton), July 24, 1841.

60. Nobody [James Cook Richmond], "No Slur, Else-slur: A Dancing Poem or Satyr," Delarue, *Fanny Elssler in America,* 55–66.

61. *Baton-Rouge* (LA) *Gazette,* June 20, 1840; Guest, *Fanny Elssler,* 132; Louis Fitzgerald Tasistro, *Random Shots and Southern Breezes* (New York: Harper and Brothers, 1842), 2:72–76; "Fools not yet Extinct," *Richmond* (VA) *Palladium,* March 27, 1841.

62. *Alexandria* (VA) *Gazette,* Dec. 11, 1841.

63. *Rutland* (VT) *Herald,* January 12, 1841.

64. Guest, *Fanny Elssler,* 217.

65. William B. Wood, *Personal Recollections of the Stage* (Philadelphia: Henry Carey Baird, 1855), 397.

66. "Memoir of Fanny Elssler," 35.

67. Ludlow, *Dramatic Life as I Found It,* 537–538.

68. Guest, *Fanny Elssler,* 185; Philip Hale, "Tom Tiddler's Ground," *Boston Symphony Orchestra Programme* (1910–1911): 263; "Memoir of Fanny Elssler," 35; "Our Last Paragraph on Fanny Elssler," *New York Herald,* July 15, 1842.

69. Allan Nevins, ed., *The Diary of Philip Hone* (New York: Dodd, Mead and Company, 1927), 546; Guest, *Fanny Elssler,* 185.

70. Christoph Irmscher, *The Poetics of Natural History: From Bartram to William James* (New Brunswick: Rutgers University Press, 1999), 123–124; P.T. Barnum, *Struggles and Triumphs: Forty Years' Recollections* (Hartford: J.B. Burr and Company, 1869), 108; Gladys Denny Shultz, *Jenny Lind: The Swedish Nightingale* (Philadelphia: J.B. Lippincott Company, 1962), 151–153; Neil Harris, *Humbug: The Art of P.T. Barnum* (Boston: Little, Brown and Company, 1973), 113, 118.

71. Harris, *Humbug,* 114; Mark C. Samples, "The Humbug and the Nightingale: P.T. Barnum, Jenny Lind, and the Branding of a Star Singer for American Reception," *Musical Quarterly* (2017): 1–35; C.G. Rosenberg, *Jenny Lind: Her Life, Her Struggles, and her Triumphs* (New York: Stringer & Townsend, 1850).

72. S.P. Avery, *The Life and Genius of Jenny Lind* (New York: W.F. Burgess, 1850), 42.

73. W. Porter Ware and Thaddeus C. Lockard, Jr., *P.T. Barnum Presents Jenny Lind: The American Tour of the Swedish Nightingale* (Baton Rouge: Louisiana State University Press, 1980), 169.

74. Harris, *Humbug,* 120–123.

75. Ware and Lockard, *P.T. Barnum Presents Jenny Lind,* 98.

76. Harris, *Humbug,* 317.

77. P.T. Barnum, *Barnum's Own Story: The Autobiography of P.T. Barnum; combined and condensed from various editions published during his lifetime by Waldo R. Browne* (New York: Peter Smith, 1972), 241.

78. Ware and Lockard, *P.T. Barnum Presents Jenny Lind,* 101; W. Porter Ware and Thaddeus C. Lockard, Jr., *The Lost Letters of Jenny Lind* (London: Victor Gollancz, LTD, 1966), 88.

79. Shultz, *Jenny Lind,* 124–129; Cavicchi, "Loving Music," 239.

80. Harris, *Humbug,* 136.

81. Shultz, *Jenny Lind,* 209.

82. Cavicchi, "Loving Music," 239; Virginia Clay-Clopton, *A Belle of the Fifties: Memoirs of Mrs. Clay, of Alabama, Covering Social and Political Life in Washington*

and the South, 1853–66 (New York: Doubleday, Page and Company, 1905), 102, 184.

83. Jenny Lind to [Amalia Wichman], October 27, 1846, Ware and Lockard, *The Lost Letters of Jenny Lind*, 40.

84. Jenny Lind to Amalia [Wichman], January 12, 1850, Ware and Lockard, *The Lost Letters of Jenny Lind*, 73.

85. Jenny Lind to My dearest [Amalia Wichman], April 27, 1846, Ware and Lockard, *The Lost Letters of Jenny Lind*, 28.

86. Barnum, *Barnum's Own Story*, 213.

87. Ednah D. Cheney, ed., *Louisa May Alcott: Her Life, Letters, and Journals* (Boston: Little, Brown, and Company, 1919), 40.

88. Shultz, *Jenny Lind*, 120, 189, 206; "Chit-Chat Upon Philadelphia Fashions for December," *Godey's Ladies Book* 41 (December 1850): 388.

89. Shultz, *Jenny Lind*, 205–206; Harris, *Humbug*, 138–139.

90. Barnum, *Barnum's Own Story*, 212.

91. Shultz, *Jenny Lind*, 210.

92. Ware and Lockard, *P.T. Barnum Presents Jenny Lind*, 105.

93. Shultz, *Jenny Lind*, 201.

94. Harris, *Humbug*, 125; Barnum, *Barnum's Own Story*, 219; Ware and Lockard, *P.T. Barnum Presents Jenny Lind*, 50, 108.

95. [William Allen Butler], "Such People I Never Have Met: A Song to be Sung Under a thin Veil of Fact," *Barnum's Parnassus: Being Confidential Disclosures of the Prize Committee on the Jenny Lind Song* (New York, D. Appleton, 1850), 20–21, 41–43.

96. Harris, *Humbug*, 130.

97. Samples "The Humbug and the Nightingale," 19.

98. Harris, *Humbug*, 317; George C.D. Odell, *Annals of the New York Stage* (New York: AMS Press, 1970), 6:57.

99. Harris, *Humbug*, 133.

100. "Our National Character—Fun and Frolic of 1852," *New York Herald*, May 14, 1852, 4.

101. Richard H. Brodhead, *Cultures of Letters: Scenes of Reading and Writing in Nineteenth-Century America* (Chicago: University of Chicago Press, 1993), 51.

102. "Our Last Paragraph on Fanny Elssler," *New York Herald*, July 15, 1842; *North Carolina Standard*, May 7, 1851; *New York Herald*, August 5, 1851.

Chapter Five

1. "The Spanish Danseuse Lola Montes, and the King of Bavaria," *New York Herald*, April 26, 1847, 2.

2. Bruce Seymour, *Lola Montez: A Life* (New Haven: Yale University Press, 1996), 1–42.

3. Seymour, *Lola Montez*, 102–105, 211–223; "European Correspondent," *Daily Union* (Washington, D.C.), April 2, 1848, 3; "The King of Bavaria, Munich, and Lola Montez," *Fraser's Magazine* 37 (January 1848): 98. This magazine was published in London but the article was widely reprinted in American periodicals.

4. "Lola Montes," *Eclectic Magazine of Foreign Literature, Science and Art* 18 (Nov. 1849): 309.

5. Seymour, *Lola Montez*, 278.

6. "Lola Montes and Kossuth," *Southern Sentinel* (Ripley, MS), Dec. 20, 1851, 2.

7. "Lola Montes," *Southern Standard* (Columbus, MS), Sept. 27, 1851, 3; Seymour, *Lola Montez*, 278.

8. "The Countess of Landsfeld—Lola Montez," *Southern Press* (Washington, D.C.), Oct. 8, 1851, 4.

9. "Movements of Lola Montes," *New York Herald*, Oct. 28, 1851, 2.

10. "Lola Montes," *Southern Standard* (Columbus, MS), Sept. 27, 1851, 3.

11. "Lola Montes," *New York Herald*, Dec. 27, 1851, 2.

12. "Lola Montez," *Alexandria* (VA) *Gazette*, Dec. 20, 1851, 2.

13. "Cant," *Daily Dispatch* (Richmond, VA), Feb. 21, 1852, 2; "More About Lola," *Daily Dispatch* (Richmond, VA), Feb. 24, 1852, 2; "Another Letter from a Lady," *Daily Dispatch* (Richmond, VA), Feb. 26, 1852, 2.

14. "Lola Montes, Unseen," *Southern Literary Messenger* 18 (March 1852): 185. Pleasants praised the poem and identified it as a parody of "Yarrow Unvisited." *Daily Dispatch* (Richmond, VA), March 10, 1852, 2.

15. "Barnum and Lola Montez—The

Great Question of the Day," *New York Herald*, November 6, 1851, 4; "Letter from Lola Montez," *New York Times*, April 1, 1852.

16. "Lola Montes among the Puritans," *New York Herald*, April 6, 1852, 4. This editorial is not signed but it does not seem to be the work of James Gordon Bennett because of the misspelling of her name and because of the style.

17. "Our National Character—Fun and Frolic of 1852," *New York Herald*, May 14, 1852, 4.

18. Seymour, *Lola Montez*, 300; Doris Foley, *The Divine Eccentric; Lola Montez and the Newspapers* (Los Angeles: Westernlore Press, 1969), 15–16.

19. Seymour, *Lola Montez*, 286, 298; Foley, *Divine Eccentric*, 163–167.

20. *Portsmouth* (OH) *Inquirer,* Jan. 2, 1852, 2; *New York Times*, February 10, 1852, 2; Seymour, *Lola Montez*, 293; Foley, *Divine Eccentric*, 37–40, 44.

21. Foley, *Divine Eccentric*, 43–44, 73.

22. Seymour, *Lola Montez*, 74, 307–309, 326; "Lola Montez in New-Orleans," *New York Times*, April 22, 1853, 8; "Lola Montez Fights an Editor," *New York Times,* Dec. 16, 1854.

23. "Outbreak of Virtuous Indignation—Letter from Lola Montez," *New York Times*, July 16, 1852, 3.

24. Seymour, *Lola Montez*, 289, 293–299; Foley, *Divine Eccentric*, 30, 164.

25. Foley, *Divine Eccentric*, 189.

26. Montez denied having an affair with Captain John Lennox, who admitted it in court, and with King Ludwig. "Lola Montez on the Witness Stand," *New York Times,* Feb. 10, 1858, 3.

27. "Jobson v. Allen," *New York Times*, Feb. 19, 1858, 8.

28. Seymour, *Lola Montez*, 374, 388; "Lecture by Lola Montez on 'Gallantry,'" *New York Times*, Feb. 11, 1858; "Lola Montez on 'Strong-Minded Women,'" *New York Times*, Feb. 16, 1858; Lola Montez, *Lectures of Lola Montez, including her Autobiography* (New York: Rudd & Carleton, 1859).

29. Seymour, *Lola Montez*, 278, 287; Fanny Fern, *Fern Leaves from Fanny's Portfolio, second series* (Auburn and Buffalo: Miller, Orton and Mulligan, 1854), 42–47; Cyrus R.K. Patell and Bryan Waterman, eds., *The Cambridge Companion to the Literature of New York* (New York: Cambridge University Press, 2010), 97.

30. Fanny Fern, *Fern Leaves from Fanny's Portfolio* (Auburn and Buffalo: Miller, Orton, and Mulligan, 1854), 39.

31. Joyce W. Warren, *Fanny Fern: an Independent Woman* (New Brunswick: Rutgers University Press, 1992), 179.

32. Warren, *Fanny Fern*, 86.

33. Laura Laffrado, "I Thought from the Way you *Writ*, that you were a Great Six Footer of a Woman: Gender and Public Voice in Fanny Fern's Newspaper Essays," in *Her Own Voice: Nineteenth-Century American Women Essayists*, ed. Sherry Lee Linkon (New York: Garland Publishing, 1997), 81.

34. "Hungry Husbands," in *Ruth Hall and Other* Writings, ed. Joyce W. Warren (New Brunswick: Rutgers University Press, 1986), 253. For an early misquoting, see "Hints to Husbands and Brothers," *Fremont* (OH) *Journal*, May 1, 1857, 4.

35. Warren, *Fanny Fern*, 104.

36. *Planters' Banner* (Franklin, LA), June 8, 1853.

37. "Woman's Rights," *Daily Dispatch* (Richmond, VA), June 8, 1853.

38. *Cecil Whig* (Elkton, MD), July 3, 1852, 3.

39. Warren, *Fanny Fern*, 100; Bonnie Carr O'Neill, *Literary Celebrity and Public Life in the Nineteenth-Century United States* (Athens: University of Georgia Press, 2017), 174.

40. Fanny Fern, *Ruth Hall: A Domestic Tale of the Present Time* (New York: Mason Brothers, 1855), 254–255, 345. Most scholars agree that the letters Fern discussed and published in her novel were probably real.

41. O'Neill, *Literary Celebrity and Public Life*, 166.

42. O'Neill, *Literary Celebrity and Public Life*, 177.

43. "The Model Minister," *Weekly National Intelligencer* (Washington, D.C.), June 9, 1852.

44. O'Neill, *Literary Celebrity and Public Life*, 177. Italics in the original.

45. O'Neill, *Literary Celebrity and Public Life*, 158, 173–175.

46. "To Fanny Fern," *Daily Evening Star*, May 2, 1853.

47. O'Neill, *Literary Celebrity and Public Life*, 172.

48. "Fun, Fact and Fancy. Who is Fanny Fern?," *Southern Standard* (Columbus, MS), Feb. 12, 1853.

49. O'Neill, *Literary Celebrity and Public Life*, 160, 176.

50. *Plymouth* (IN) *Banner*, May 5, 1853.

51. *Daily Union* (Washington, D.C.), Aug. 30, 1853.

52. *Grand River Times* (Grand Haven, MI), June 15, 1853.

53. "Woman's Rights," *Daily Dispatch* (Richmond, VA), June 8, 1853.

54. "Female Physicians," *Monongalia Mirror* (Morgantown, VA), Feb. 19, 1853.

55. "Female Physicians," *Fremont* (OH) *Journal*, March 19, 1853, 2.

56. *Daily Evening Star* (Washington, D.C.), May 31, 1853.

57. For example see, the *Camden* (SC) *Journal*, Oct. 8, 1852 and the *Miners' Express* (Dubuque, IA), Feb. 2, 1853.

58. Original must be from early Feb. or late Jan. *Southerner* (Tarboro, NC), Feb. 5, 1853.

59. Warren, *Fanny Fern*, 123.

60. Patell and Waterman, *Cambridge Companion*, 97; Warren, *Fanny Fern*, 117.

61. Warren, *Ruth Hall and other Writings*, 251–252.

62. Mary F. W. Gibson and Daniel Cohen, eds., *'Hero Strong' and Other Stories: Tales of Girlhood Ambition, Female Masculinity, and Women's Worldly Achievement in Antebellum America* (Knoxville: University of Tennessee Press, 2014), vii–viii, 1, 10–19, 108.

63. Ruth Rustic [Cornelia Orme], *Forget-me-nots from Dew Drop Dale* (Washington: Taylor and Maury, 1855), 174–176.

64. "Lady Like," *Nashville* (TN) *Union*, April 27, 1853.

65. "The Pilgrim Mothers!," *Weekly Lancaster* (OH) *Gazette*, March 3, 1853.

66. Ada Sterling, ed., *A Belle of the Fifties: Memoirs of Mrs. Clay, of Alabama, Covering Social and Political Life in Washington and the South, 1853–66* (New York: Doubleday, Page and Company, 1905), 58; Fern, *Fern Leaves from Fanny's Portfolio*, 387.

67. "Hungry Husbands," *Ruth Hall and Other Writings*, 253; "Hints to Husbands and Brothers," *Fremont* (OH) *Journal*, May 1, 1857, 4.

68. "Ladies Dresses," *Preble County Democrat* (Eaton, OH), Jan. 29, 1857, 3.

69. *Indiana American* (Brookville), Feb. 6, 1857.

70. Fanny Fern, "Lady Doctors" in *Fresh Leaves* (New York: Mason Brothers, 1857), 111–112.

71. Sharon Harris, *Dr. Mary Walker: An American Radical, 1832–1919* (New Brunswick: Rutgers University Press, 2009), 20.

72. *Southern Enterprise* (Greenville, SC), March 5, 1857, 2.

73. Fanny Fern, "Fair Play; or, Both Sides of the Story" in *Fresh Leaves*, 302–304.

74. Fanny Fern, "To a Correspondents," *New York Ledger*, March 7, 1857, 4.

75. Fanny Fern, "Answers to Fern Correspondents," *New York Ledger*, Nov. 15, 1856, 4.

76. Fanny Fern, "Answers to Fern Correspondents," *New York Ledger* Nov. 15, 1856, 4; Fern, *Ruth Hall*, 294–297, 312–316, 356–357.

77. Nancy A. Walker, *Fanny Fern* (New York: Maxwell Macmillan International, 1993), 100; Fern, *Fresh Leaves*, 56–58; O'Neill, *Literary Celebrity and Public Life*, 181; Warren, *Fanny Fern*, 179.

78. Warren, *Ruth Hall and other Writings*, 368–369; Laffrado, "I thought from the Way you *Writ*," 81; Nicole Tonkovich, *Domesticity with a Difference* (Jackson: University Press of Mississippi, 1997), 47–48.

79. Seymour, *Lola Montez*, 390.

80. Renee M. Sentilles, *Performing Menken: Adah Isaacs Menken and the Birth of American Celebrity* (Cambridge: Cambridge University Press, 2003), 7–10.

81. Seymour, *Lola Montez*, 394–395.

82. Sentilles, *Performing Menken*, 138–139; Adah Isaacs Menken, *Infelicia* (New York: H.L. Williams, 1868), 46–49. In this collection of poems published just after she died, the poem is titled "Myself" but it was titled "Now and Then" when it appeared in the New York *Sunday Mercury* February 10, 1861.

83. Sentilles, *Performing Menken*, 91–92.

84. Montez, *Lectures of Lola Montez*, 12–13.

85. Sentilles, *Performing Menken*, 188; Menken, *Infelicia*, 140–141. In this collection of poems published just after she died, the poem is titled "Infelix" but it was titled "El Suspiro" when it appeared in the *Golden Era* January 3, 1864.

86. Sentilles, *Performing Menken*, 19.

87. Sentilles, *Performing Menken*, 216–219, 229.

88. Sentilles, *Performing Menken*, 2, 254, 259–265.

89. Sentilles, *Performing Menken*, 266.

Chapter Six

1. "Hardly Consistent," *State Rights Democrat* (Albany, OR), June 28, 1872, 2.

2. Joan Hedrick, *Harriet Beecher Stowe: A Life* (New York: Oxford University Press, 1994), 206.

3. Charles Edward Stowe, *Life of Harriet Beecher Stowe* (Boston: Houghton Mifflin, 1889), 145–146.

4. Harriet Beecher Stowe, "The Freeman's Dream: A Parable," *National Era* (Washington, D.C.), Aug. 1, 1850, 121.

5. Stowe, *Life of Harriet Beecher Stowe*, 148–149, 156.

6. The book actually has 45 chapters. Moira Davison Reynolds, *Uncle Tom's Cabin and Mid-Nineteenth Century United States: Pen and Conscience* (Jefferson, NC: McFarland, 2012), 8–9.

7. Reynolds, *Uncle Tom's Cabin*, 11–12; Stowe, *Life of Harriet Beecher Stowe*, 160.

8. Hedrick, *Harriet Beecher Stowe*, 216–217.

9. Elizabeth Ammons, ed., *Harriet Beecher Stowe's Uncle Tom's Cabin: A Casebook* (New York: Oxford University Press, 2007), 9.

10. Stephen A. Hirsch, "Uncle Tom-itudes: The Popular Reaction to 'Uncle Tom's Cabin,'" *Studies in the American Renaissance* (1978): 316–320.

11. Stowe, *Life of Harriet Beecher Stowe*, 164–165.

12. Reynolds, *Uncle Tom's Cabin*, 10, 151.

13. Forrest Wilson, *Crusader in Crinoline: The Life of Harriet Beecher Stowe* (Philadelphia: JB Lippincott Company, 1941), 308; David S. Reynolds, *Mightier*

than the Sword (New York: WW Norton, 2011), 125–126.

14. Joseph Roppolo, "Harriet Beecher Stowe and New Orleans: A Study in Hate," *New England Quarterly* 30 (Sept. 1957): 354.

15. "Uncle Tom's Cabin," *Lancaster* (SC) *Ledger*, Oct. 20, 1852, 2.

16. Thomas Chase Hagood, "'Oh, what a slanderous book': Reading *Uncle Tom's Cabin* in the Antebellum South" *Southern Quarterly* 49 (Summer 2012): 71–93; "Uncle Tom's Cabin in Alabama," Uncle Tom's Cabin and American Culture, accessed March 10, 2020, http://utc.iath.virginia.edu/notices/noar08jt.html.

17. Clement Eaton, *The Freedom of Thought Struggle in the Old South* (Durham: Duke University Press, 1940), 123–131; "Slave Laws of Maryland," *Anti-Slavery Bugle* (New Lisbon, OH), Dec. 11, 1858.

18. Carolyn Karcher, *The First Woman in the Republic: A Cultural Biography of Lydia Maria Child* (Durham: Duke University Press, 1994), 208.

19. Stowe, *Life of Harriet Beecher Stowe*, 171–172.

20. *Daily Dispatch* (Richmond, VA), August 28, 1852, 4.

21. J.C. Furnas, *Goodbye to Uncle Tom* (New York: W. Sloane Associates, 1956), 61; Hagood, "'Oh, what a slanderous book,'" 84.

22. D.D. Hall, "A Yankee Tutor in the Old South," *New England Quarterly* 33 (March 1960): 89–90.

23. *Daily Dispatch* (Richmond, VA), August 25, 1852, 2.

24. *Anti-Slavery Bugle* (New Lisbon, OH), August 14, 1852.

25. *Camden* (SC) *Journal*, Oct. 26, 1852.

26. Charles Grandison Parsons, *Inside View of Slavery: or, A Tour among the Planters* (Boston: Jewett, 1855), 292.

27. Wilson, *Crusader in Crinoline*, 297.

28. *Daily Comet* (Baton Rouge, LA), Oct. 24, 1852, 2; T.J. Carty, *A Dictionary of Literary Pseudonyms in the English Language* (New York: Routledge, 2014).

29. William Still, *Still's Underground Railroad Records* (Philadelphia: Still, 1886), 246–250; "Barbaric Despotism," *Anti-Slavery Bugle* (New Lisbon, OH), Nov. 6, 1858, 2; Richard Albert Blondo,

"Samuel Green: A Black Life in Antebellum Maryland," (University of Maryland, MA thesis, 1988), 32; "Out of Jail: The Black Man who was Imprisoned for Reading Uncle Tom's Cabin," *Uncle Tom's Cabin and American Culture*, accessed March 10, 2020, http://utc.iath.virginia.edu/notices/noar02bmt.html.

30. Ammons, *Uncle Tom's Cabin*, 445.

31. Wilson, *Crusader in Crinoline*, 294; Stowe, *Life of Harriet Beecher Stowe*, 182–183.

32. Joyce W. Warren, *Fanny Fern: an Independent Woman* (Rutgers University Press, 1992), 31; Hedrick, *Harriet Beecher Stowe*, 56.

33. Joyce W. Warren, ed., *Ruth Hall and other Writings* (New Brunswick: Rutgers University Press, 1986), 255–257.

34. Hedrick, *Harriet Beecher Stowe*, 357.

35. "The True Story of Lady Byron's Life," *Atlantic Monthly* 24 (Sept. 1869): 295–313. Stowe expanded the article into a book: *Lady Byron Vindicated: A History of the Byron Controversy, from Its Beginnings in 1816 to the Present Time* (Boston: Fields, Osgood, and Company, 1870).

36. Reynolds, *Uncle Tom's Cabin*, 148; Wilson, *Crusader in Crinoline*, 427–429, 534–536.

37. Hedrick, *Harriet Beecher Stowe*, 349–351.

38. "The Last of the American Female Ghoul," *Old Guard* 7 (Dec. 1869): 889–890.

39. Wilson, *Crusader in Crinoline*, 539.

40. Wilson, *Crusader in Crinoline*, 583.

41. Amanda Frisken, *Victoria Woodhull's Sexual Revolution: Political Theater and the Popular Press in Nineteenth Century America* (Philadelphia: University of Pennsylvania Press, 2004), 46.

42. Victoria Woodhull to Mrs. Bladen, June 22, 1871, in *Selected Writings of Victoria Woodhull: Suffrage, Free Love, and Eugenics*, ed. Cari M. Carpenter (Lincoln: University of Nebraska Press, 2010), 38.

43. Harriet Beecher Stowe, *My Wife and I: or, Harry Henderson's History* (New York: J.B. Ford and Company, 1871), 240–246, 257–261.

44. Frisken, *Victoria Woodhull's Sexual Revolution*, 6–8.

45. Frisken, *Victoria Woodhull's Sexual Revolution*, 15–16.

46. Frisken, *Victoria Woodhull's Sexual Revolution*, 8, 24; Mrs. Miller who was with them voted. "Women at the Polls," *Harper's Weekly*, Nov. 25, 1871, 1109.

47. Frisken, *Victoria Woodhull's Sexual Revolution*, 13, 28.

48. Mary Gabriel, *Notorious Victoria: the Life of Victoria Woodhull, Uncensored* (Chapel Hill: Algonquin Books of Chapel Hill, 1998), 156; Frisken, *Victoria Woodhull's Sexual Revolution*, 37–38, 46, 48.

49. Frisken, *Victoria Woodhull's Sexual Revolution*, 55.

50. Barbara Goldsmith, *Other Powers: The Age of Suffrage, Spiritualism, and the Scandalous Victoria Woodhull* (New York: Alfred A. Knopf, 1998), 316–320.

51. Frisken, *Victoria Woodhull's Sexual Revolution*, 90; Theodore Tilton, *Victoria C. Woodhull: A Biographical Sketch* (New York: The Golden Age, 1871), 8–9, 27.

52. Victoria Woodhull, "Tried as by Fire; or, the True and the False, Socially" in Carpenter, ed., *Selected Writings of Victoria Woodhull*, 217.

53. Goldsmith, *Other Powers*, 337, 343.

54. Wilson, *Crusader in Crinoline*, 583.

55. Frisken, *Victoria Woodhull's Sexual Revolution*, 94.

56. Amy Werbel, *Lust on Trial: Censorship and the Rise of American Obscenity in the Age of Anthony Comstock* (New York: Columbia University Press, 2018), 63.

57. Helen Lefkowitz Horowitz, "Victoria Woodhull, Anthony Comstock, and the Conflict over Sex in the United States in the 1870s," *Journal of American History* 87 (September 2000): 431.

58. Frisken, *Victoria Woodhull's Sexual Revolution*, 102.

59. Frisken, *Victoria Woodhull's Sexual Revolution*, 99.

60. Frisken, *Victoria Woodhull's Sexual Revolution*, 105–106; Woodhull's speech was published as "Mrs. Woodhull's Address" in the January 25, 1873 *Woodhull and Claflin Weekly* and later as "The Naked Truth; or, the Situation Reviewed!" in ed. Carpenter, *Selected Writings of Victoria Woodhull*, 125–126.

61. Frisken, *Victoria Woodhull's Sexual Revolution*, 107–108.

62. Frisken, *Victoria Woodhull's Sexual Revolution*, 111, 116–117.

63. Leon Oliver, *The Great Sensation: A Full, Complete and Reliable History of the Beecher-Tilton-Woodhull Scandal [also A Clear and Concise Statement of the Views of 'The Woodhull' upon Social Reform, Free-Love, etc., etc.]* (Chicago: The Beverly Company, 1873), 33.

64. Frisken, *Victoria Woodhull's Sexual Revolution*, 116–117, 125–126.

65. Reynolds, *Uncle Tom's Cabin*, 148; Frisken, *Victoria Woodhull's Sexual Revolution*, 9.

Chapter Seven

1. Nell Irvin Painter, *Sojourner Truth: A Life, A Symbol* (New York: WW Norton, 1996), 74–75.

2. Painter, *Sojourner Truth*, 114.

3. Suzanne Pullon Fitch and Roseann M. Mandziuk, *Sojourner Truth As Orator: Wit, Story, and Song* (Westport, CT: Greenwood Press, 1997), 139.

4. "Affairs in New York; Political and Local," *Southern Press* (Washington, D.C.), Oct. 29, 1850, 3.

5. Painter, *Sojourner Truth*, 98.

6. *Oxford Democrat* (Paris, ME), July 18, 1851, 2.

7. Fitch and Mandziuk, *Sojourner Truth as Orator*, 107–108.

8. Fitch and Mandziuk, *Sojourner Truth as Orator*, 31–46, 115.

9. Painter, *Sojourner Truth*, 110; Fitch and Mandziuk, *Sojourner Truth as Orator*, 109.

10. Fitch and Mandziuk, *Sojourner Truth as Orator*, 94; M.E.B., "Sojourner Truth: Further Reminiscences of the Career of the African Sibyl," *Chicago Daily Tribune*, Dec. 5, 1880, 18.

11. Harriet Beecher Stowe, "Sojourner Truth, the Libyan Sibyl," *Atlantic Monthly* 11 (April 1863): 474.

12. Painter, *Sojourner Truth*, 130; Sojourner Truth, *Narrative of Sojourner Truth, A Northern Slave, Emancipated from Bodily Servitude by the State of New York, in 1828* (New York: n.p., 1853), iii–iv.

13. Jessica Janecki and Lauren Reno, "Sojourner Truth's Narrative" The Devil's Tale, last modified Feb. 14, 2018, https://blogs.library.duke.edu/rubenstein/2018/02/14/sojourner-

truths-narrative/. The book is located in the David M. Rubenstein Rare Book and Manuscript Library, Duke University.

14. Darcy Grimaldo Grigsby, *Enduring Truths: Sojourner's Shadows and Substance* (Chicago: University of Chicago Press, 2015), 42.

15. Stowe, "Sojourner Truth," 480.

16. Joseph P. Thompson, *The Theology of Christ, From His Own Words* (New York: Charles Scribner and Co., 1870): 118.

17. Kay Siebler, "Far from the Truth: Teaching the Politics of Sojourner Truth's 'Ain't I a Woman?'" *Pedagogy Critical Approaches to Teaching Literature Language Composition and Culture* 10 (Sept. 2010): 528–529.

18. Grigsby, *Enduring Truths*, 42; Stowe, "Sojourner Truth," 473, 476–477; Siebler, "Far from the Truth," 529.

19. "Woman's Work," *Chicago Daily Tribune*, Oct. 15, 1874, 7.

20. "Amusements," *Stark County Democrat*, Feb. 12, 1880, 5; Lizzie W. Champney, *Entertainments. Comprising Directions for Holiday Merry-Makings, New Programmes for Amateur Performances, and Many Novel Sunday-School Exercises* (Boston: D. Lothrop and Company, 1879), 343.

21. Fitch and Mandziuk, *Sojourner Truth as Orator*, 175.

22. *Our Young Folks* 7 (June 1871): 384.

23. Fitch and Mandziuk, *Sojourner Truth as Orator*, 9.

24. "Knox County Shearing," *Prairie Farmer* (Chicago), June 23, 1866, 431.

25. Letter CX in *Soldiers' Letters from Camp, Battle-Field and Prison*, ed. Lydia Minturn Post (New York: Bunce and Huntington, Publishers, 1865), 232.

26. Robert B. Taber, "Gas Stoves for Cooking and Heating," read at the "Semi-Annual Meeting of the New England Association of Gas Engineers" *American Gas Light Journal*, Sept. 2, 1882, 107.

27. "'Sojourner Truth' Sharp as Ever," *Portland* (ME) *Daily Press*, Feb. 17, 1864, 3.

28. "Woman's Right to a Womanly Dress," *Health Reformer* 5 (January 1871): 124.

29. "Sojourner Truth," *Anti-slavery Bugle* (New Lisbon, OH), Jan. 21, 1860, 2.

30. "Sojourner Truth," *Friends' Intelligencer* (Philadelphia), December 25, 1880, 709–710.

31. "Sojourner Truth," *Household Reading: Selections from the Congregationalist, 1849–1867* (Boston: W. L. Greene and Co., 1868), 150.

32. Fitch and Manziuk, *Sojourner Truth as Orator,* 181–182.

33. Nell Irvin Painter, ed., *Narrative of Sojourner Truth* (New York: Penguin Books, 1998), 208–209.

34. Fitch and Manziuk, *Sojourner Truth as Orator,* 221–222.

35. "Sojourner Truth's Lecture, Last Night," *Wilmington* (DE) *Daily Commercial,* July 1, 1874, 4.

36. Grigsby, *Enduring Truths,* 172.

37. "Sojourner Truth," *Watertown* (WI) *Republican,* May 20, 1874, 6.

38. Joanna Cohan Scherer, "The Public Faces of Sarah Winnemucca," *Cultural Anthropology* 3 (May 1988): 196.

39. Sally Zanjani, *Sarah Winnemucca* (Lincoln: University of Nebraska Press, 2001), 6, 38, 71.

40. Zanjani, *Sarah Winnemucca,* 71–75, 199, 251.

41. Zanjani, *Sarah Winnemucca,* 75–77; Cari M. Carpenter and Carolyn Sorisio, eds., *The Newspaper Warrior: Sarah Winnemucca Hopkin's Campaign for American Indian Rights, 1864–1891* (Lincoln: University of Nebraska Press, 2015), 35–38.

42. Carpenter and Sorisio, *Newspaper Warrior,* 34–36.

43. Cari Carpenter, "Choking off that Angel Mother: Sarah Winnemucca Hopkins's Strategic Humor," *Studies in American Indian Literature* (Fall 2014): 5; "Winnemucca and His Daughters," *Gold Hill* (Nevada, Terr.) *Daily News,* Oct. 24, 1864, 2.

44. Zanjani, *Sarah Winnemucca,* 85, 101; Carpenter and Sorisio, *Newspaper Warrior,* 38–42.

45. Zanjani, *Sarah Winnemucca,* 109, 111, 124; Carpenter and Sorisio, *Newspaper Warrior,* 47, 55.

46. Carpenter and Sorisio, *Newspaper Warrior,* 42–44.

47. Zanjani, *Sarah Winnemucca,* 111–113.

48. Zanjani, *Sarah Winnemucca,* 120.

49. Carpenter and Sorisio, *Newspaper Warrior,* 72, 77.

50. Sarah Winnemucca Hopkins, *Life Among the Piutes: Their Wrongs and Claims* (Boston: Cupples, Upham and Co., 1883), 164.

51. Carpenter and Sorisio, *Newspaper Warrior,* 77–78.

52. Carpenter and Sorisio, *Newspaper Warrior,* 74; Zanjani, *Sarah Winnemucca,* 290.

53. Zanjani, *Sarah Winnemucca,* 6, 199–200; J.J.F. Haine, "A Belgian in the Gold Rush: California Indians," *California Historical Society Quarterly* 38 (1959): 153; Carpenter and Sorisio, *Newspaper Warrior,* 99.

54. Carpenter and Sorisio, *Newspaper Warrior,* 101, 104; Carpenter, "Choking off that Angel Mother," 4, 14–15.

55. "Table Gossip," *Boston Daily Globe,* Feb. 14, 1880, 2.

56. "Washington Letter," *Somerset* (PA) *Herald,* Feb. 18, 1880, 5.

57. Carpenter and Sorisio, *Newspaper Warrior,* 121–122.

58. Zanjani, *Sarah Winnemucca,* 207.

59. Zanjani, *Sarah Winnemucca,* 203–206, 209, 216–217.

60. *Chicago Tribune,* March 15, 1871, 2.

61. Painter, *Sojourner Truth,* 181.

62. Grigsby, *Enduring Truths,* 63, 165, 177, 197–198.

63. Carleton Mabee, *Sojourner Truth: Slave, Prophet, Legend* (New York: New York University Press, 1993), 129–138; "Sojourner Truth on 'Yelping,'" *Democrat* (Weston, WV), May 8, 1871, 1.

64. C.P.O., "Correspondence—Letter from Washington," *Harper's Weekly,* Feb. 4, 1865, 76–78.

65. "Letter from Sojourner Truth," *Friends' Intelligencer* (Philadelphia), 28 (April 8, 1871), 93; Painter, *Sojourner Truth,* 231–232, 239–241, 245.

66. The book is in the Western Michigan University Archives and Regional Historical Collections, Kalamazoo. Fitch and Mandziuk, *Sojourner Truth as Orator,* 26.

67. *Chicago Daily Tribune,* Jan. 2, 1880, 8.

68. "How Sojourner Truth Earned Five Dollars in Washington," *Portland* (ME) *Daily Press,* Oct. 9, 1872.

69. *National Republican* (Washington, D.C.), Sept. 7, 1875.

70. Fitch and Mandziuk, *Sojourner Truth as Orator*, 201.

71. G.W. Amadon, "A Relic of New York Slavery," *Good Health* 18 (Feb. 1883): 52.

72. Painter, *Narrative of Sojourner Truth*, 233.

73. Scherer, "Public Faces of Sarah Winnemucca," 192; Zanjani, *Sarah Winnemucca*, 244, 251.

74. Carpenter and Sorisio, *Newspaper Warrior*, 151, 170–171, 176, 187, 188.

75. Sarah Winnemucca, "The Pah-utes," *Californian* 6 (September 1882): 256.

76. Carpenter, "Choking off that Angel Mother," 813.

77. Carpenter and Sorisio, *Newspaper Warrior*, 188.

78. Carpenter, "Choking off that Angel Mother," 8.

79. Zanjani, *Sarah Winnemucca*, 252; Carpenter and Sorisio, *Newspaper Warrior*, 176, 215.

80. Zanjani, *Sarah Winnemucca*, 260–262.

Chapter Eight

1. Matthew Gallman, *America's Joan of Arc: The Life of Anna Elizabeth Dickinson* (Oxford: Oxford University Press, 2006), 2, 52; Peter Cherches, *Star Course: Nineteenth-Century Lecture Tours and the Consolidation of Modern Celebrity* (Rotterdam: Sense Publishers, 2017), 15; Nell Painter, ed., *Narrative of Sojourner Truth* (New York: Penguin Books, 1998), 174.

2. Janet Robertson, *The Magnificent Mountain Women: Adventures in the Colorado Rockies* (Lincoln: University of Nebraska Press, 2003), 9–11.

3. Gregory Kent Stanley, *The Rise and Fall of the Sportswoman: Women's Health, Fitness, and Athletics, 1860–1940* (New York: Peter Lang Publishing, 1996), 25, 26, 41; Catharine Beecher, *Physiology and Calisthenics: For Schools and Families* (New York: Harper, 1858), 11; Catharine Beecher, *Woman Suffrage and Woman's Profession* (Hartford, CT: Brown and Gross, 1871), 121–122, 129.

4. Stanley, *The Rise and Fall of the Sportswoman*, 42, 48, 75; Dio Lewis, *Our Girls* (New York: Harper and Brothers, 1871), 92; Dio Lewis, *Five Minute Chats with Young Women, and Certain Other Parties* (New York: Harper and Brothers, 1874), 182.

5. Richard Etulain, *The Life and Legends of Calamity Jane* (Norman: University of Oklahoma Press, 2014).

6. "A Woman Ready to Risk her Life," *Evening Star*, April 25, 1876; "Spelterini at Niagara," *New York Herald*, June 22, 1876; Henry Collins Brown, ed., *Valentine's Manual of the City of New York, 1917–1918* (New York: The Old Colony Press, 1917), 155–156; "Amusements," *New York Herald*, June 9, 1876, 2.

7. Sherman Zavitz, "Life of Lady Wire Walker Shrouded in Mystery," *Niagara Falls* (NY) *Review*, Feb. 22, 2003, 7; Albert Parkes, "The Only Woman to Cross Niagara on a Rope," *Theatre Magazine* 7 (June 1907): 168.

8. Zavitz, "Life of Lady Wire Walker Shrouded in Mystery," 7; *New North-West* (Deer Lodge, MT), August 11, 1876, 2; *National Republican* (Washington, D.C.), July 10, 1876, 2; *Eaton* (OH) *Democrat*, Aug. 3, 1876.

9. "Over Niagara," *New York Herald*, July 13, 1876, 5.

10. "Spelterini Crossing Niagara," *New York Herald*, July 28, 1876, 6.

11. "Crossing Niagara on a Tight Rope," *Elk County Advocate* (Ridgway, PA), Aug. 10, 1876, 4.

12. "Speltarini," *Public Ledger* (Memphis, TN), Aug. 7, 1876; Orrin E. Dunlap, "Women who Dared Death in the Wild Waters of Niagara," *Scrap Book* 5 (May 1908): 846.

13. W.S. Caine, M.P., *A Trip Round the World in 1887–8* (London: George Routledge and Sons, 1888), 31–32; "Dragged into the Air by the Teeth," *Lexington* (MO) *Weekly Intelligencer*, Aug. 21, 1886.

14. Lady Aeronaut, Carlotta, *Aerial Adventures of Carlotta, or Sky-Larking in Cloudland, Being Hap-Hazard Accounts of the Perils and Pleasures of Aerial Navigation* (Mohawk, NY: C.E. Myers, 1883), 5–8.

15. Carlotta, *Aerial Adventures*, 24–26.

16. Carlotta, *Aerial Adventures*, 56, 58, 66, 85; "Gymnastics a Mile Above Earth,"

Fairfield News and Herald (Winnsboro, SC), July 25, 1888, 4; Joseph Nathan Kane, *Famous First Facts, Fifth Edition* (New York: H.W. Wilson Company, 1997), 47.

17. *American Engineer and Railroad Journal* 68 (December 1894): xxx; Carlotta, *Aerial Adventures*, 74.

18. "Falling Two Miles," *Wheeling* (WV) *Register,* July 20, 1883, 3.

19. "Careers of Danger and Daring," *St. Nicholas* 28 (March 1901):397.

20. Carlotta, *Aerial Adventures*, 124; "Up in the Air," *Wichita* (KS) *Eagle,* Aug. 18, 1889, 9.

21. Carlotta, *Aerial Adventures*, 33.

22. Carlotta, *Aerial Adventures*, 72.

23. "Carlotta, *Aerial Adventures*, 102; Falling Two Miles," *Wheeling* (WV) *Register,* July 20, 1883; "Miss Carlotta and Her Balloon," *Sun* (New York), July 6, 1888.

24. Christine Hamelin, "She Soared to Fame in a Balloon: Mary Myers 1849–1930s," *Kingston Whig—Standard,* Oct 11, 1997, 14.

25. Matthew Algeo, *Pedestrianism: When Watching People Walk was America's Favorite Spectator Sport* (Chicago: Chicago Review Press, 2014), 22.

26. Algeo, *Pedestrianism*, 105–107.

27. Algeo, *Pedestrianism*, 107–108; "On the Track," *New York Herald,* December 17, 1878, 5.

28. "Madame Anderson's Plucky Walk," *Frank Leslie's Illustrated Newspaper,* February 1, 1879, 389, 393.

29. "On the Track," *New York Herald,* December 17, 1878, 5.

30. "Mme. Anderson's Walk," *New York Herald,* Dec. 23, 1878, 8.

31. Algeo, *Pedestrianism*, 106, 109, 113; "The Female Walker," *Wheeling* (WV) *Daily Intelligencer,* Dec. 30, 1878.

32. Algeo, *Pedestrianism*, 108, 112.

33. Algeo, *Pedestrianism*, 113.

34. See for instance "Madame Anderson Still on the Tramp," *New Orleans Democrat,* Dec. 27, 1878.

35. Lewis, *Five Minute Chats,* 197, 353–356.

36. Algeo, *Pedestrianism*, 108.

37. Algeo, *Pedestrianism*, 112.

38. "Madame Anderson the Walkist," *Wheeling* (WV) *Daily Intelligencer,* Jan. 6, 1879.

39. "Pluck," *Chicago Daily Tribune,* Jan. 14, 1879, 5.

40. Algeo, *Pedestrianism*, 115; "Mme. La Chapelle's Great Walk," *New York Herald,* Feb. 26, 1879, 5.

41. Algeo, *Pedestrianism*, 116.

42. "Ada Anderson Achievements," *Baltimore American and Commercial Advertiser,* May 16, 1880.

43. "Miss Howard Wins the Belt," *New York Tribune,* Dec. 21, 1879.

44. *Cincinnati Daily Star,* March 20, 1880, 6.

45. "Ada Anderson Achievements"; Algeo, *Pedestrianism,* 116–118.

46. Glenda Riley, *The Life and Legacy of Annie Oakley* (Norman: University of Oklahoma Press, 1994), 3–26.

47. Shirl Kasper, *Annie Oakley* (Norman: University of Oklahoma Press, 1992), 33.

48. Riley, *Life and Legacy,* 34–35; Kasper, *Annie Oakley,* 64.

49. Riley, *Life and Legacy,* 51–54, 58, 113; Glenda Riley, "Annie Oakley: Creating the Cowgirl," *Montana, Magazine of the West* 45 (Summer 1995): 40.

50. "Earned it with Her Rifle," *Topeka* (KS) *State Journal,* July 3, 1894, 6.

51. Advertisement for Allen's Foot-Ease, *Evening Journal* (Wilmington, DE), Sept. 22, 1896, 4.

52. Kasper, *Annie Oakley,* 76.

53. Riley, *Life and Legacy,* 86; "Annie Oakley's Speech," *Evening World* (NY), Aug. 11, 1894, 2.

54. Annie Oakley, "Women with Guns" *Times* (Owosso, MI) Aug. 31, 1894, 7.

55. Riley, *Life and Legacy,* 199.

56. Riley, "Annie Oakley," 37.

57. Riley, *Life and Legacy,* 44, 85, 131, 136.

58. Kasper, *Annie Oakley,* 101; Will Wildwood, *Sportsman's Directory and Yearbook* (Milwaukee, WI: Pond and Goldey, 1892), 78.

59. "Women in Athletics," *Roanoke* (VA) *Times,* Sept. 2, 1893, 6.

60. "Champion Woman Shot," *Eddy Current* (Carlsbad, NM), May 14, 1898, 6.

61. Riley, "Annie Oakley," 37; Riley, *Life and Legacy,* 66.

62. Riley, "Annie Oakley," 43.

63. Kasper, *Annie Oakley,* 173–175.

64. Riley, *Life and Legacy,* 76–82; Kasper, *Annie Oakley,* 179.

65. Kasper, *Annie Oakley,* 179–180.

66. Riley, *Life and Legacy*, 61; Kasper, *Annie Oakley*, 205–206.

67. Annie Oakley, "A Brief Sketch of Her Career and Notes on Shooting," in *Heart Shots*, ed. Mary Zeiss Stange (London: Stackpole Books, 2018), 273. Riley dates this pamphlet to around 1899.

68. Kasper, *Annie Oakley*, 205–206; Riley, *Life and Legacy*, 188.

69. Riley, *Life and Legacy*, 138–139; Roger Gilles, *Women on the Move: The Forgotten Era of Women's Bicycle Racing* (Lincoln: University of Nebraska Press, 2018), xii.

70. Gilles, *Women on the Move*, 6, 13, 58.

71. Gilles, *Women on the Move*, 11.

72. Gilles, *Women on the Move*, xii–xiii, 3–5.

73. Gilles, *Women on the Move*, 7, 52, 55, 194–195; Clare Simpson, "Capitalising on Curiousity: Women's Professional Cycle Racing in the Late-Nineteenth Century," in *Cycling and Society*, ed. Paul Rosen (New York: Routledge, 2016), 55; Ron Spreng, "The 1890s Bicycling Craze in the Red River Valley," *Minnesota History* 54 (Summer 1995): 273.

74. Gilles, *Women on the Move*, 153.

75. Gilles, *Women on the Move*, 9–10, 16, 26–27.

76. Gilles, *Women on the Move*, 40, 50, 52, 54, 80, 102.

77. Gilles, *Women on the Move*, 108, 157.

78. Gilles, *Women on the Move*, 80.

79. Gilles, *Women on the Move*, 84.

80. Gilles, *Women on the Move*, 101.

81. Gilles, *Women on the Move*, 205, 210.

82. Gilles, *Women on the Move*, 211–213.

83. Gilles, *Women on the Move*, 221.

84. Gilles, *Women on the Move*, 223, 239.

85. Gilles, *Women on the Move*, 225.

86. Gilles, *Women on the Move*, 226–227.

87. Gilles, *Women on the Move*, 236.

88. Gilles, *Women on the Move*, 117, 249.

89. Gilles, *Women on the Move*, 281; "Dottie Farnsworth Dies in New York," *Minneapolis Tribune*, June 7, 1902.

Chapter Nine

1. "The Star's Daily Pictorial Page," *Evening Star* (Washington, D.C.), June 29, 1922, 17; "Annie Oakley Hits High Balls at Fred Stone's Society Circus," *New York Tribune*, July 4, 1922, 5; *Washington (D.C.) Times*, July 3, 1922, 7; Shirl Kasper, *Annie Oakley* (Norman: University of Oklahoma Press, 1992), 226.

2. Gioia Diliberto, *A Useful Woman: The Early Life of Jane Addams* (New York: Scribner, 1999), 85, 147.

3. Allen F. Davis, *American Heroine: The Life and Legend of Jane Addams* (New York: Oxford University Press, 1973), 109, 159.

4. "Jane Addams Best American," *New York Times*, January 10, 1913; "Jane Addams Chrysanthemum," *Lawrence* (KS) *Daily Journal*, November 3, 1908, 2; Mary Stoyell Stimpson, *The Child's Book of American Biography* (Boston: Little, Brown and Company, 1915), 222–228.

5. Davis, *American Heroine*, 205, 208; "Jane Addams," *Pearson's Magazine* 26 (October 1911): 401.

6. "Rose N. Cullen to Jane Addams, Dec. 12, 1911," Jane Addams Digital Edition, accessed March 11, 2020, https://digital.janeaddams.ramapo.edu/items/show/3959.

7. "Grace Raymond Hebard to Jane Addams, Feb. 1, 1913," Jane Addams Digital Edition, accessed March 11, 2020, https://digital.janeaddams.ramapo.edu/items/show/5975.

8. "Hannah O. Lislerude to Jane Addams, March 24, 1912," Jane Addams Digital Edition, accessed March 11, 2020, https://digital.janeaddams.ramapo.edu/items/show/4346.

9. Jane Addams, *A New Conscience and an Ancient Evil* (New York: MacMillan Company, 1912), 111, 153–154.

10. Jane Addams, *Twenty Years at Hull-House with Autobiographical Notes* (New York: The Macmillan Company, 1912), 385–386.

11. Jane Addams, *The Spirit of Youth and the City Streets* (1909; repr., New York: The MacMillan Company, 1930), 86, 93.

12. Addams, *Spirit of Youth*, 77, 80, 92–93.

13. "Letter Vachel Lindsay to Sara

Teasdale, August 2, 1913," Annotated Letters, accessed March 11, 2020, http://vachellindsay.org/wp-content/uploads/2017/01/intro_and_vl_letters_1_21-1.pdf; "The Most Famous Girl in America," *Ladies' World* (December 1912), 39.

14. "Local Woman Wins Literary Prize," *Daily Palo Alto* (CA) *Times*, Sep. 20, 1912. Scholars call this fandom. See Jessica L. Whitehead, "The Historical Process of Fandom as a Participatory Pastime: Film Discourse in Newspapers from 1911 to 1918," (MA thesis, York University, 2012), 10.

15. "The 'Mary' Answer that Wins the Prize and Some of the Others," *Ladies' World* (October 1912), 38.

16. Nan Enstad, *Ladies of Labor, Girls of Adventure* (New York: Columbia University Press, 1999), 174; "The Editor and the Reader: A Review and a Promise," *Ladies' World* (December 1912), 1; "'Mary' the Prize Winner," *Ladies' World* (November 1912), 40; "'Mary' the October Contest," *Ladies' World* (January 1913), 25; "'Mary' the Prize Winner," *Ladies' World* (February 1913), 30; "The Old Mary—A New Mary and a Prize Contest," *Ladies' World* (July 1913), 1.

17. "New Kozy," *Chickasha* (Indian Terr.) *Daily Express*, April 17, 1913, 5; "Empire," *Bridgeport* (CT) *Evening Farmer*, 2 July 1913, 12; "Miss Mary Fuller Wearing the 'Mary' Hat," *Ladies' World* (June 1913), 4; "Things are happening to Mary," *Edison Kinetogram* 8 (April 15, 1913): 17; Enstad *Ladies of Labor*, 174; "The Activities of Mary: How She Appeared in Moving Pictures, in a Song, a Puzzle, a Game and on the Stage," *Ladies' World* (March 1913), 11; "What Happened to Mary," Frances G. Spencer Collection of American Popular Sheet Music, accessed March 11, 2020, http://digitalcollections.baylor.edu/cdm/ref/collection/fa-spnc/id/83687.

18. There is a debate about whether it is a series of films or an actual serial. The episodes do not have cliff hangers, but I chose to portray it as a serial. See Raymond William Stedman, *The Serials: Suspense and Drama by Installment* (Norman: University of Oklahoma Press, 1971), 6–7.

19. Angela Firkus, "What Happened to Mary" in *Reforming America: A Thematic Encyclopedia and Document Collection of the Progressive Era*, ed. Jeffrey Johnson (Santa Barbara: ABC-CLIO, 2017), 743–744.

20. "A Few Comments on 'What Happened to Mary,'" *Edison Kinetogram* 8 (May 15, 1913): 18; *Cape County* (Cape Girardeau, MO) *Herald*, May 16, 1913; *Hattiesburg* (MS) *News*, April 17, 1913, 8; "What Happened to Mary at the Kozy Sunday," *Chickasha* (Indian Terr.) *Daily Express*, June 21, 1913, 4; "Empire," *Bridgeport (CT) Evening Farmer*, May 28, 1913, 5; "Alone in New York," *Laurens* (SC) *Advertiser*, November 13, 1912; *Evening Capital and Maryland Gazette* (Annapolis), January 11, 1913.

21. "New Cozy," *Chickasha* (Indian Terr.) *Daily Express*, January 25, 1913, 3; "Performances for Flood Sufferers," *Daily Capital* (Salem, OR), March 27, 1913, 8; "Ran 'Mary' Anyway," *Edison Kinetogram* 8 (Feb. 1, 1913): 18.

22. *Motion Picture Story Magazine* 4 (January 1913): 162; "East Belfast," *Republican Journal* (Belfast, ME), March 20, 1913.

23. "What Happened to Mary, Beaten: Girl who Seems to have more Trouble than a Bumble Bee on Fly Paper," *Daily Gate City* (Keokuk, IA), August, 17, 1913.

24. "They were elected in August," *Roundup* (MT) *Record*, October 18, 1912, 4.

25. Samantha Barbas, *Movie Crazy: Fans, Stars, and the Cult of Celebrity* (New York: Palgrave Macmillan, 2002), 10–11.

26. Diliberto, *Useful Woman*, 172; Robert S. Birchard, "What Happened to Mary?," Hollywood Heritage, accessed March 11, 2020, http://archive.is/fnacj; Mary Fuller and Bailey Millard, "My Adventures as a Motion-Picture Heroine," *Collier's* 48 (December 30, 1911): 16–17.

27. *Motion Picture Story Magazine*, 5 (July 1913): 131; "What Really Happened to Mary," *Evening Standard* (Ogden City, UT), April 4, 1913, 6; "Extracts from the Diary of Mary Fuller," *Motion Picture Story Magazine*, 8 (August 1914): 97.

28. "What Happened to Mary," *Lexington* (MS) *Advertiser*, November 28, 1913; "Mary Fuller Perfume Advertisement," *Photoplay Magazine* 6 (November 1914):

183; "Extracts from the Diary of Mary Fuller," *Motion Picture Story Magazine* 8 (August 1914): 98–99; *Motion Picture Story Magazine* 7 (April 1914): 125.

29. *Motion Picture Story Magazine* 6 (October 1913): 114; *Motion Picture Story Magazine* 4 (October 1912): 133; *Motion Picture Story Magazine* 3 (June 1912): 141; *Motion Picture Story Magazine* 5 (March 1913): 125.

30. "The Varied Experiences of Pretty Mary Fuller told in Entertaining Chat," *Ogden (UT) Standard,* August 23, 1913; Mary Fuller, "My Summer Vacation," *Photoplay Magazine* 6 (November 1914): 114.

31. *Motion Picture Story Magazine* 8 (August 1914): 166; *Motion Picture Story Magazine* 8 (October 1914): 165; *Motion Picture Story Magazine* 5 (April 1913): 122; *Motion Picture Story Magazine* 7 (June 1914): 173.

32. *Motion Picture Story Magazine* 8 (October 1914): 165; Fuller and Millard, "My Adventures as a Motion-Picture Heroine," 16–17; "The Varied Experiences"; Mary Fuller, "How I Became a Photoplayer," *Motion Picture Story Magazine* 8 (December 1914): 107–108; "Extracts from the Diary of Mary Fuller," *Motion Picture Story Magazine* 7 (July 1914): 80–84; "Extracts from the Diary of Mary Fuller," *Motion Picture Story Magazine* 8 (August 1914): 97–99; "Greenroom Jottings," *Motion Picture Story Magazine* 6 (December 1913): 123; "Chats with Players—Mary Fuller," *Motion Picture Story Magazine* 7 (February 1914): 99.

33. *Motion Picture Story Magazine* 7 (May 1914): 159; *Motion Picture Story Magazine* 6 (December 1913): 124.

34. *Motion Picture Story Magazine* 6 (November 1913): 144; *Motion Picture Story Magazine* 4 (January 1913): 136.

35. *Motion Picture Story Magazine* 6 (October 1913): 114.

36. "Statement on Henry Leunker, Oct. 29, 1913," Jane Addams Digital Edition, accessed March 11, 2020, https://digital.janeaddams.ramapo.edu/items/show/9728; "Annoys Jane Addams, Held," *Chicago Tribune,* October 30, 1913.

37. Diliberto, *Useful Woman,* 138, 149, 186, 243.

38. Daniel Levine, *Jane Addams and the Liberal Tradition* (Madison: University of Wisconsin Press, 1971), 186; "Suffrage Via Biography," *New York Tribune,* June 1, 1912, 3; Diliberto, *Useful Woman,* 261.

39. Diliberto, *Useful Woman,* 260; "Part Played by Women," *Evening Star* (Washington, D.C.), November 3, 1912, 13.

40. "Chats with Players—Mary Fuller," *Motion Picture Story Magazine* 3 (July 1912): 132–133.

41. Elshtain, *Jane Addams,* 226–235.

42. Diliberto, *Useful Woman,* 261; Davis, *American Heroine,* 245.

43. Elshtain, Jane Addams, 211, 233–235.

44. Davis, *American Heroine,* 229, 240.

45. Davis, *American Heroine,* 263–265.

46. Levine, *Jane Addams and the Liberal Tradition,* 234, 236.

47. Davis, *American Heroine,* 260.

48. Birchard, "What Happened to Mary?"; "Answer Department," *Motion Picture Story Magazine* 12 (November 1916): 164; *Motion Picture Story Magazine* 8 (December 1914): 123.

49. "Photoplay Finds Mary Fuller," *Photoplay Magazine* 26 (August 1924): 58–59, 125.

50. "Chats with Players—Mary Fuller," *Motion Picture Story Magazine* (July 1912): 133.

51. Mary Pickford, *Sunshine and Shadow* (New York: Double Day, 1955), 210–213, 267–274.

52. Davis, *American Heroine,* 284; Helen Josephine Ferris, *When I was a Girl; the Stories of Five Famous Women as Told by Themselves* (New York: The Macmillan Company, 1930); Robin Berson, *Jane Addams: A Biography* (Westport, CT: Greenwood Press, 2004), 118; *America's Twelve Great Women Leaders* (1933; repr., New York: Books for Libraries Press, 1969), 8.

53. Birchard, "What Happened to Mary?"

54. "Extracts from the Diary of Mary Fuller," *Motion Picture Story Magazine* 7 (July 1914): 81.

Index

www.ingramcontent.com/pod-product-compliance
Lightning Source LLC
Chambersburg PA
CBHW031131270326
41929CB00011B/1579